THE FUSE ™

VOL 1 · THE RUSSIA SHIFT

WRITER · ANTONY JOHNSTON

ARTIST · JUSTIN GREENWOOD

COLORIST · SHARI CHANKHAMMA

LETTERER · ED BRISSON

fusecomic.com

FUSE CREATED BY JOHNSTON & GREENWOOD

Cover earth image: NASA archive # AS17-148-22727

IMAGE COMICS, INC.
Robert Kirkman – Chief Operating Officer
Erik Larsen – Chief Financial Officer
Todd McFarlane – President
Marc Silvestri – Chief Executive Officer
Jim Valentino – Vice-President

Eric Stephenson – Publisher
Ron Richards – Director of Business Development
Jennifer de Guzman – Director of Trade Book Sales
Kat Salazar – Director of PR & Marketing
Jeremy Sullivan – Director of Digital Sales
Emilio Bautista – Sales Assistant
Branwyn Bigglestone – Senior Accounts Manager
Emily Miller – Accounts Manager
Jessica Ambriz – Administrative Assistant
Tyler Shainline – Events Coordinator
David Brothers – Content Manager
Jonathan Chan – Production Manager
Drew Gill – Art Director
Meredith Wallace – Print Manager
Monica Garcia – Senior Production Artist
Jenna Savage – Production Artist
Addison Duke – Production Artist
Tricia Ramos – Production Assistant
IMAGECOMICS.COM

THE FUSE VOL 1: THE RUSSIA SHIFT. First printing. August 2014.

ISBN: 978-1-63215-008-0. Contains material originally published in magazine form as THE FUSE #1-6.
Published by Image Comics, Inc. Office of publication: 2001 Center Street, 6th Floor, Berkeley, CA 94704.

PART 1

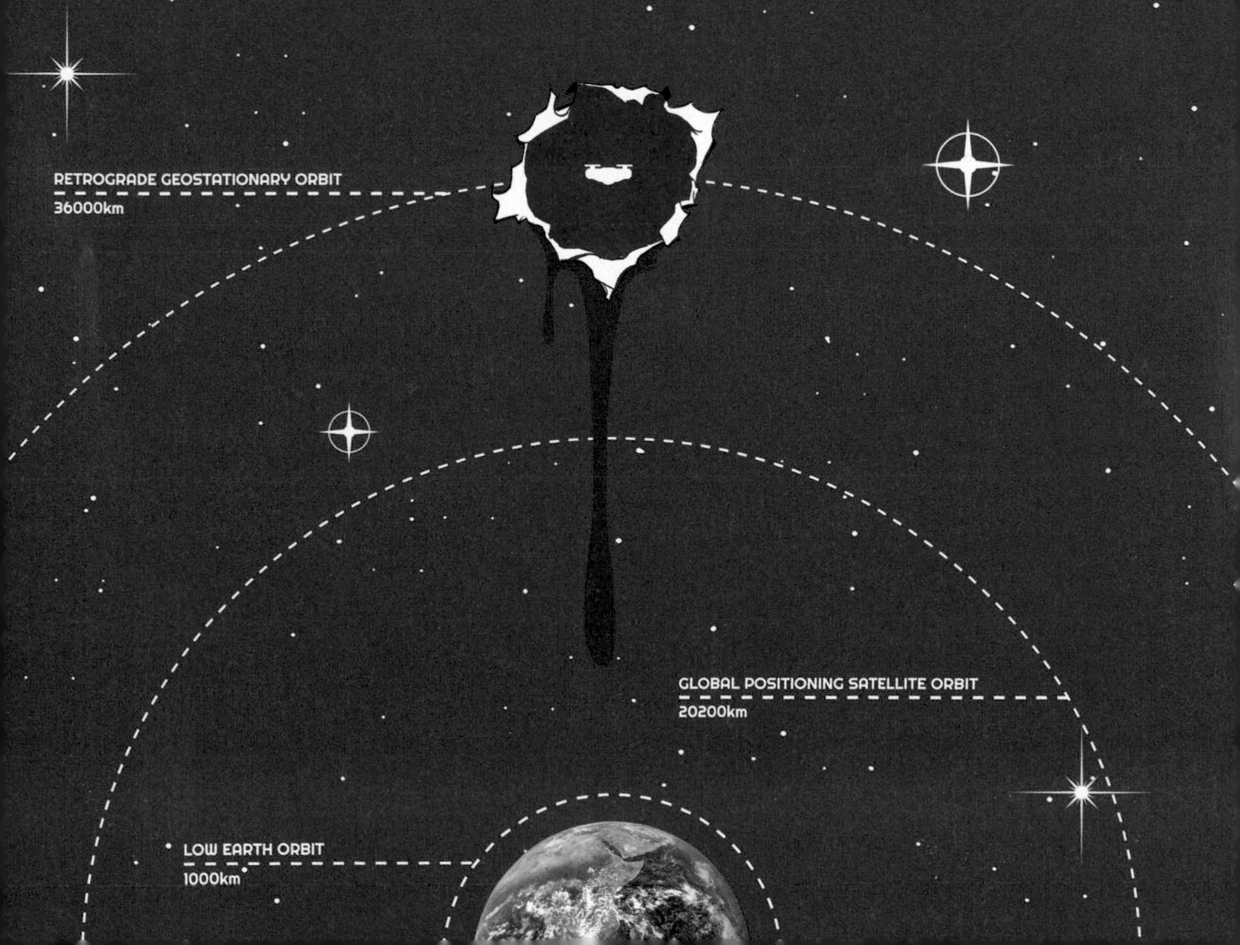
RETROGRADE GEOSTATIONARY ORBIT
36000km
GLOBAL POSITIONING SATELLITE ORBIT
20200km
LOW EARTH ORBIT
1000km

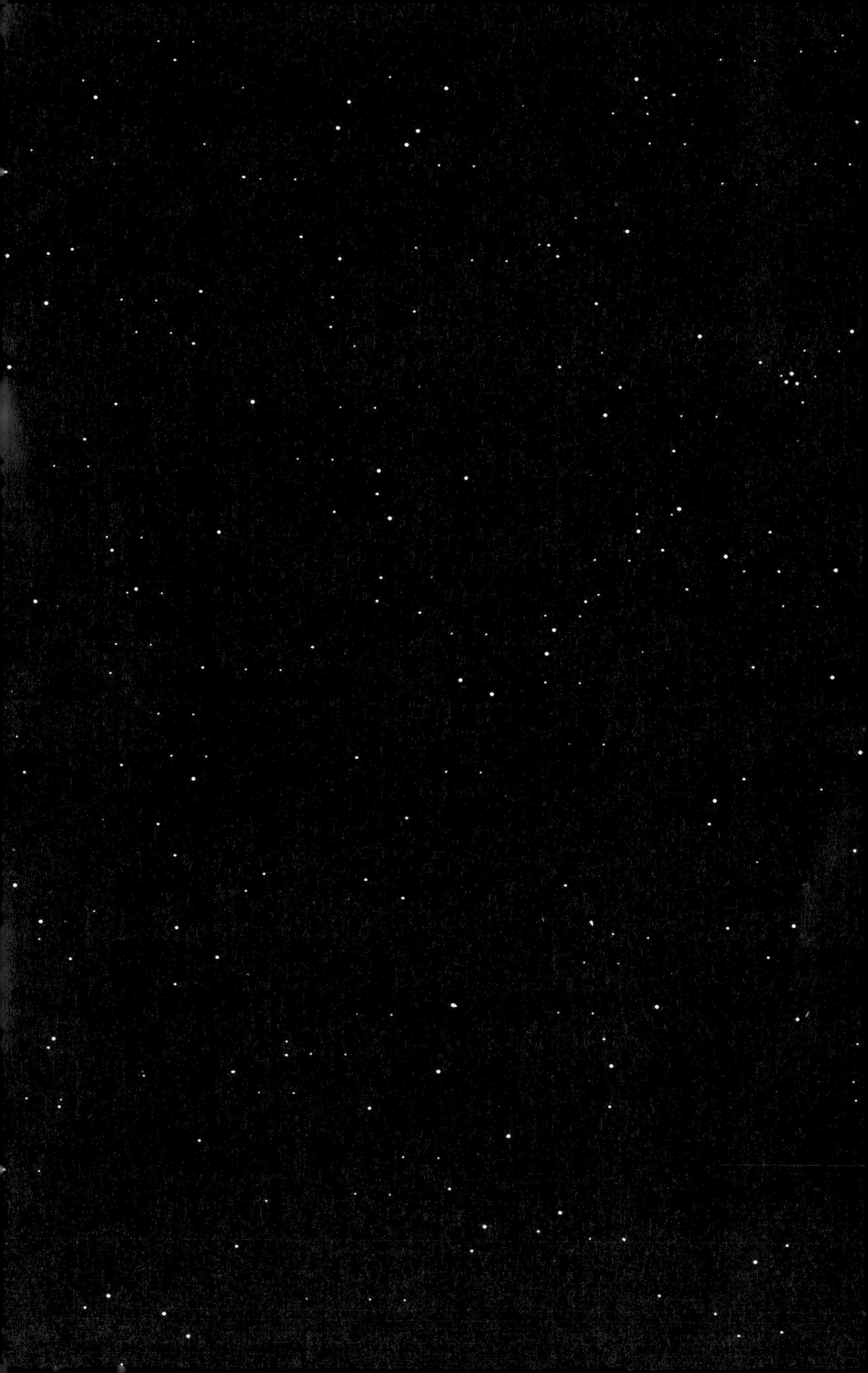

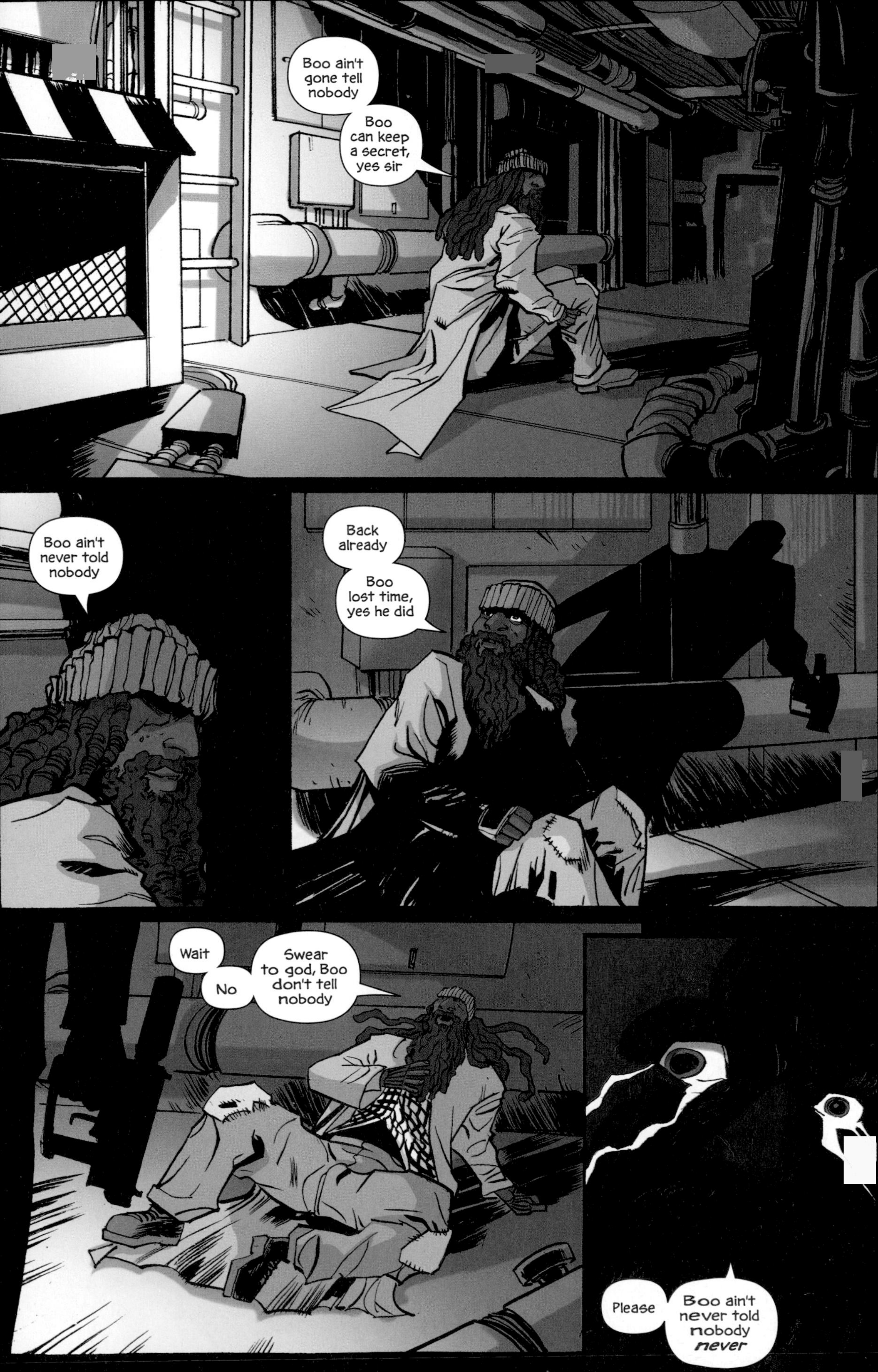
Boo ain't gone tell nobody
Boo can keep a secret, yes sir
Boo ain't never told nobody
Back already
Boo lost time, yes he did
Wait
No
Swear to god, Boo don't tell nobody
Please
Boo ain't never told nobody *never*

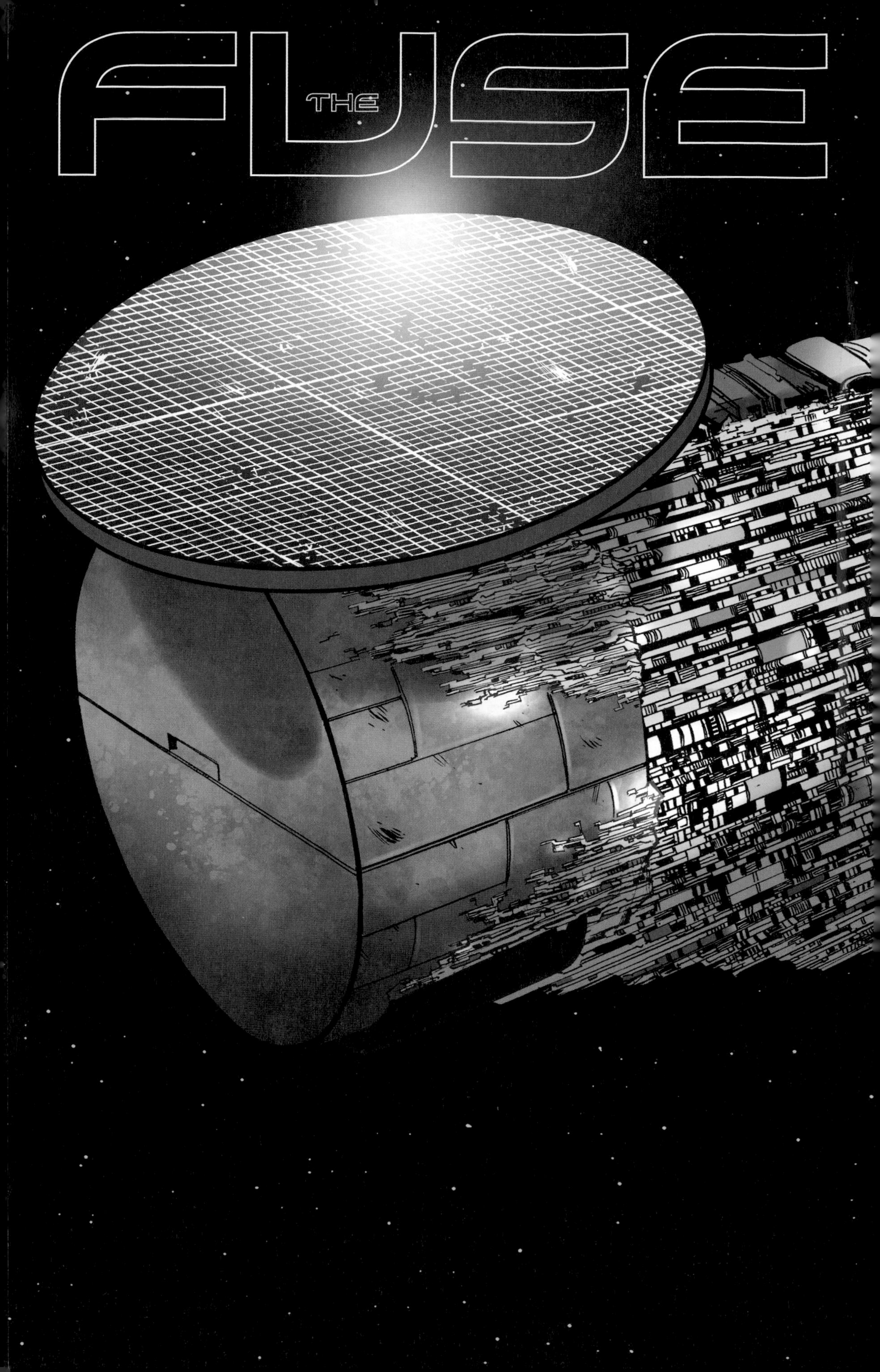
THE FUSE

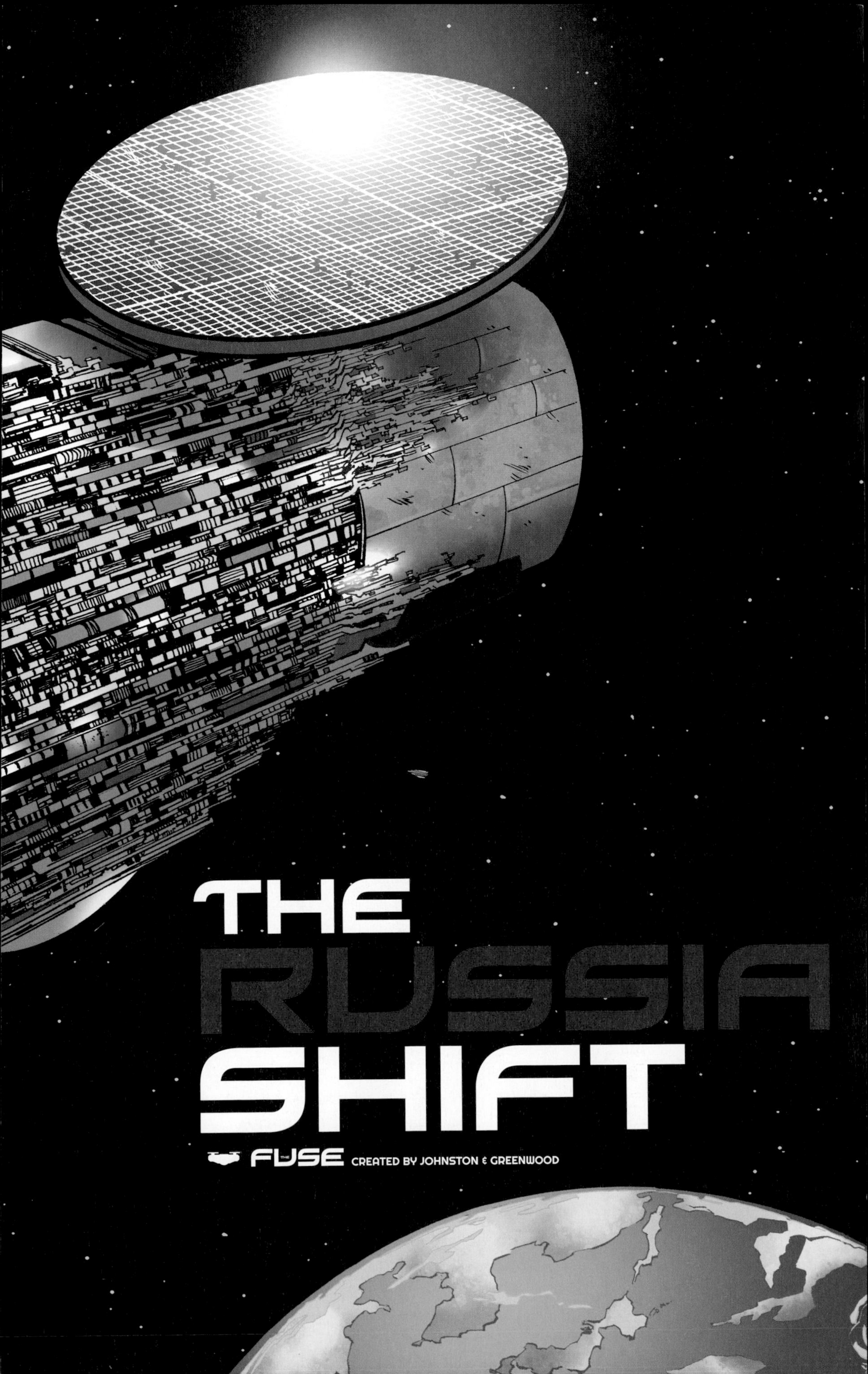
THE
RUSSIA
SHIFT
THE FUSE CREATED BY JOHNSTON & GREENWOOD

MIDWAY CITY SHUTTLEPORT • GAGARIN & 30TH • LEVEL 18

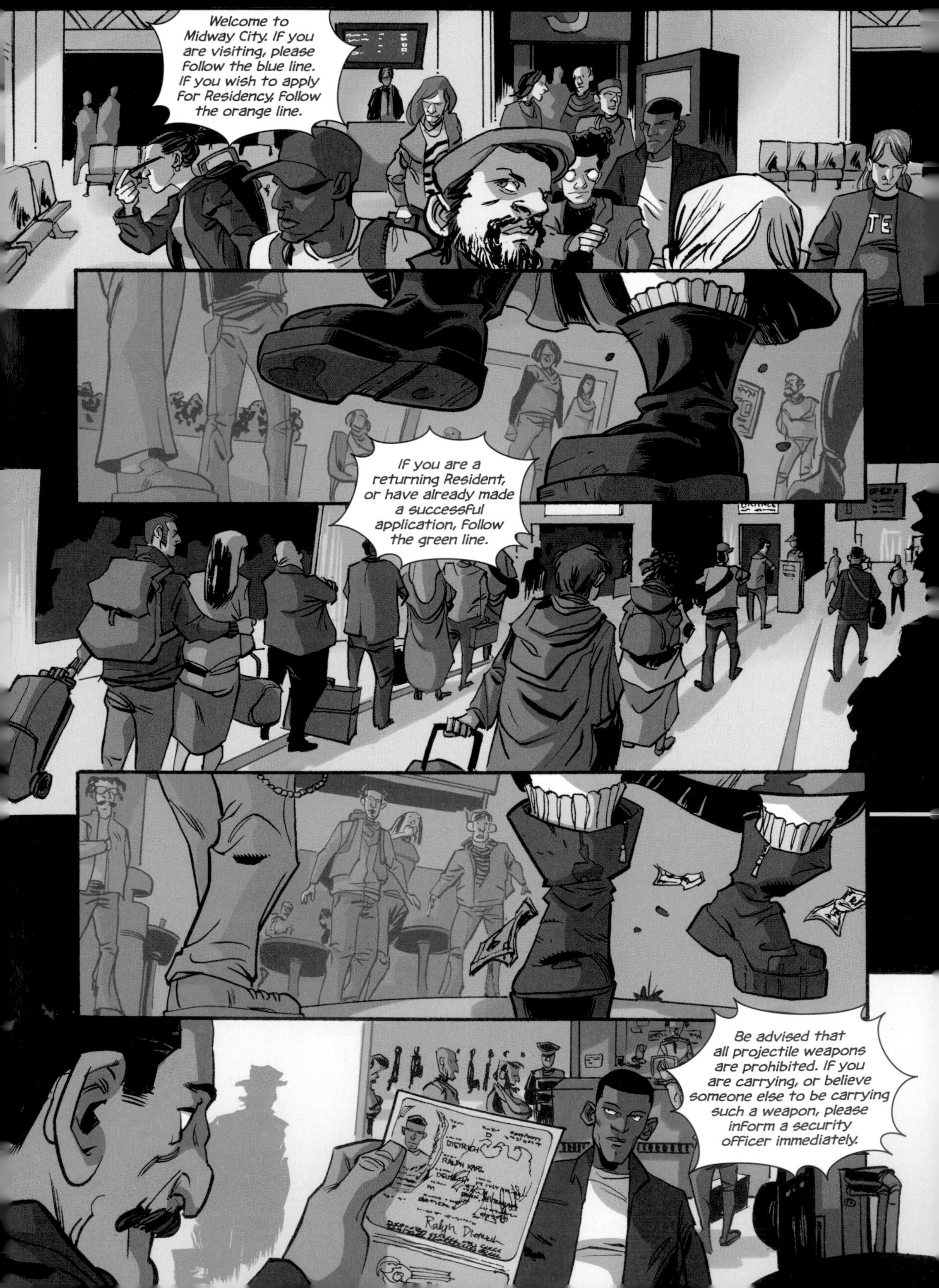

Welcome to Midway City. If you are visiting, please follow the blue line. If you wish to apply for Residency, follow the orange line.
If you are a returning Resident, or have already made a successful application, follow the green line.
Be advised that all projectile weapons are prohibited. If you are carrying, or believe someone else to be carrying such a weapon, please inform a security officer immediately.

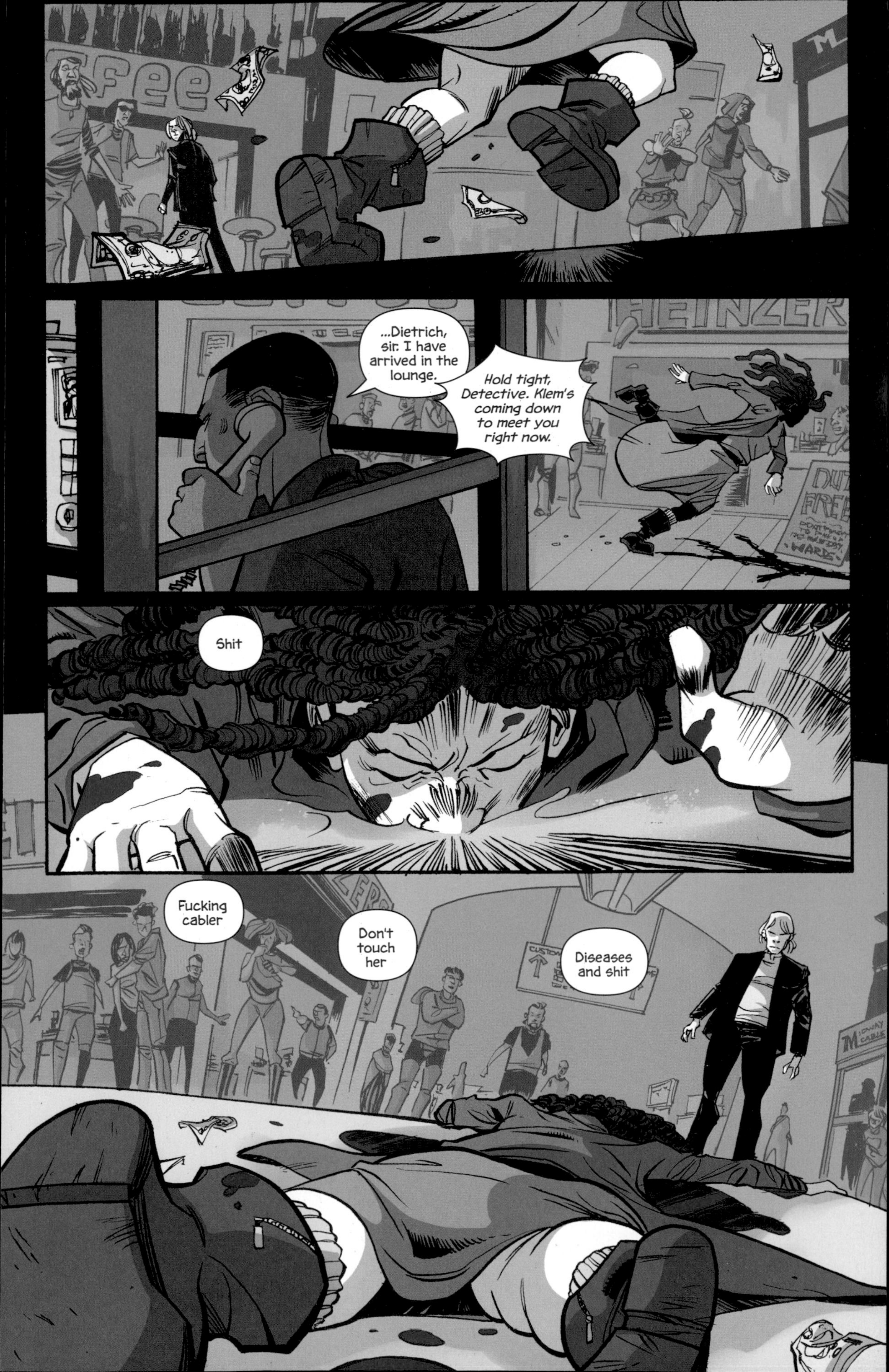
...Dietrich, sir. I have arrived in the lounge.
Hold tight, Detective. Klem's coming down to meet you right now.
Shit
Fucking cabler
Don't touch her
Diseases and shit

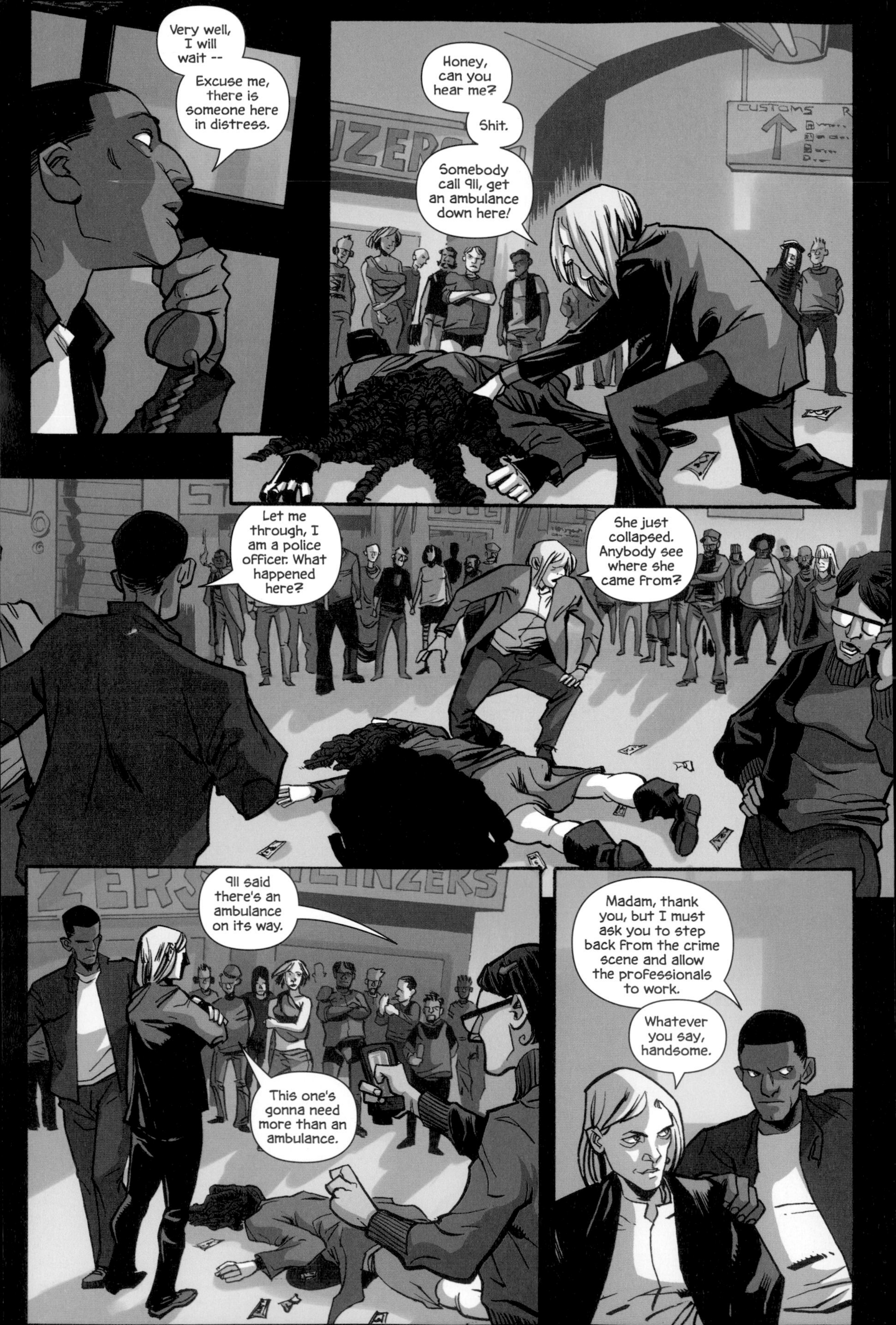
Very well, I will wait --
Excuse me, there is someone here in distress.
CUSTOMS
Honey, can you hear me?
Shit.
Somebody call 911, get an ambulance down here!
Let me through, I am a police officer. What happened here?
She just collapsed. Anybody see where she came from?
911 said there's an ambulance on its way.
This one's gonna need more than an ambulance.
Madam, thank you, but I must ask you to step back from the crime scene and allow the professionals to work.
Whatever you say, handsome.

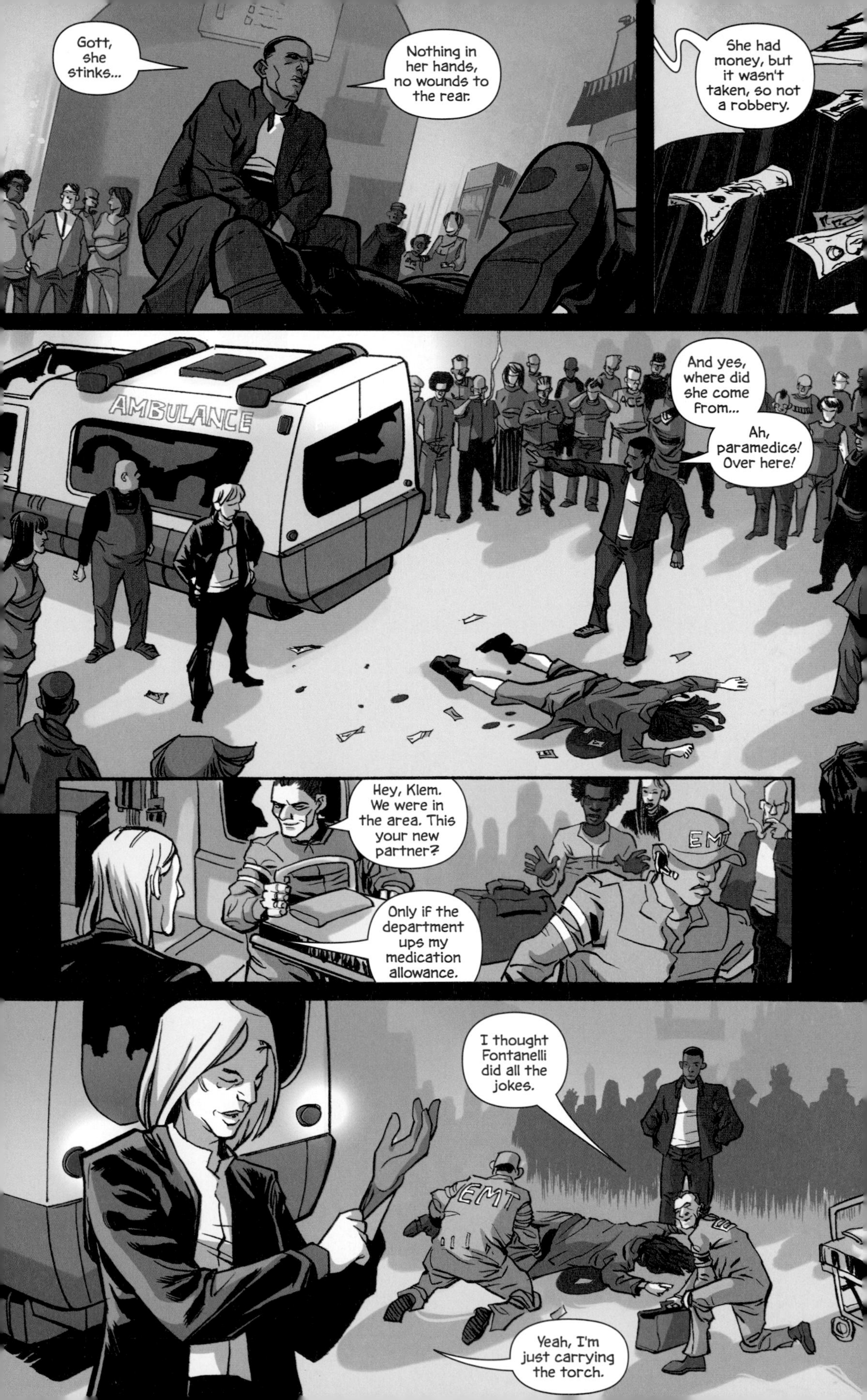

Gott, she stinks...
Nothing in her hands, no wounds to the rear.
She had money, but it wasn't taken, so not a robbery.
AMBULANCE
And yes, where did she come from...
Ah, paramedics! Over here!
Hey, Klem. We were in the area. This your new partner?
Only if the department ups my medication allowance.
EMT
I thought Fontanelli did all the jokes.
EMT
Yeah, I'm just carrying the torch.

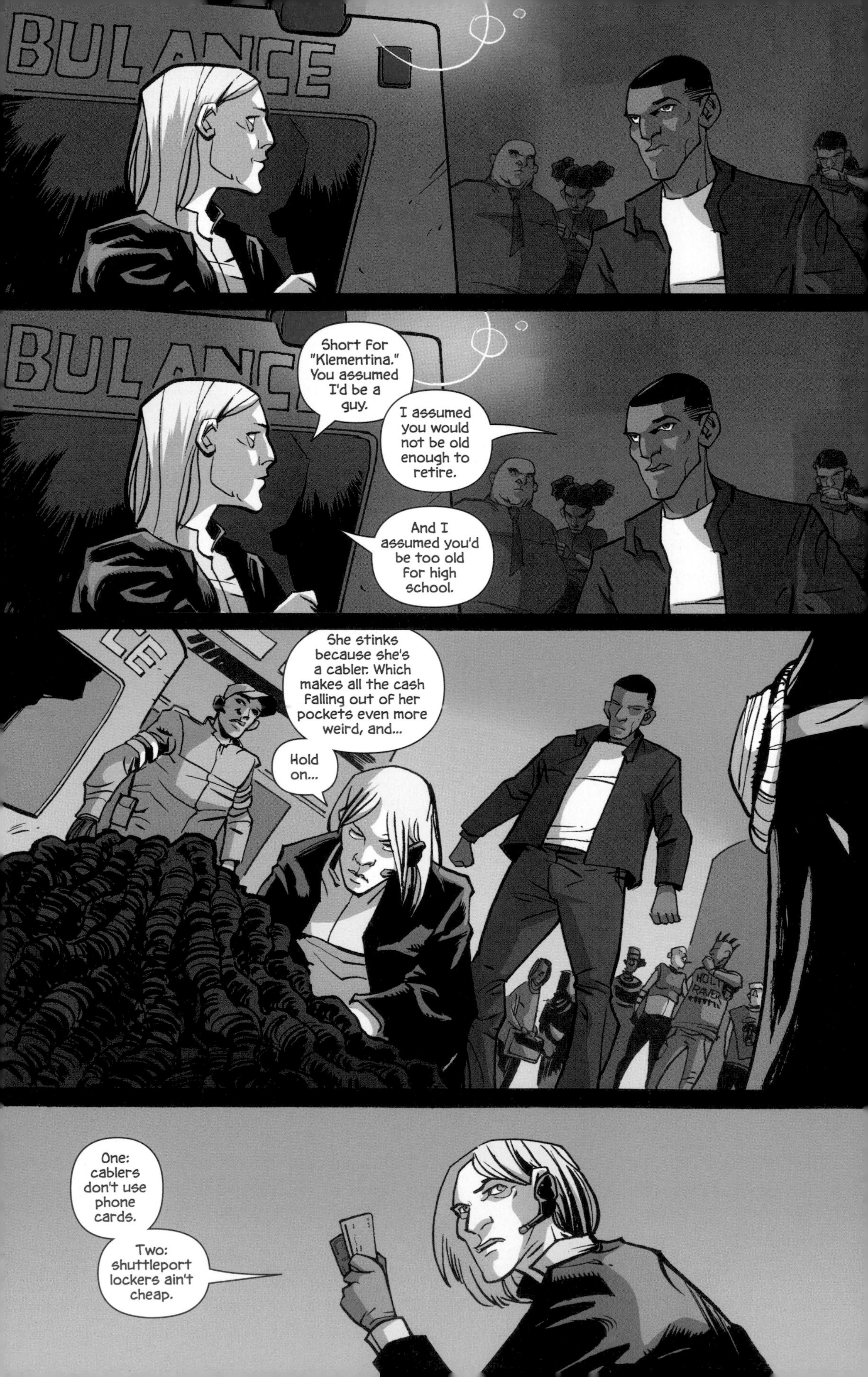
BULANCE
BULANCE
Short for "Klementina." You assumed I'd be a guy.
I assumed you would not be old enough to retire.
And I assumed you'd be too old for high school.
She stinks because she's a cabler. Which makes all the cash falling out of her pockets even more weird, and...
Hold on...
One: cablers don't use phone cards.
Two: shuttleport lockers ain't cheap.

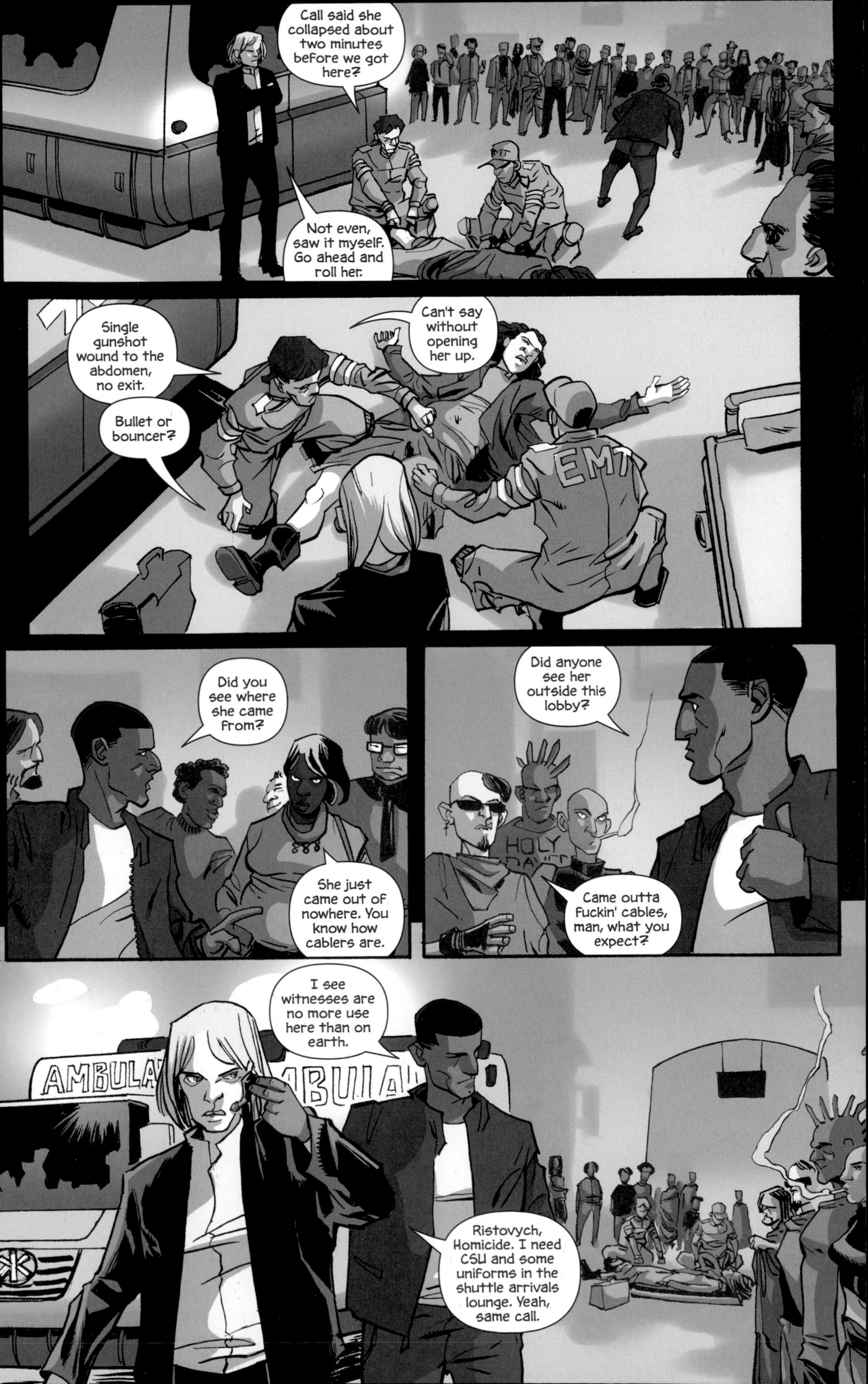
Call said she collapsed about two minutes before we got here?
Not even, saw it myself. Go ahead and roll her.
Single gunshot wound to the abdomen, no exit.
Bullet or bouncer?
Can't say without opening her up.
Did you see where she came from?
She just came out of nowhere. You know how cablers are.
Did anyone see her outside this lobby?
Came outta fuckin' cables, man, what you expect?
I see witnesses are no more use here than on earth.
Ristovych, Homicide. I need CSU and some uniforms in the shuttle arrivals lounge. Yeah, same call.

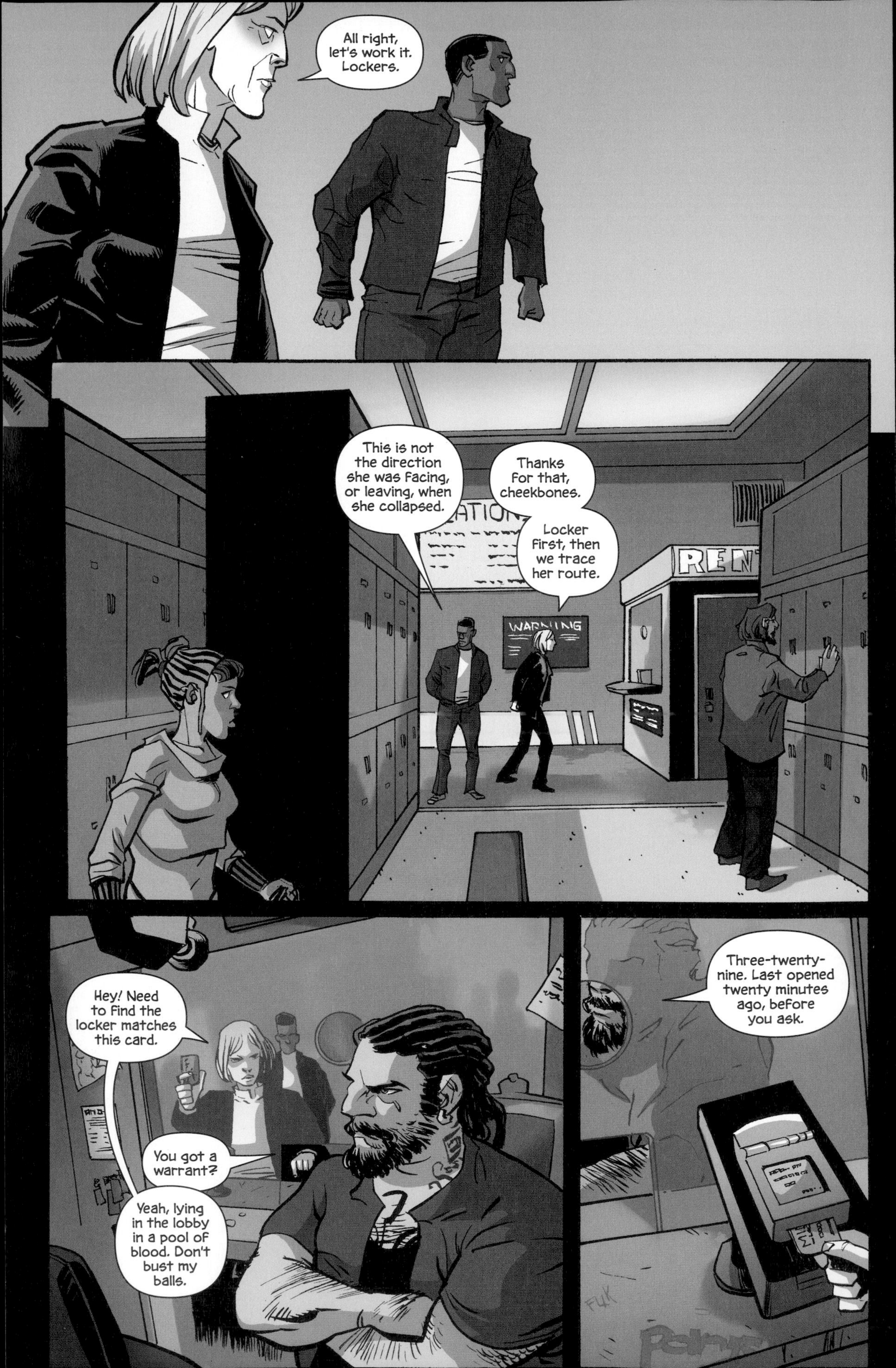
All right, let's work it. Lockers.
This is not the direction she was facing, or leaving, when she collapsed.
Thanks for that, cheekbones.
Locker first, then we trace her route.
WARNING
Hey! Need to find the locker matches this card.
You got a warrant?
Yeah, lying in the lobby in a pool of blood. Don't bust my balls.
Three-twenty-nine. Last opened twenty minutes ago, before you ask.

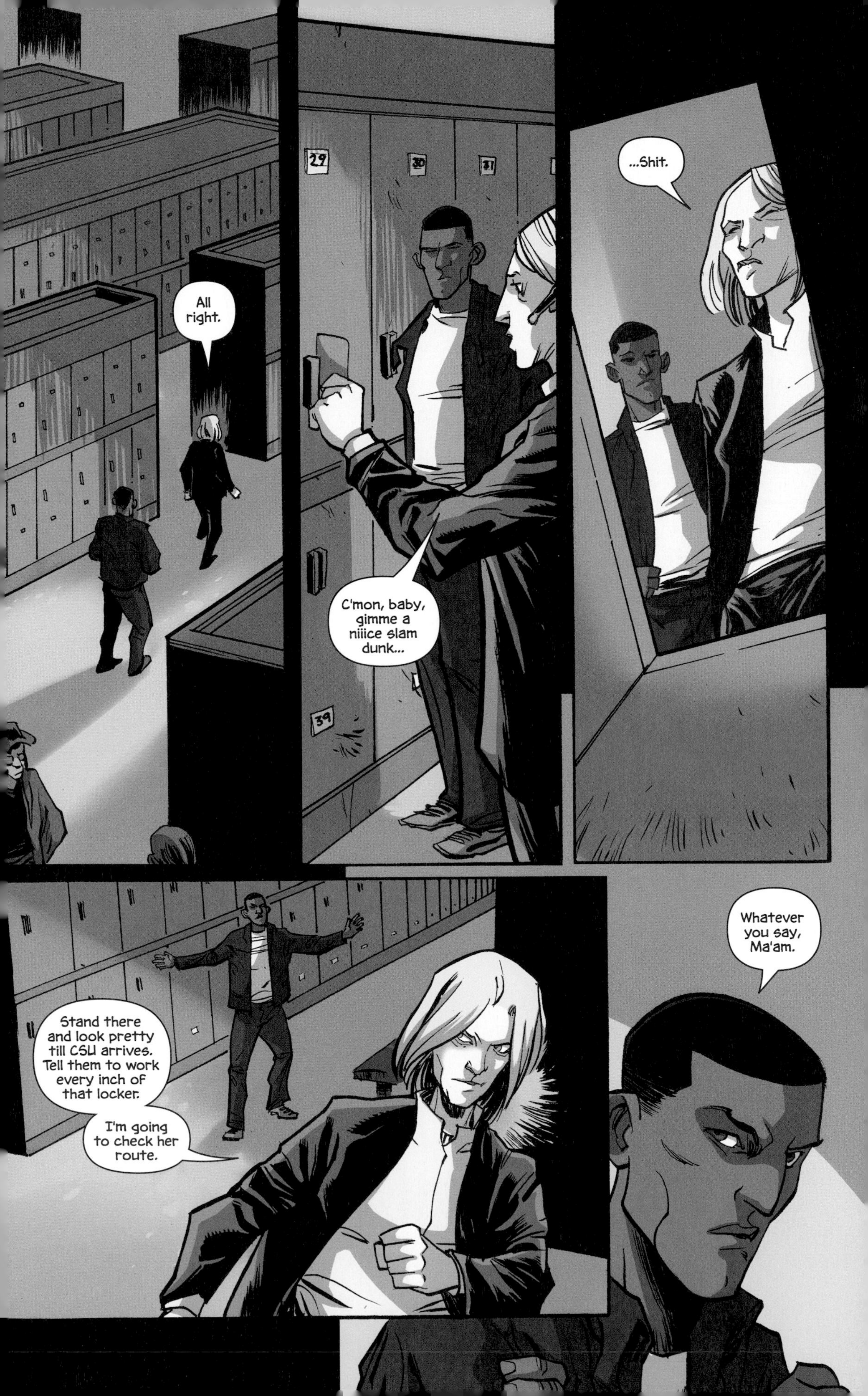
All right.
29
30
31
C'mon, baby, gimme a niiice slam dunk...
39
...Shit.
Whatever you say, Ma'am.
Stand there and look pretty till CSU arrives. Tell them to work every inch of that locker.
I'm going to check her route.

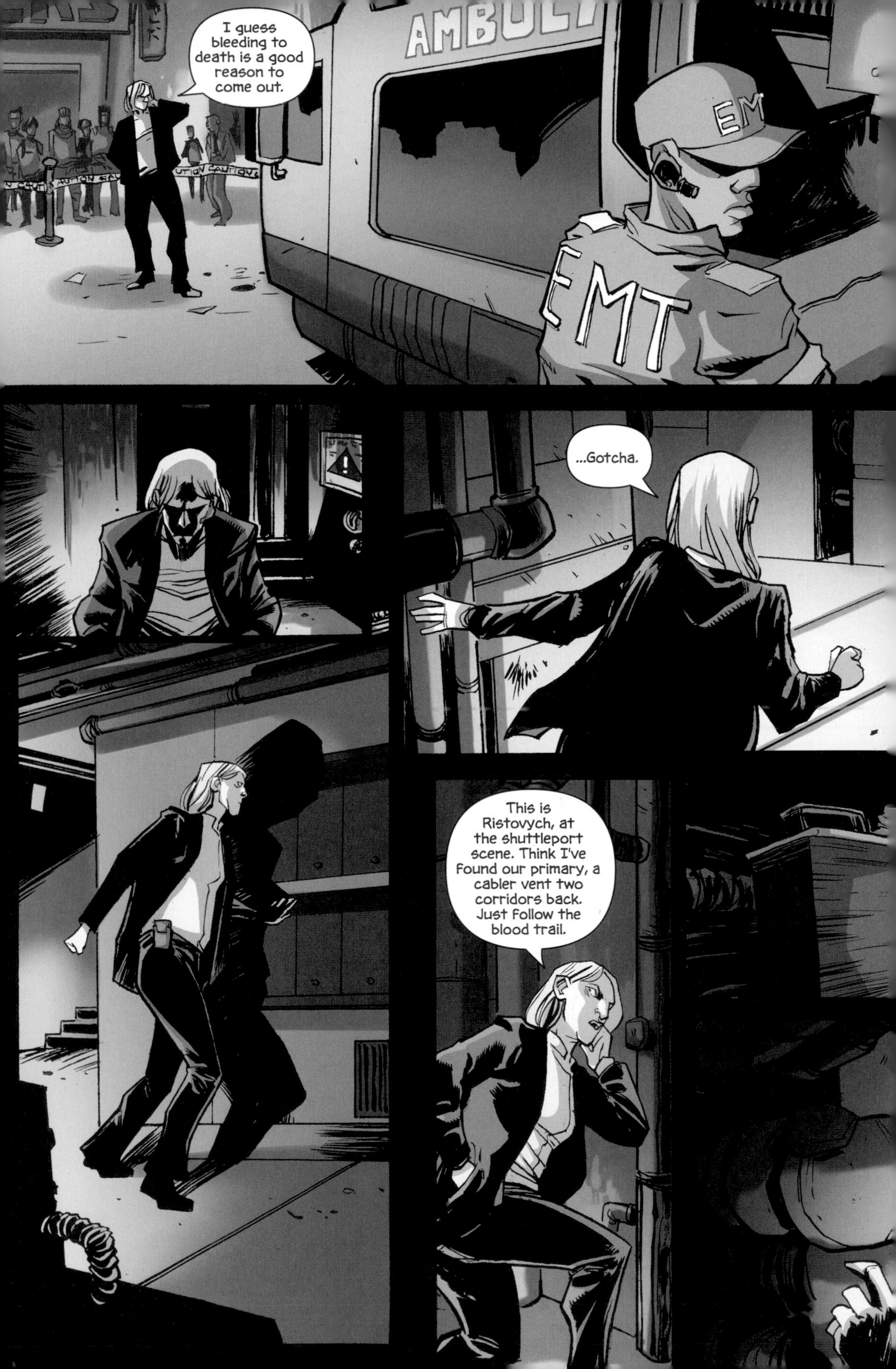

AMBUL
I guess bleeding to death is a good reason to come out.
EMT
EMT
...Gotcha.
This is Ristovych, at the shuttleport scene. Think I've found our primary, a cabler vent two corridors back. Just follow the blood trail.

Not enough for anyone to help you, though...

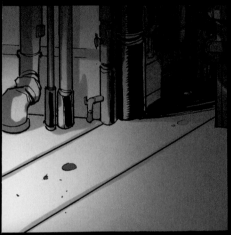

≥Snf≤

Huh.

Explains the smell, I guess.

...Maybe this is a slam dunk after all.

Hello...

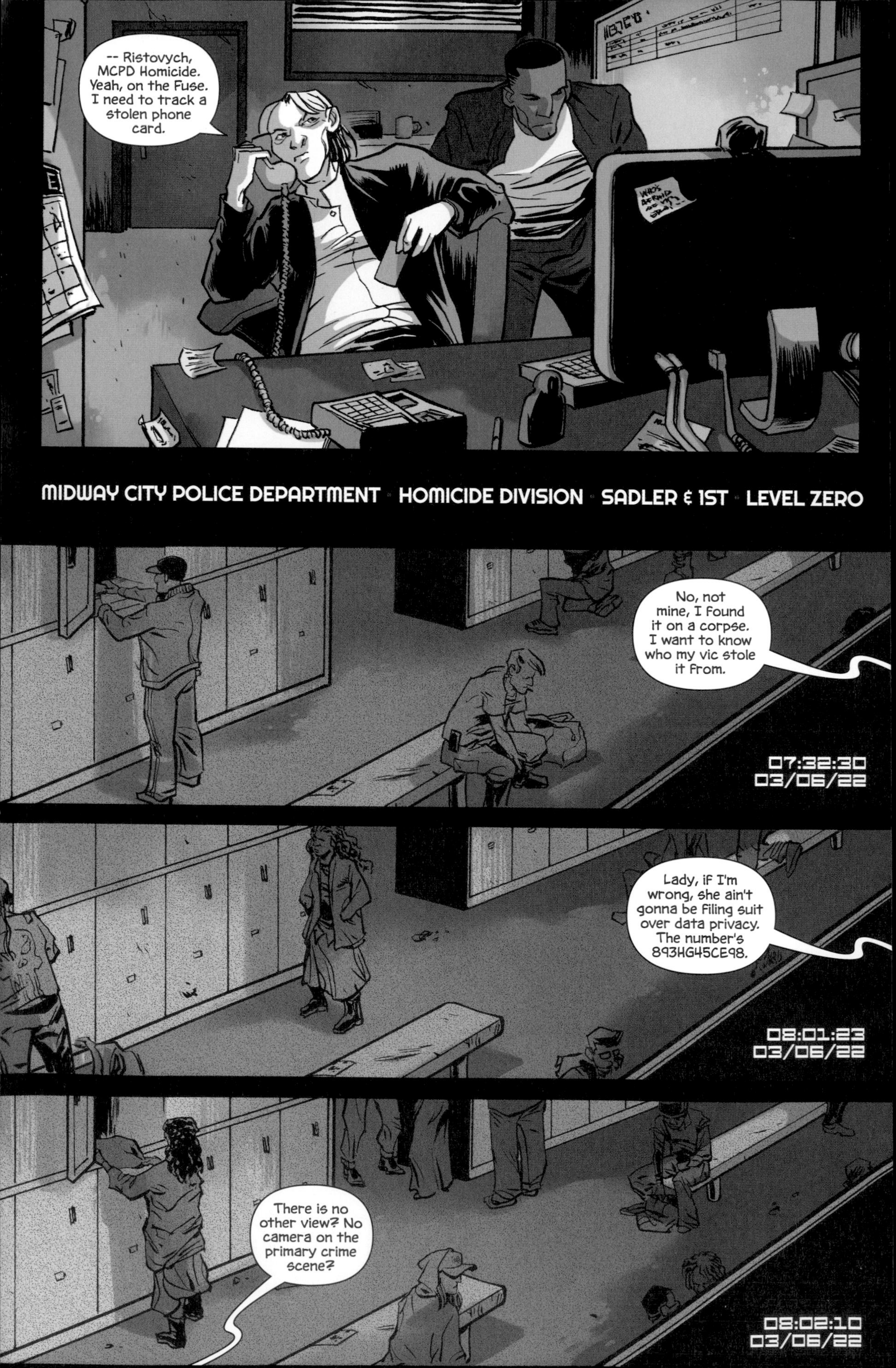
-- Ristovych, MCPD Homicide. Yeah, on the Fuse. I need to track a stolen phone card.
MIDWAY CITY POLICE DEPARTMENT · HOMICIDE DIVISION · SADLER & 1ST · LEVEL ZERO
No, not mine, I found it on a corpse. I want to know who my vic stole it from.
07:32:30
03/06/22
Lady, if I'm wrong, she ain't gonna be filing suit over data privacy. The number's 893HG45CE98.
08:01:23
03/06/22
There is no other view? No camera on the primary crime scene?
08:02:10
03/06/22

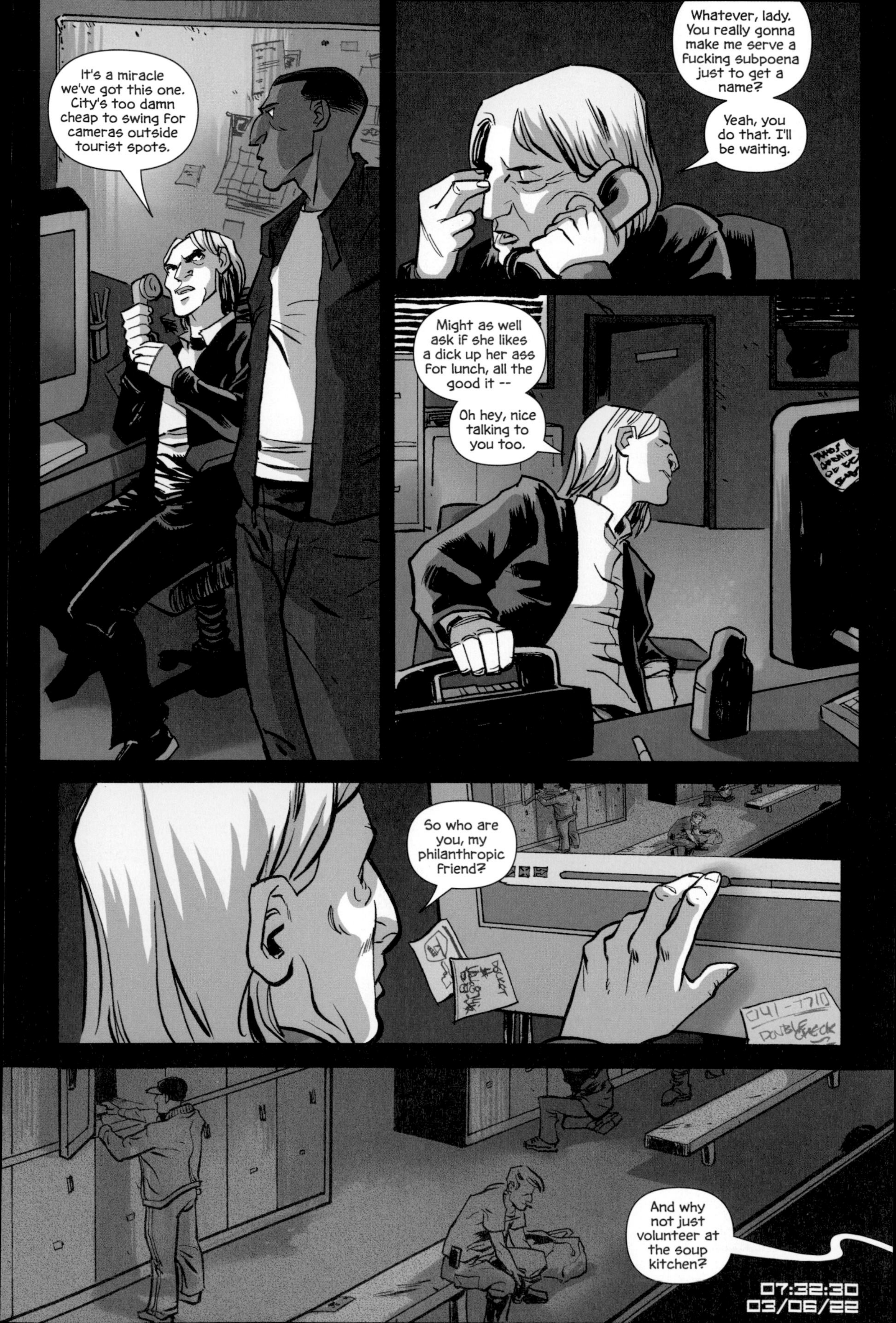
It's a miracle we've got this one. City's too damn cheap to swing for cameras outside tourist spots.
Whatever, lady. You really gonna make me serve a fucking subpoena just to get a name?
Yeah, you do that. I'll be waiting.
Might as well ask if she likes a dick up her ass for lunch, all the good it --
Oh hey, nice talking to you too.
So who are you, my philanthropic friend?
DOCKET
041-7710
DOUBLE CHECK
And why not just volunteer at the soup kitchen?
07:32:30
03/06/22

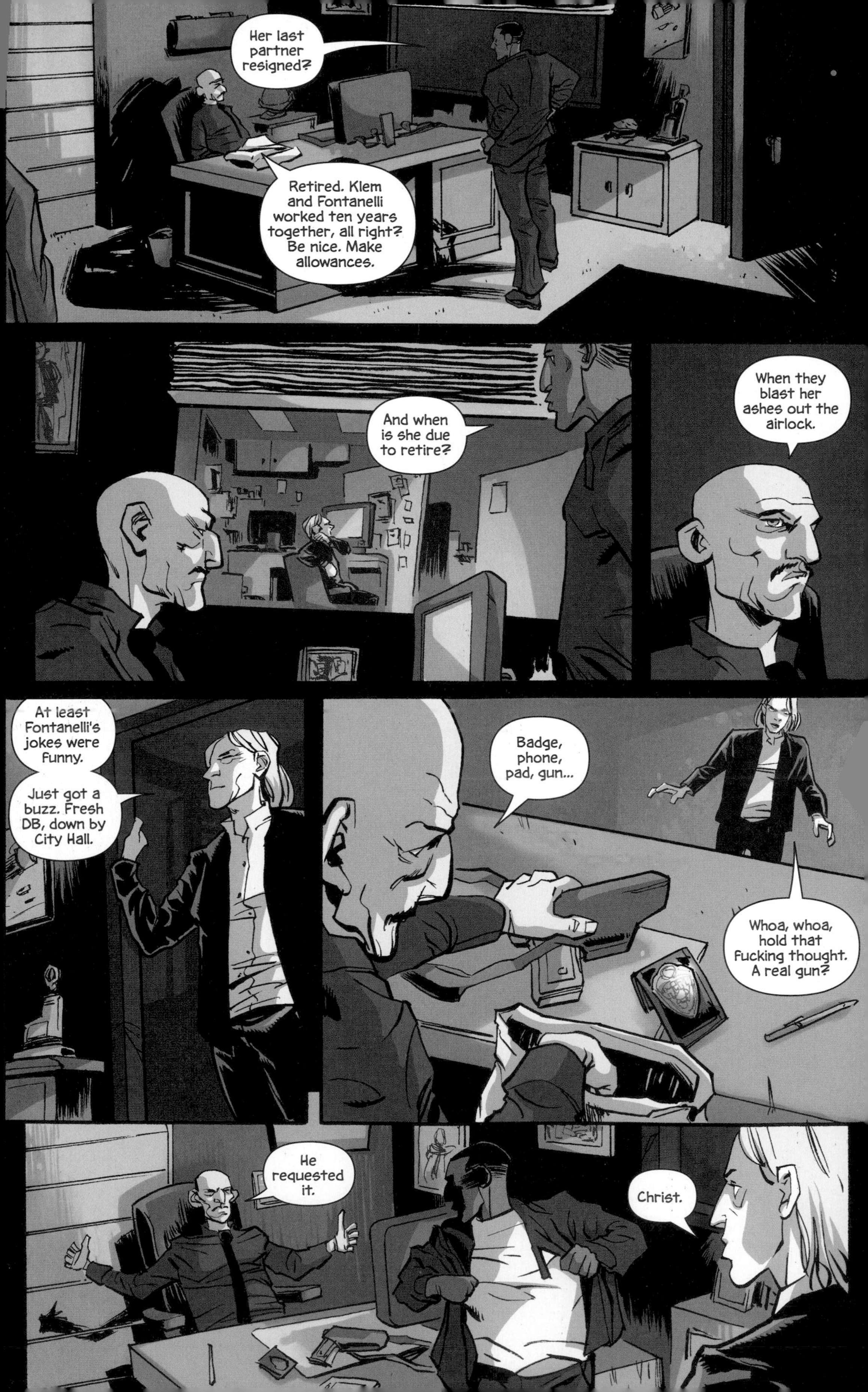
Her last partner resigned?
Retired. Klem and Fontanelli worked ten years together, all right? Be nice. Make allowances.
And when is she due to retire?
When they blast her ashes out the airlock.
At least Fontanelli's jokes were funny.
Just got a buzz. Fresh DB, down by City Hall.
Badge, phone, pad, gun...
Whoa, whoa, hold that fucking thought. A real gun?
He requested it.
Christ.

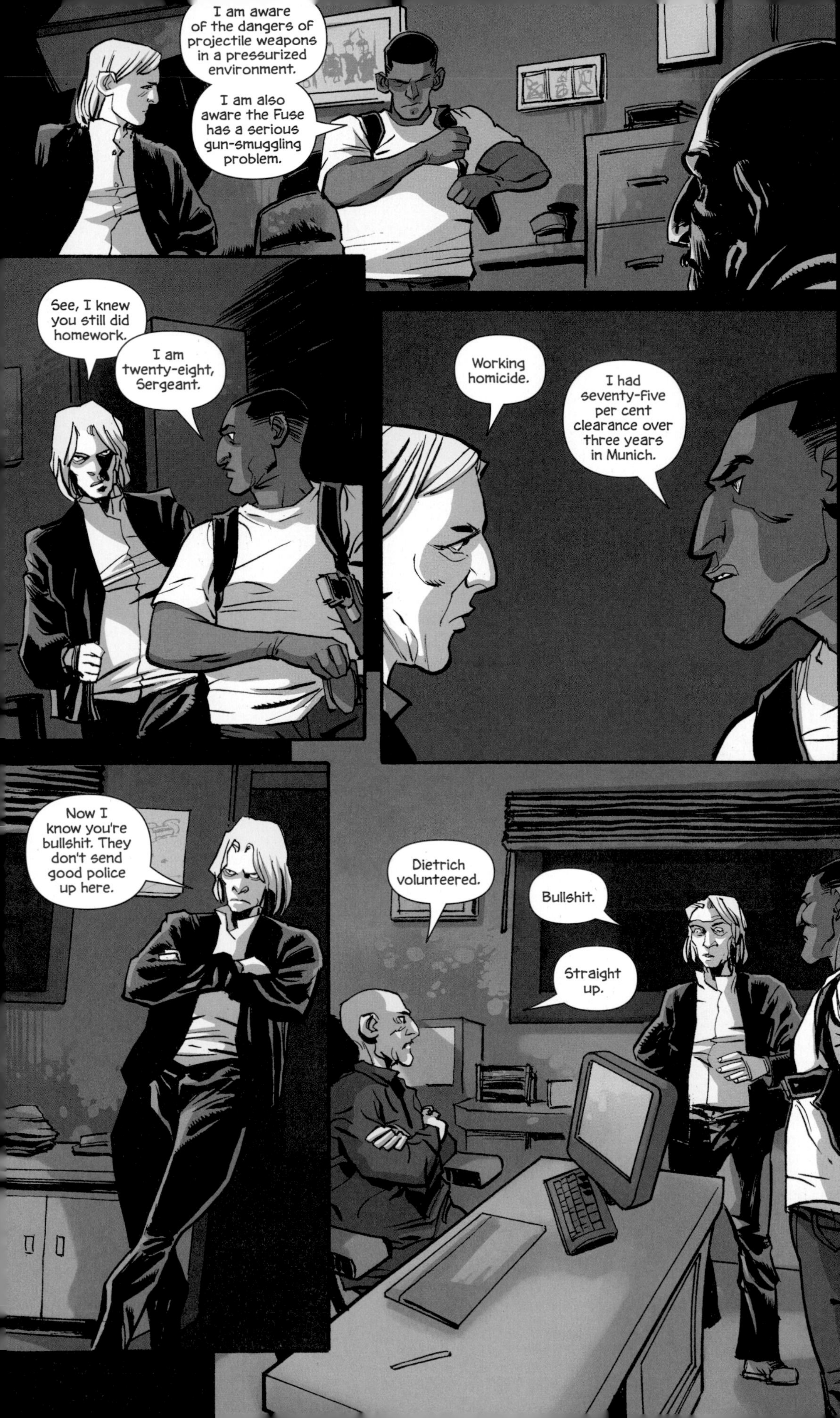
I am aware of the dangers of projectile weapons in a pressurized environment.
I am also aware the Fuse has a serious gun-smuggling problem.
See, I knew you still did homework.
I am twenty-eight, Sergeant.
Working homicide.
I had seventy-five per cent clearance over three years in Munich.
Now I know you're bullshit. They don't send good police up here.
Dietrich volunteered.
Bullshit.
Straight up.

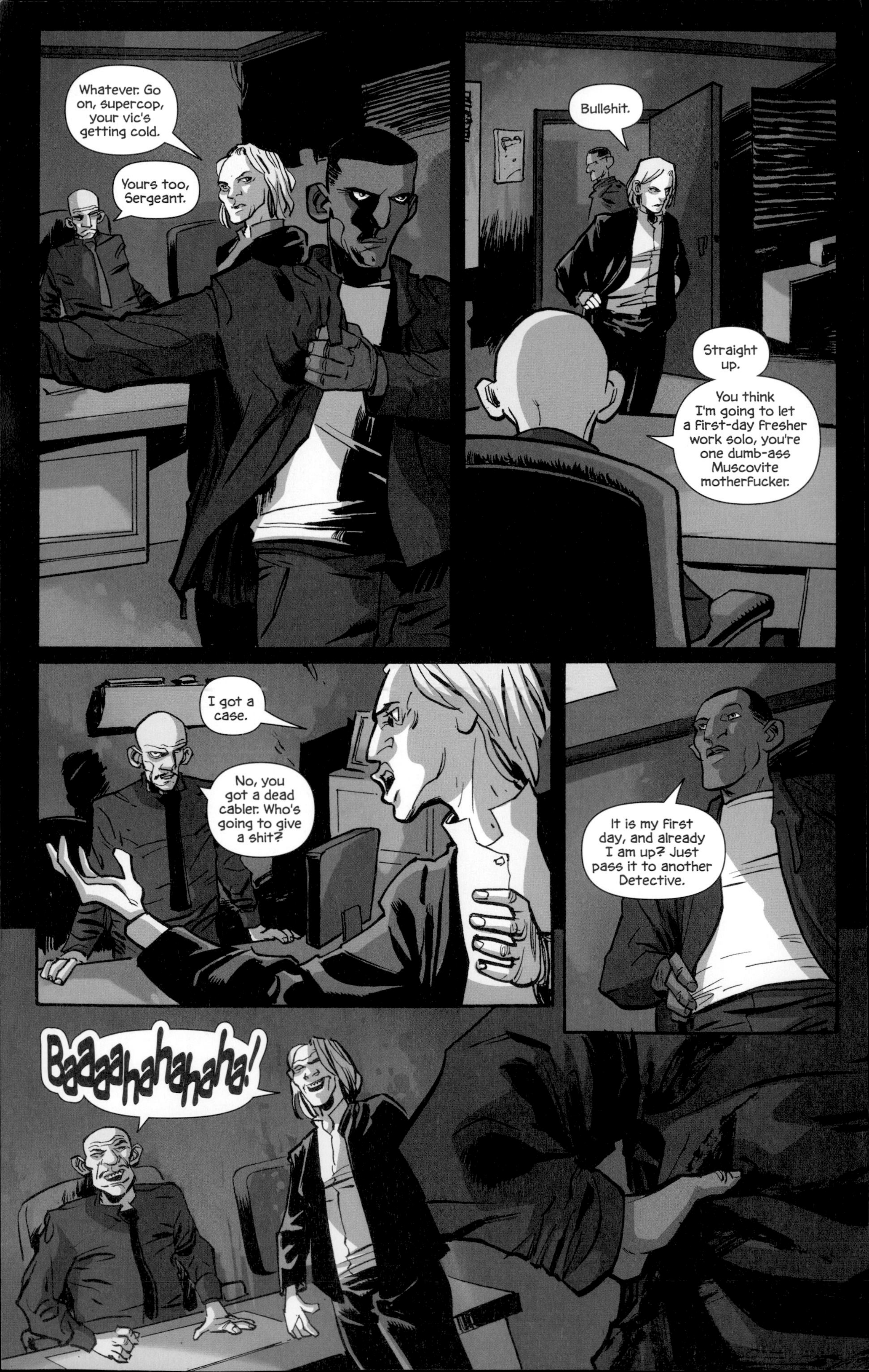
Whatever. Go on, supercop, your vic's getting cold.
Yours too, Sergeant.
Bullshit.
Straight up.
You think I'm going to let a first-day fresher work solo, you're one dumb-ass Muscovite motherfucker.
I got a case.
No, you got a dead cabler. Who's going to give a shit?
It is my first day, and already I am up? Just pass it to another Detective.
Baaaahahahaha!

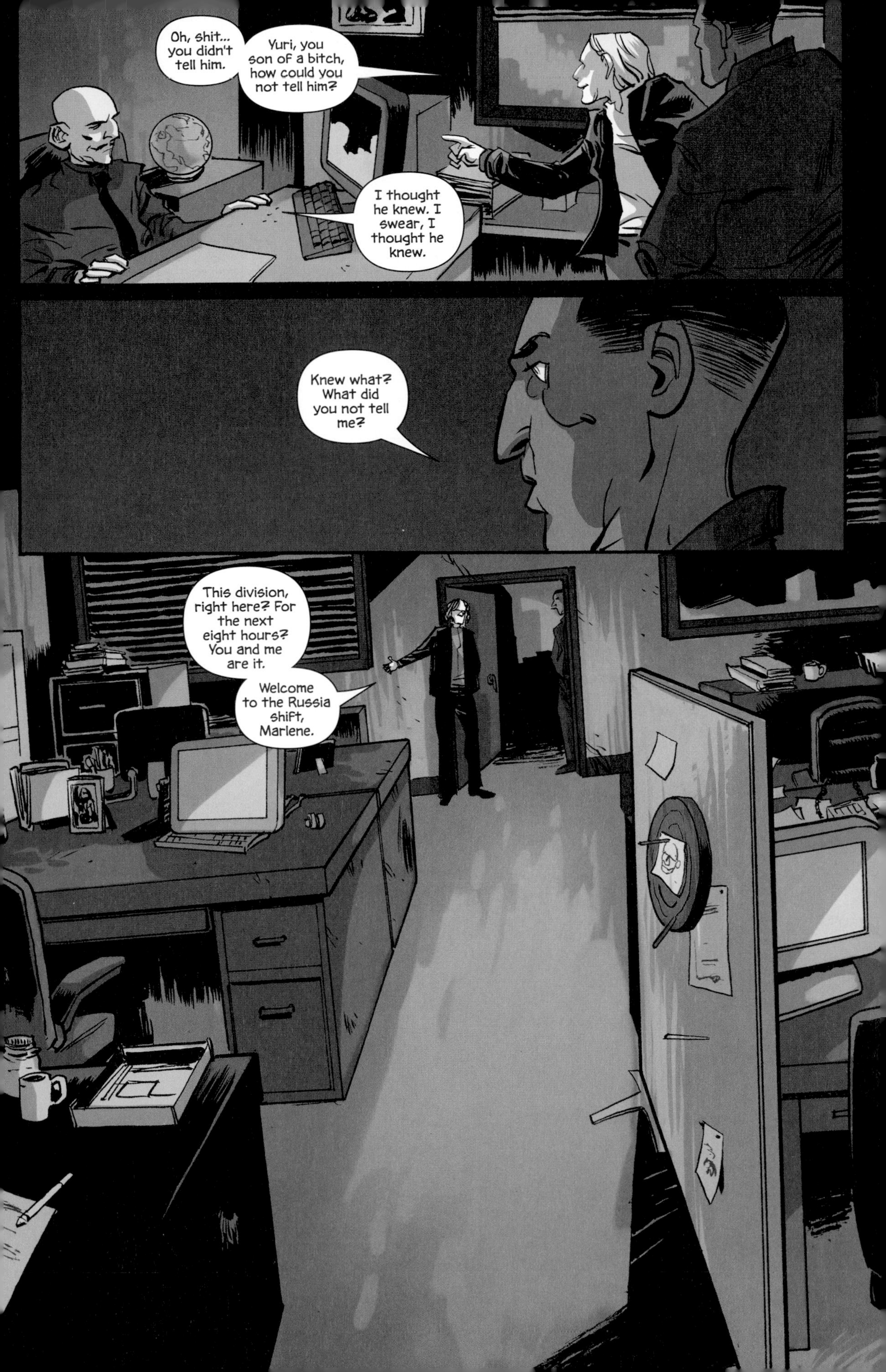
Oh, shit... you didn't tell him.
Yuri, you son of a bitch, how could you not tell him?
I thought he knew. I swear, I thought he knew.
Knew what? What did you not tell me?
This division, right here? For the next eight hours? You and me are it.
Welcome to the Russia shift, Marlene.

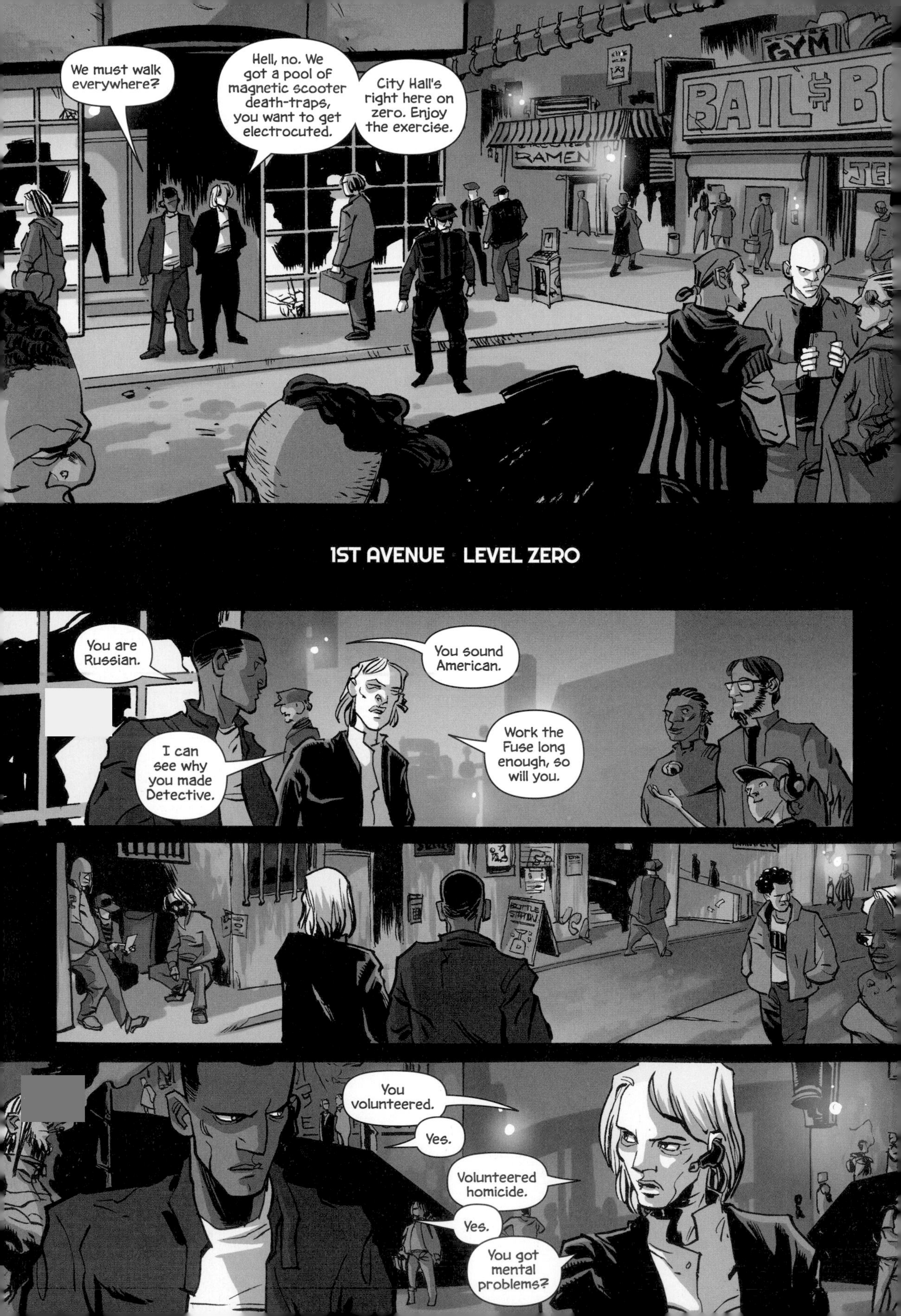
GYM
RAMEN
We must walk everywhere?
Hell, no. We got a pool of magnetic scooter death-traps, you want to get electrocuted.
City Hall's right here on zero. Enjoy the exercise.
1ST AVENUE LEVEL ZERO
You are Russian.
You sound American.
I can see why you made Detective.
Work the Fuse long enough, so will you.
You volunteered.
Yes.
Volunteered homicide.
Yes.
You got mental problems?

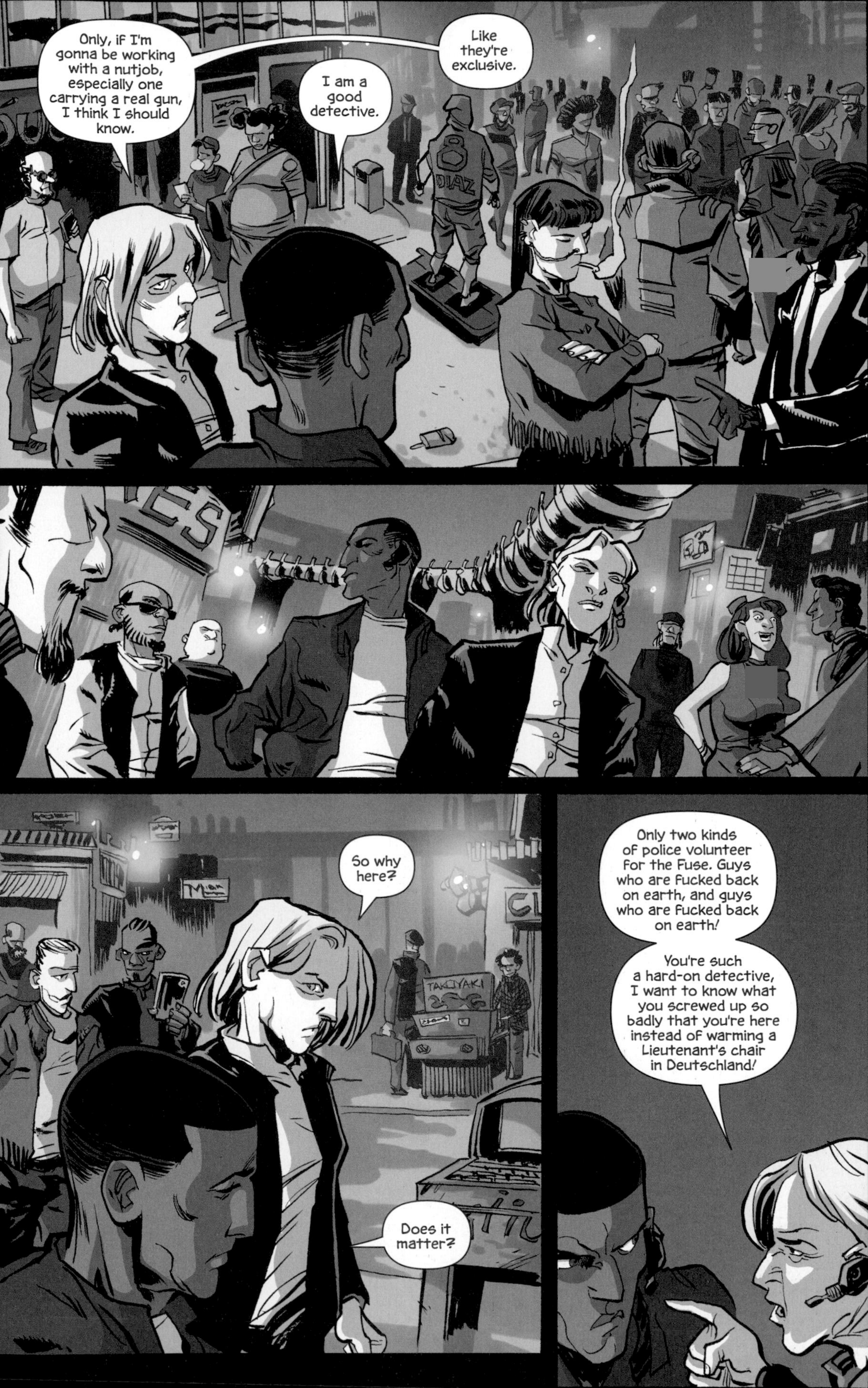
Only, if I'm gonna be working with a nutjob, especially one carrying a real gun, I think I should know.
Like they're exclusive.
I am a good detective.
DIAZ
So why here?
TAKOYAKI
Does it matter?
Only two kinds of police volunteer for the Fuse. Guys who are fucked back on earth, and guys who are fucked back on earth!
You're such a hard-on detective, I want to know what you screwed up so badly that you're here instead of warming a Lieutenant's chair in Deutschland!

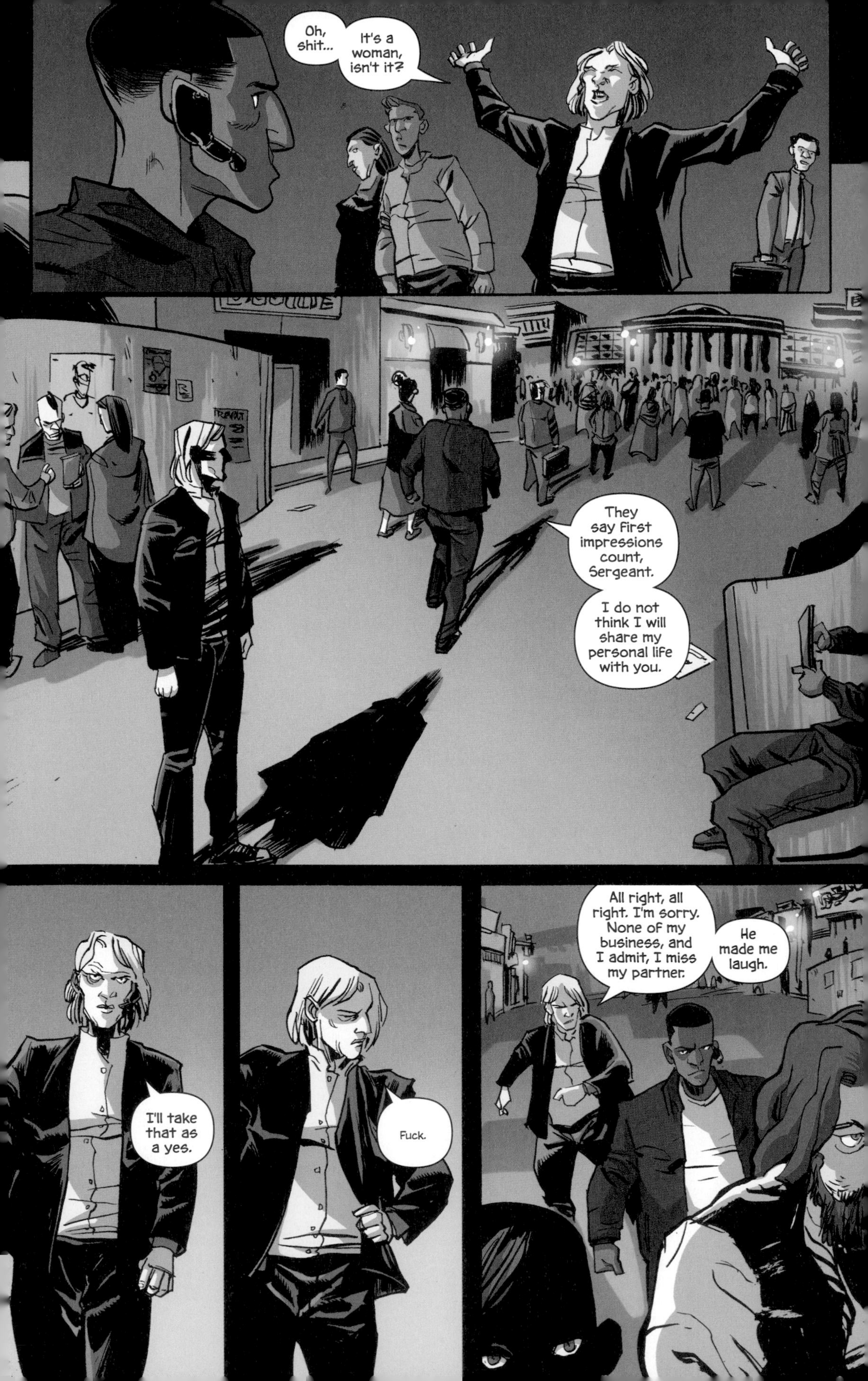
Oh, shit...
It's a woman, isn't it?
They say first impressions count, Sergeant.
I do not think I will share my personal life with you.
I'll take that as a yes.
Fuck.
All right, all right. I'm sorry. None of my business, and I admit, I miss my partner.
He made me laugh.

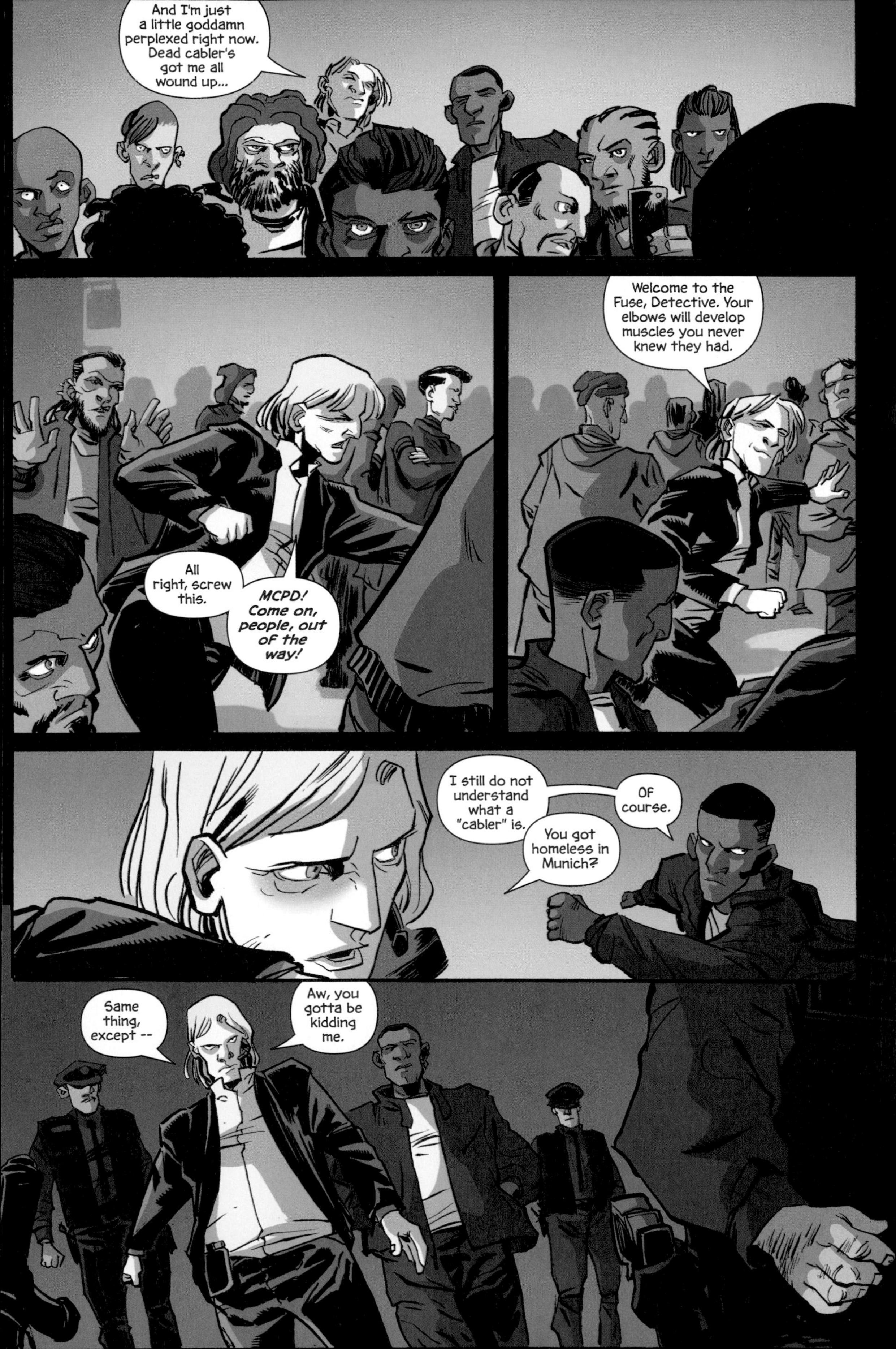
And I'm just a little goddamn perplexed right now. Dead cabler's got me all wound up...
All right, screw this.
MCPD! Come on, people, out of the way!
Welcome to the Fuse, Detective. Your elbows will develop muscles you never knew they had.
I still do not understand what a "cabler" is.
Of course.
You got homeless in Munich?
Same thing, except --
Aw, you gotta be kidding me.

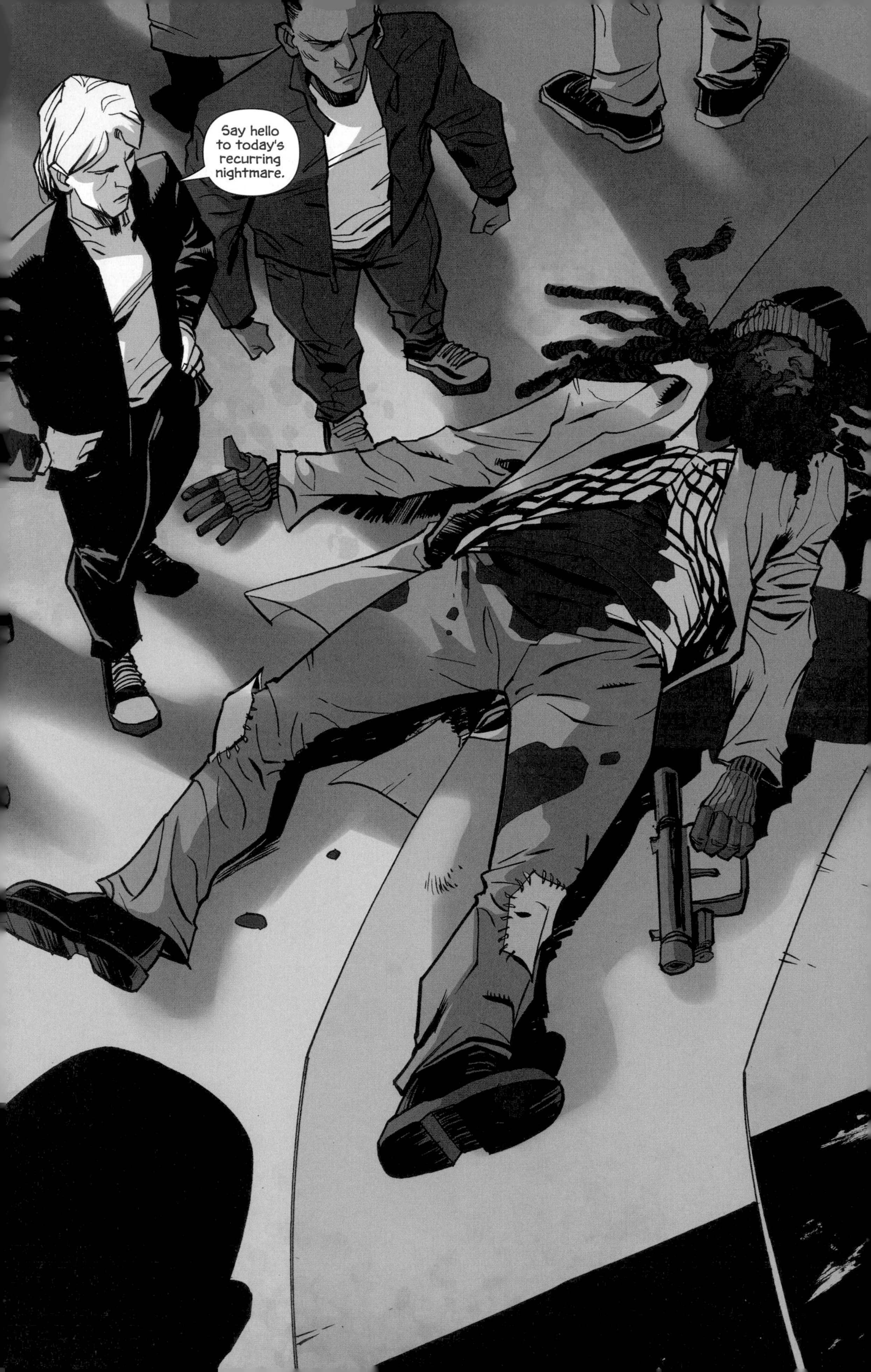
Say hello to today's recurring nightmare.

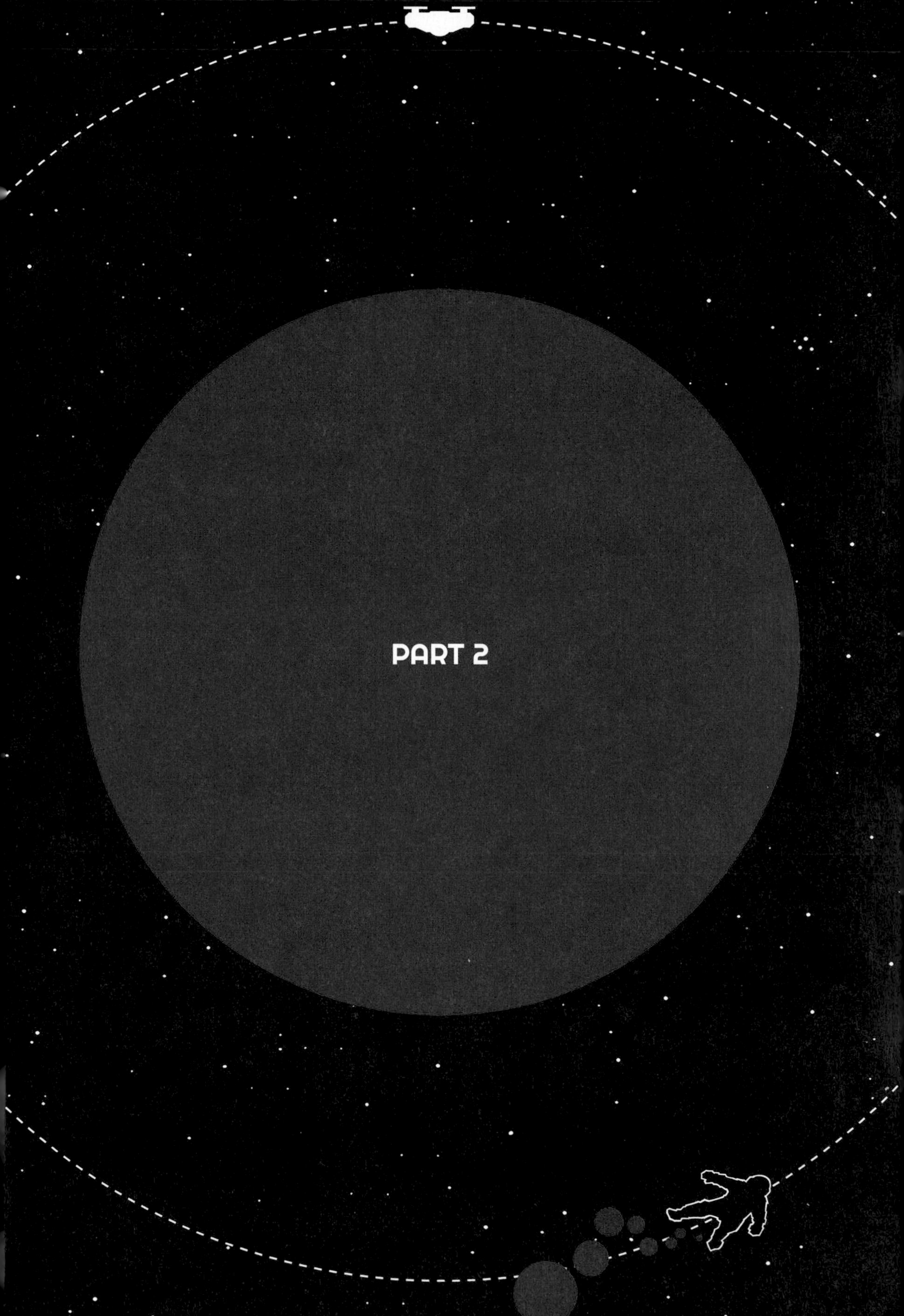

PART 2

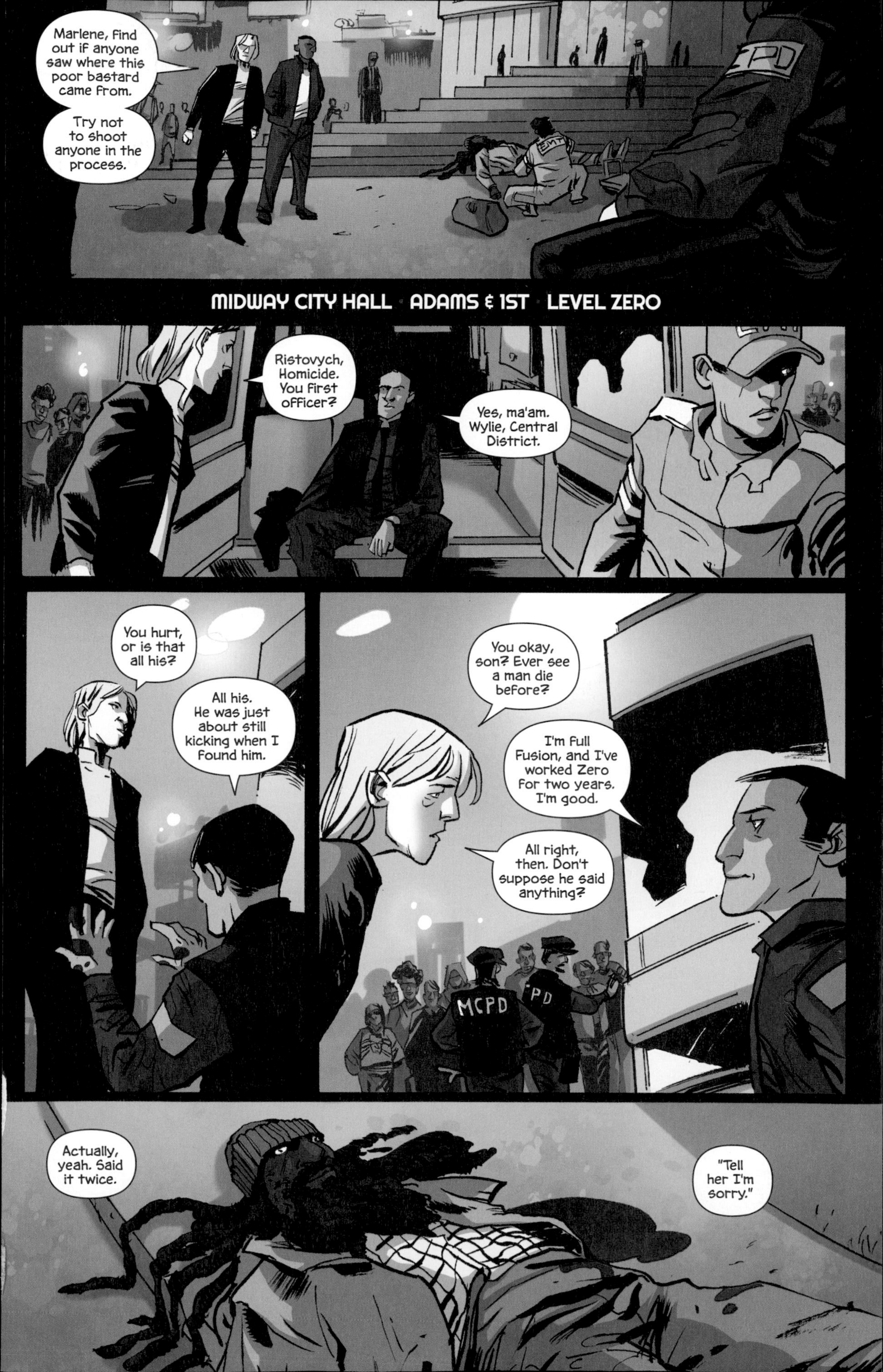

Marlene, find out if anyone saw where this poor bastard came from.
Try not to shoot anyone in the process.
MIDWAY CITY HALL ADAMS & 1ST LEVEL ZERO
Ristovych, Homicide. You first officer?
Yes, ma'am. Wylie, Central District.
You hurt, or is that all his?
All his. He was just about still kicking when I found him.
You okay, son? Ever see a man die before?
I'm full Fusion, and I've worked Zero for two years. I'm good.
All right, then. Don't suppose he said anything?
MCPD
Actually, yeah. Said it twice.
"Tell her I'm sorry."

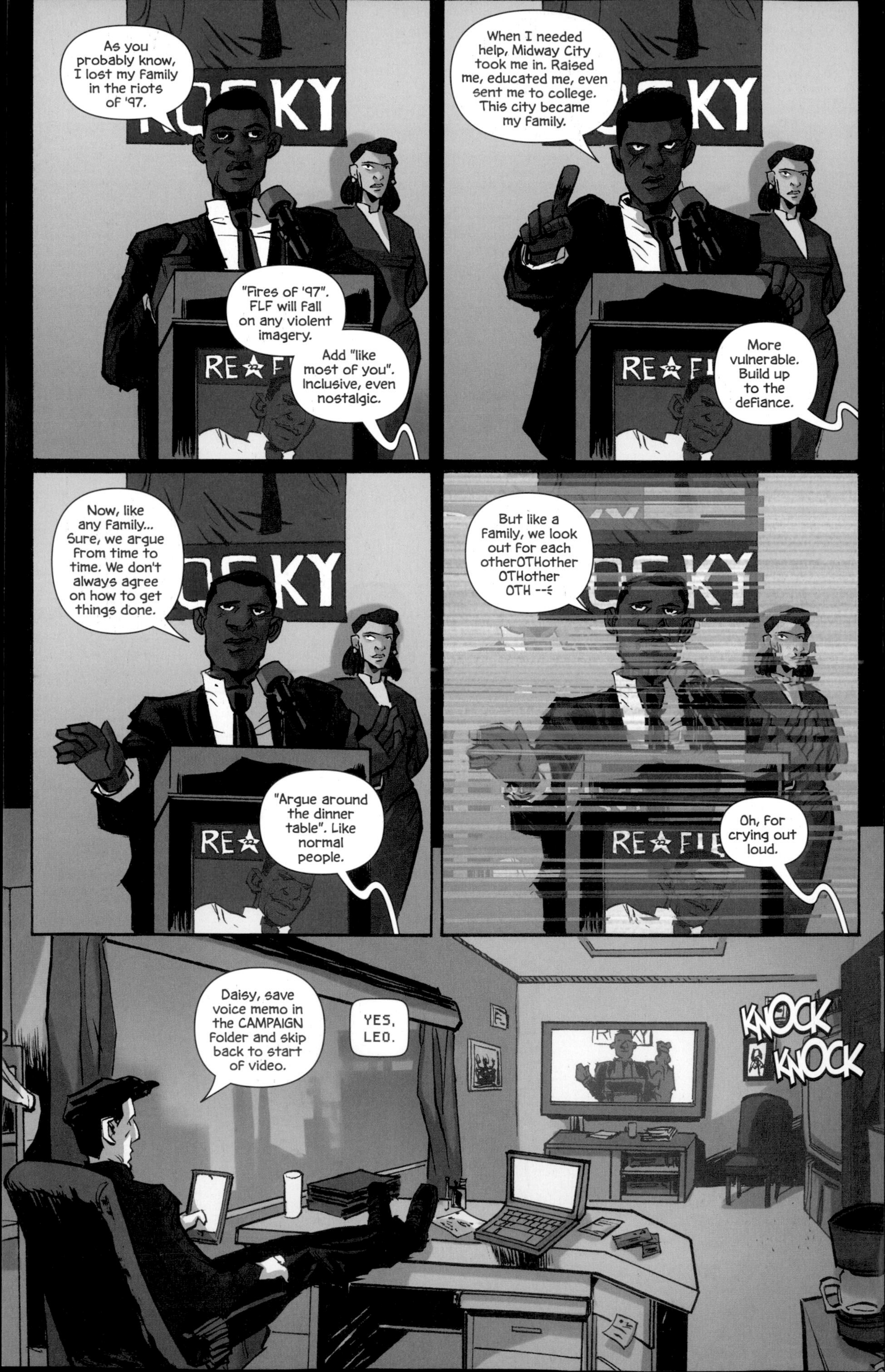

As you probably know, I lost my family in the riots of '97.
"Fires of '97". FLF will fall on any violent imagery.
Add "like most of you". Inclusive, even nostalgic.
When I needed help, Midway City took me in. Raised me, educated me, even sent me to college. This city became my family.
More vulnerable. Build up to the defiance.
Now, like any family... Sure, we argue from time to time. We don't always agree on how to get things done.
"Argue around the dinner table". Like normal people.
But like a family, we look out for each otherOTHother OTHother OTH --
Oh, for crying out loud.
Daisy, save voice memo in the CAMPAIGN folder and skip back to start of video.
YES, LEO.
KNOCK KNOCK

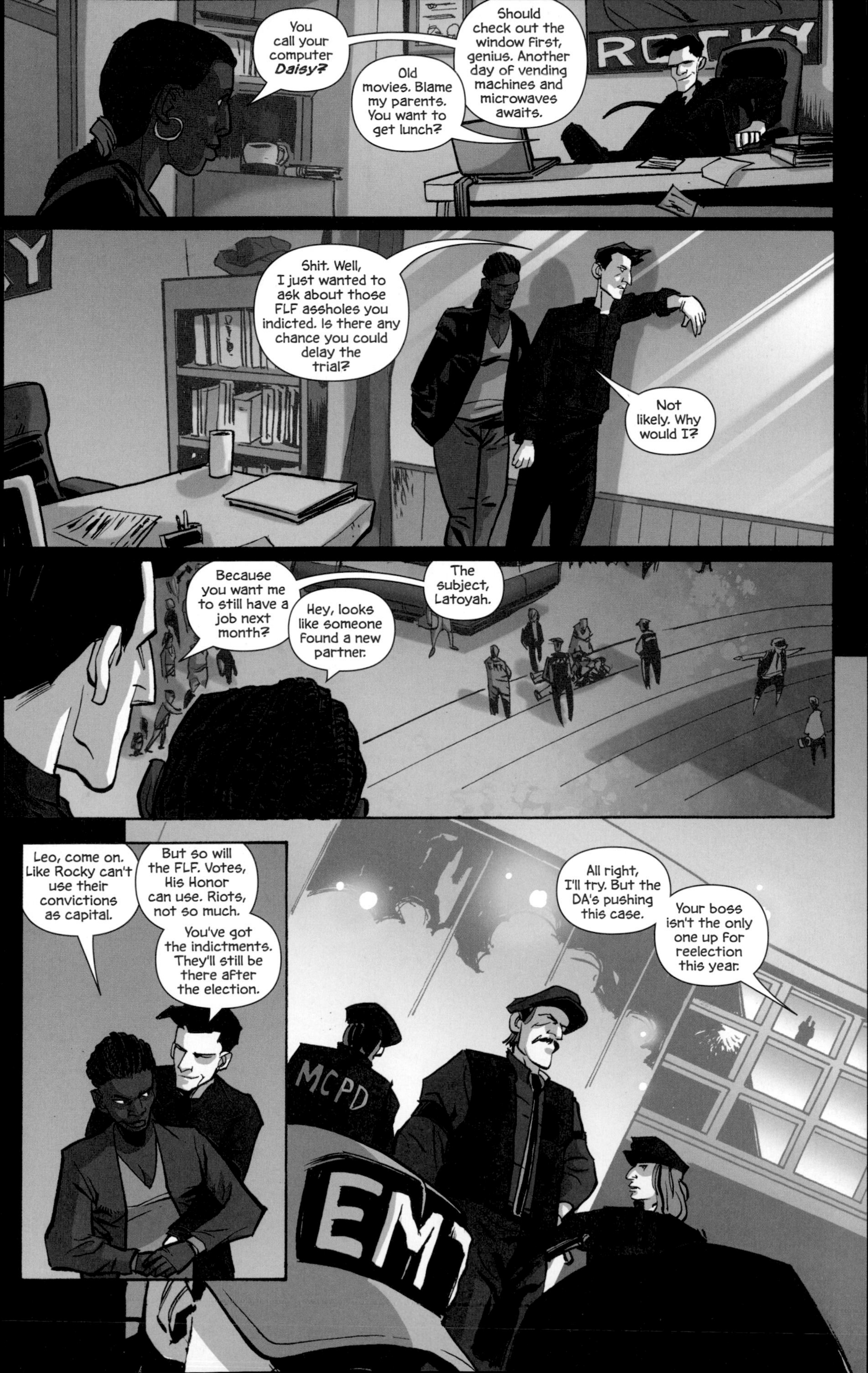
You call your computer Daisy?
Should check out the window first, genius. Another day of vending machines and microwaves awaits.
Old movies. Blame my parents. You want to get lunch?
ROCKY
Shit. Well, I just wanted to ask about those FLF assholes you indicted. Is there any chance you could delay the trial?
Not likely. Why would I?
Because you want me to still have a job next month?
The subject, Latoyah.
Hey, looks like someone found a new partner.
Leo, come on. Like Rocky can't use their convictions as capital.
But so will the FLF. Votes, His Honor can use. Riots, not so much.
You've got the indictments. They'll still be there after the election.
All right, I'll try. But the DA's pushing this case.
Your boss isn't the only one up for reelection this year.
MCPD

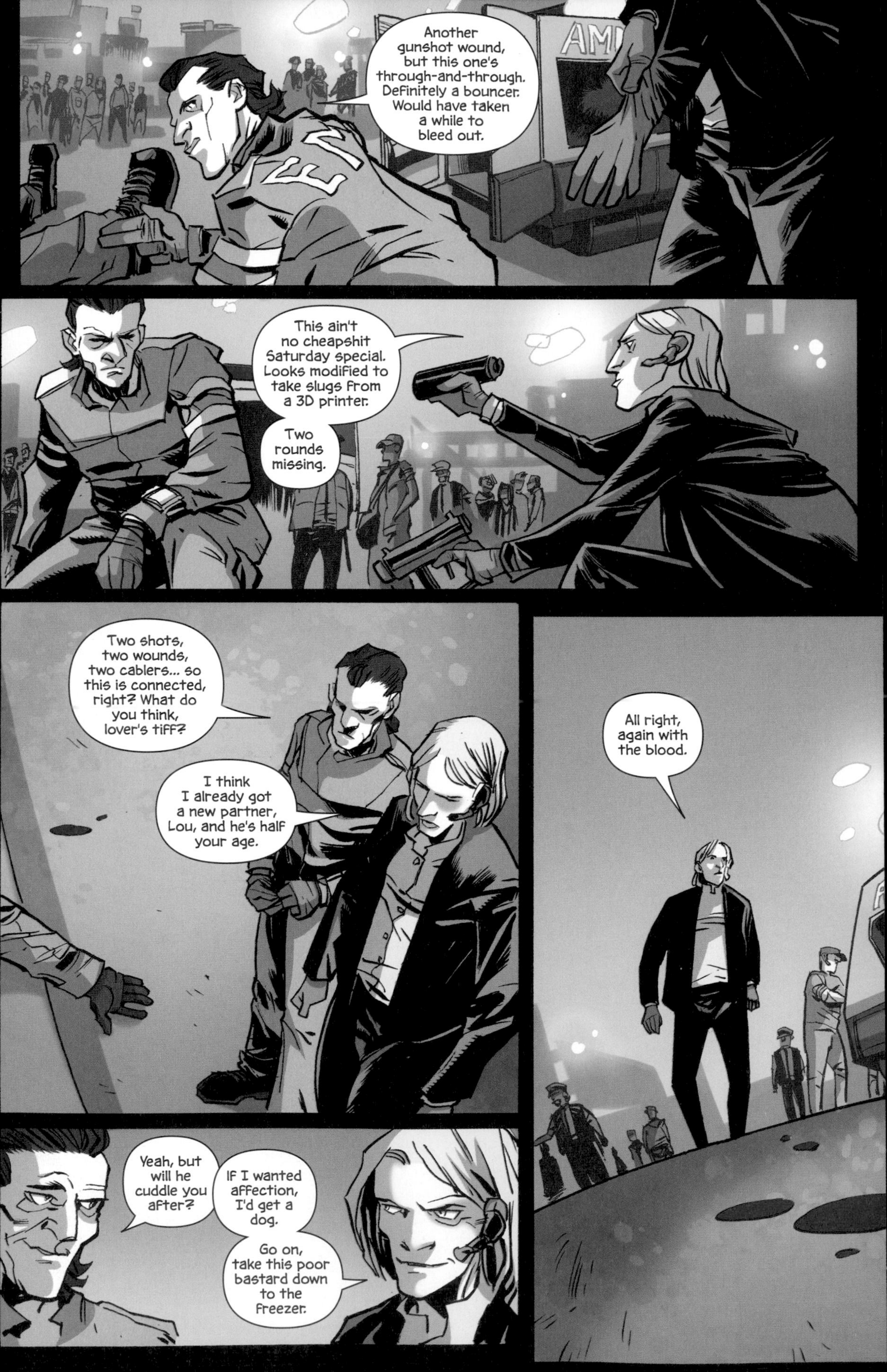
Another gunshot wound, but this one's through-and-through. Definitely a bouncer. Would have taken a while to bleed out.
AM
This ain't no cheapshit Saturday special. Looks modified to take slugs from a 3D printer.
Two rounds missing.
Two shots, two wounds, two cablers... so this is connected, right? What do you think, lover's tiff?
I think I already got a new partner, Lou, and he's half your age.
Yeah, but will he cuddle you after?
If I wanted affection, I'd get a dog.
Go on, take this poor bastard down to the freezer.
All right, again with the blood.

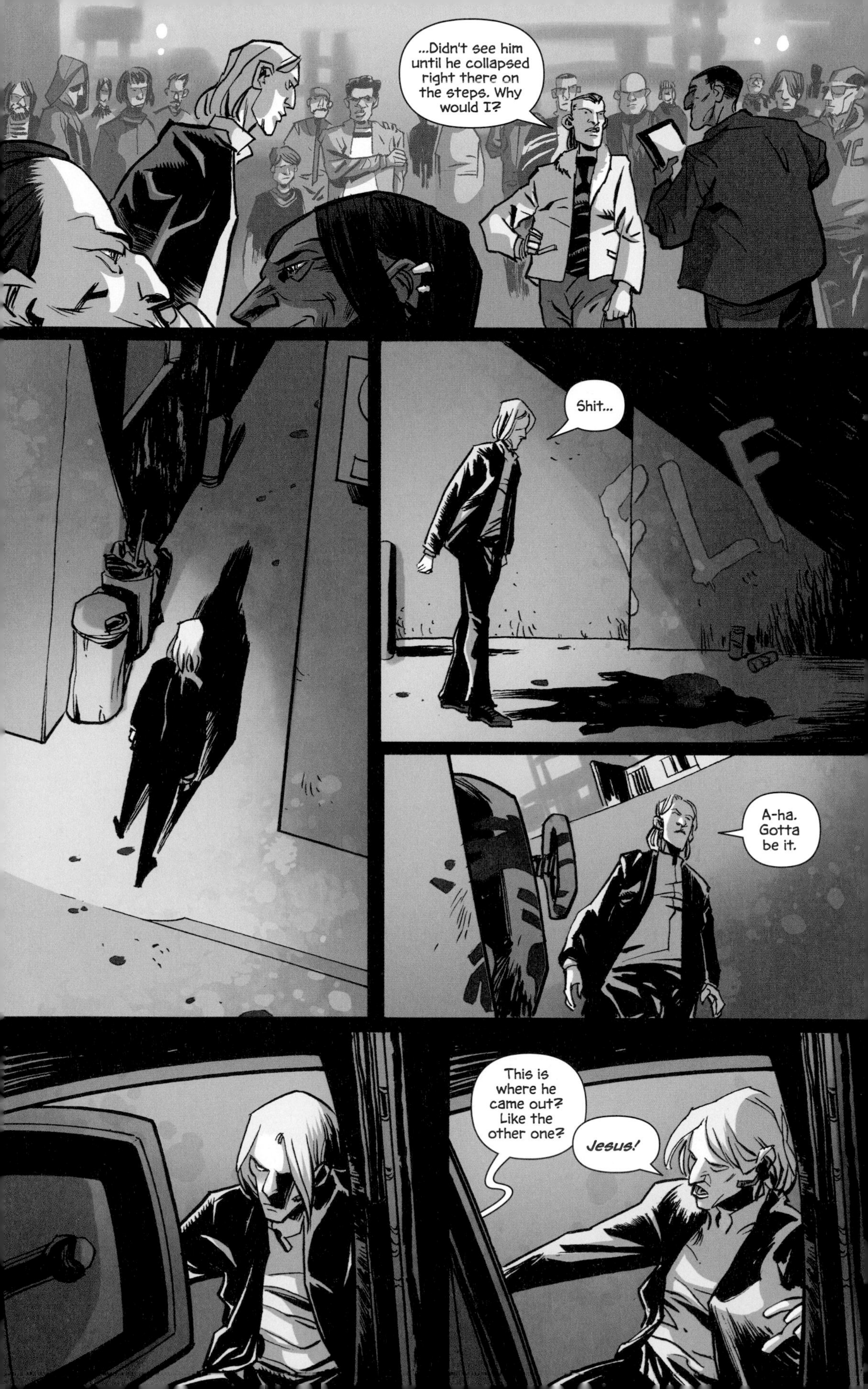
...Didn't see him until he collapsed right there on the steps. Why would I?
Shit...
A-ha. Gotta be it.
This is where he came out? Like the other one?
Jesus!

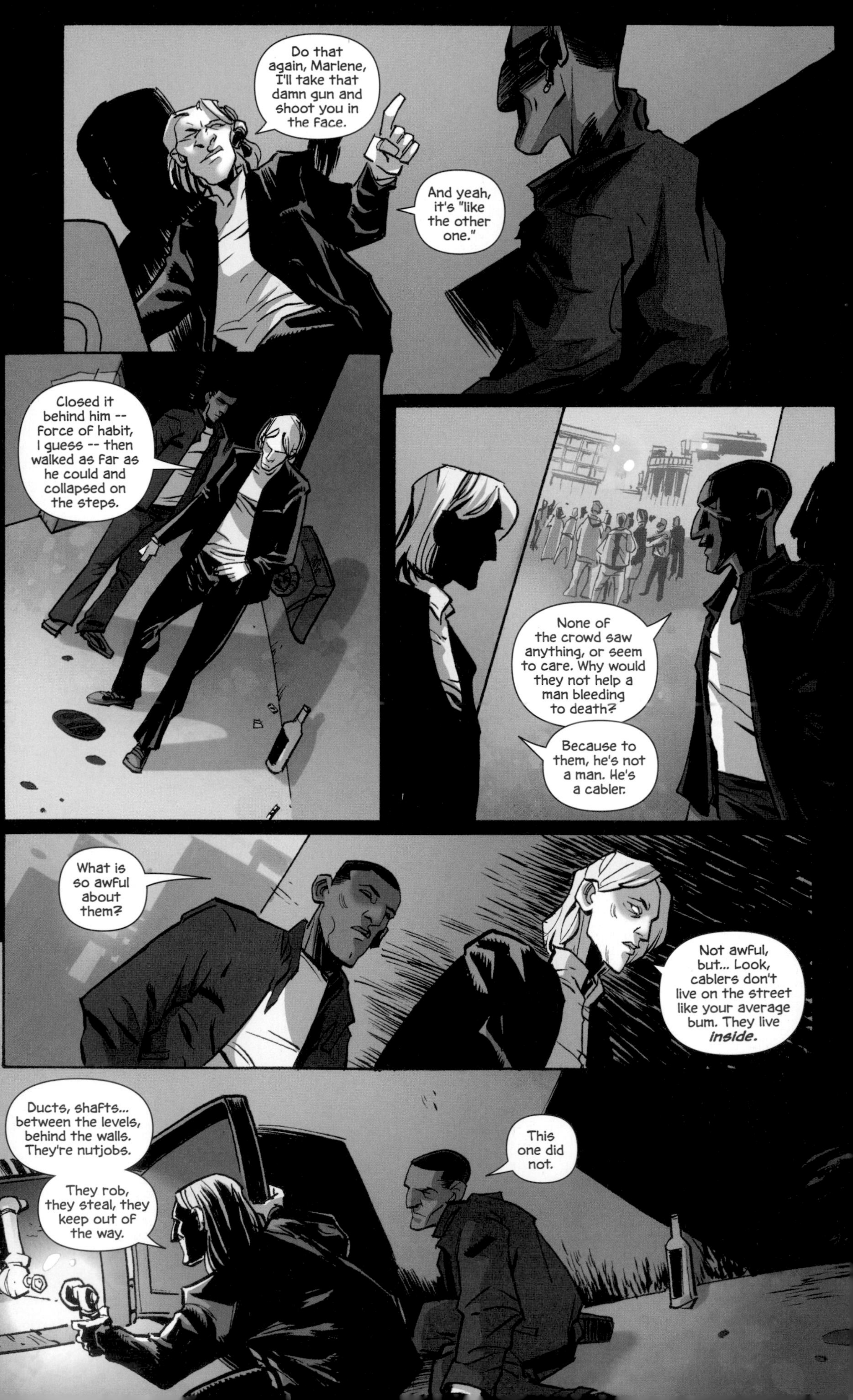
Do that again, Marlene, I'll take that damn gun and shoot you in the face.
And yeah, it's "like the other one."
Closed it behind him -- force of habit, I guess -- then walked as far as he could and collapsed on the steps.
None of the crowd saw anything, or seem to care. Why would they not help a man bleeding to death?
Because to them, he's not a man. He's a cabler.
What is so awful about them?
Not awful, but... Look, cablers don't live on the street like your average bum. They live *inside.*
Ducts, shafts... between the levels, behind the walls. They're nutjobs.
They rob, they steal, they keep out of the way.
This one did not.

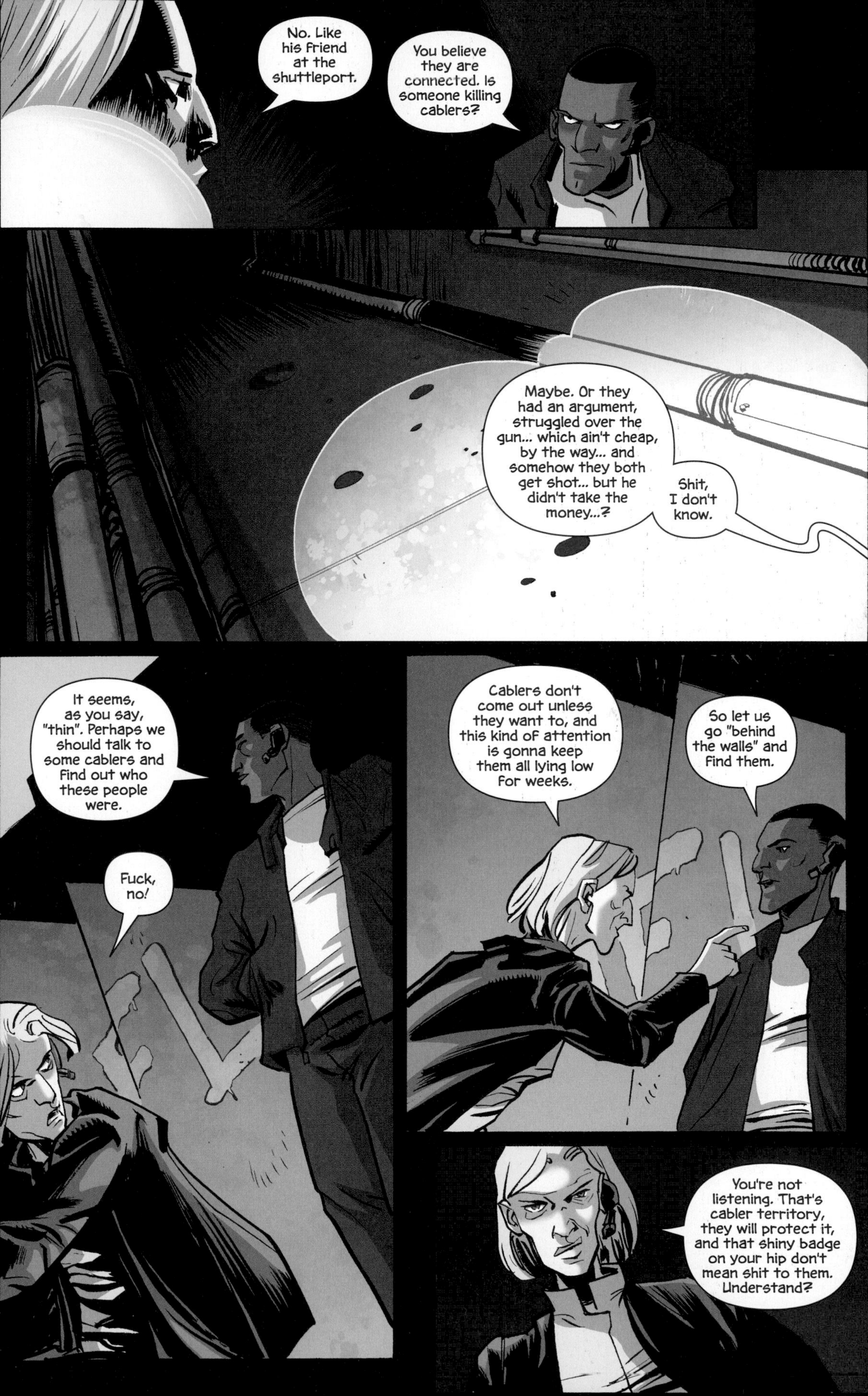
No. Like his friend at the shuttleport.
You believe they are connected. Is someone killing cablers?
Maybe. Or they had an argument, struggled over the gun... which ain't cheap, by the way... and somehow they both get shot... but he didn't take the money...?
Shit, I don't know.
It seems, as you say, "thin". Perhaps we should talk to some cablers and find out who these people were.
Fuck, no!
Cablers don't come out unless they want to, and this kind of attention is gonna keep them all lying low for weeks.
So let us go "behind the walls" and find them.
You're not listening. That's cabler territory, they will protect it, and that shiny badge on your hip don't mean shit to them. Understand?

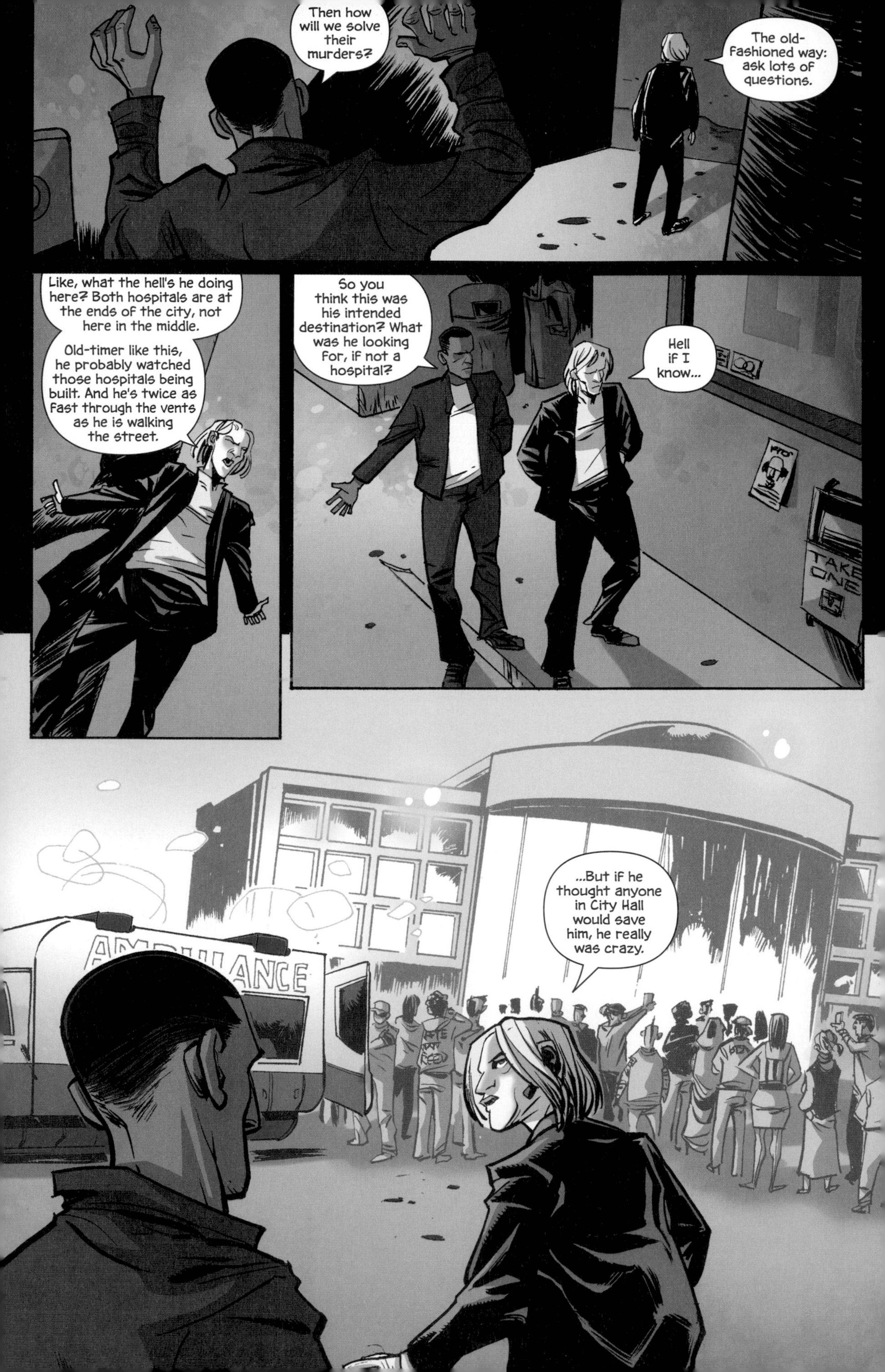
Then how will we solve their murders?
The old-fashioned way: ask lots of questions.
Like, what the hell's he doing here? Both hospitals are at the ends of the city, not here in the middle.
Old-timer like this, he probably watched those hospitals being built. And he's twice as fast through the vents as he is walking the street.
So you think this was his intended destination? What was he looking for, if not a hospital?
Hell if I know...
TAKE ONE
AMBULANCE
...But if he thought anyone in City Hall would save him, he really was crazy.

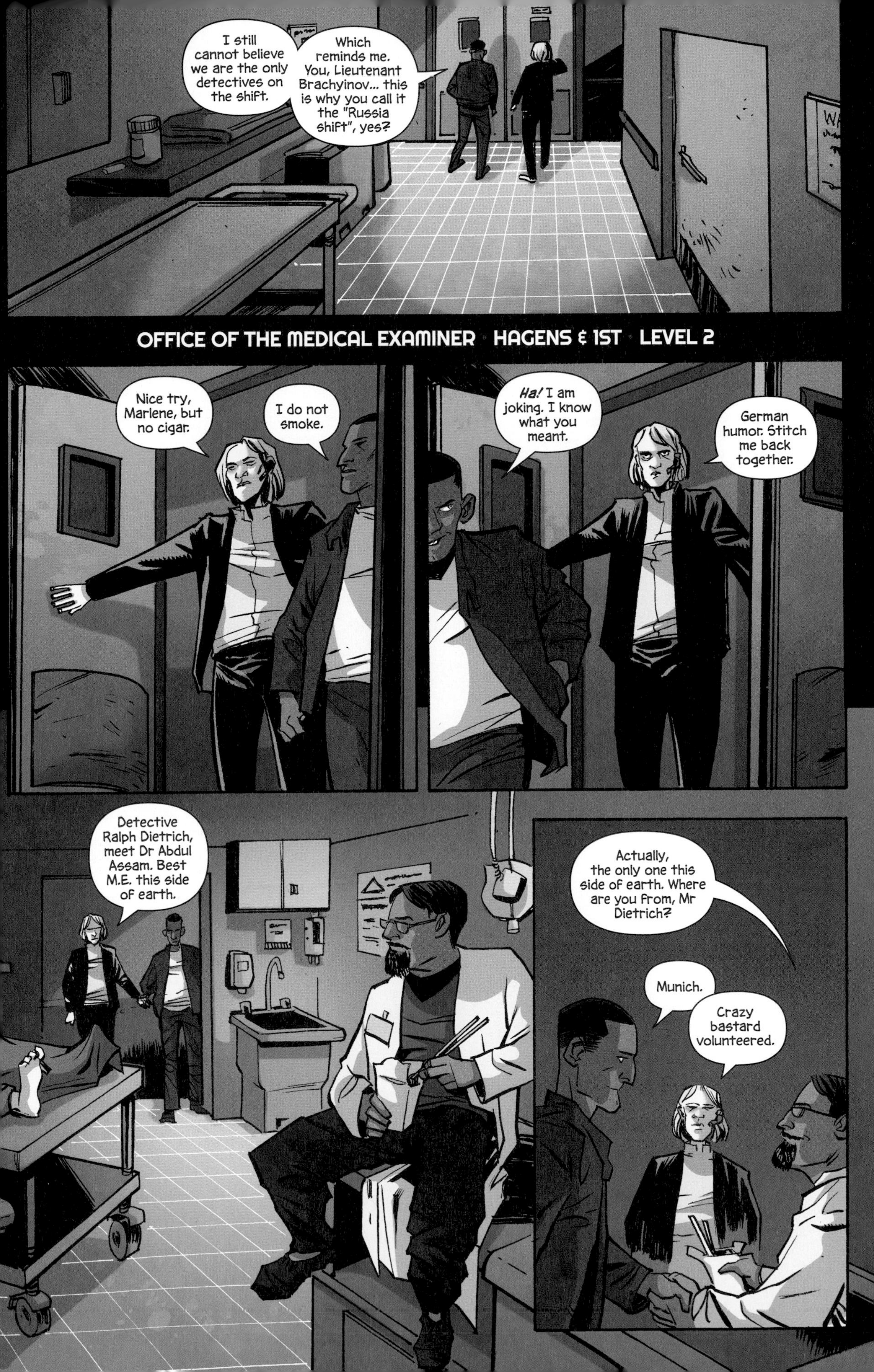
I still cannot believe we are the only detectives on the shift.
Which reminds me. You, Lieutenant Brachyinov... this is why you call it the "Russia shift", yes?
OFFICE OF THE MEDICAL EXAMINER · HAGENS & 1ST · LEVEL 2
Nice try, Marlene, but no cigar.
I do not smoke.
Ha! I am joking. I know what you meant.
German humor. Stitch me back together.
Detective Ralph Dietrich, meet Dr Abdul Assam. Best M.E. this side of earth.
Actually, the only one this side of earth. Where are you from, Mr Dietrich?
Munich.
Crazy bastard volunteered.

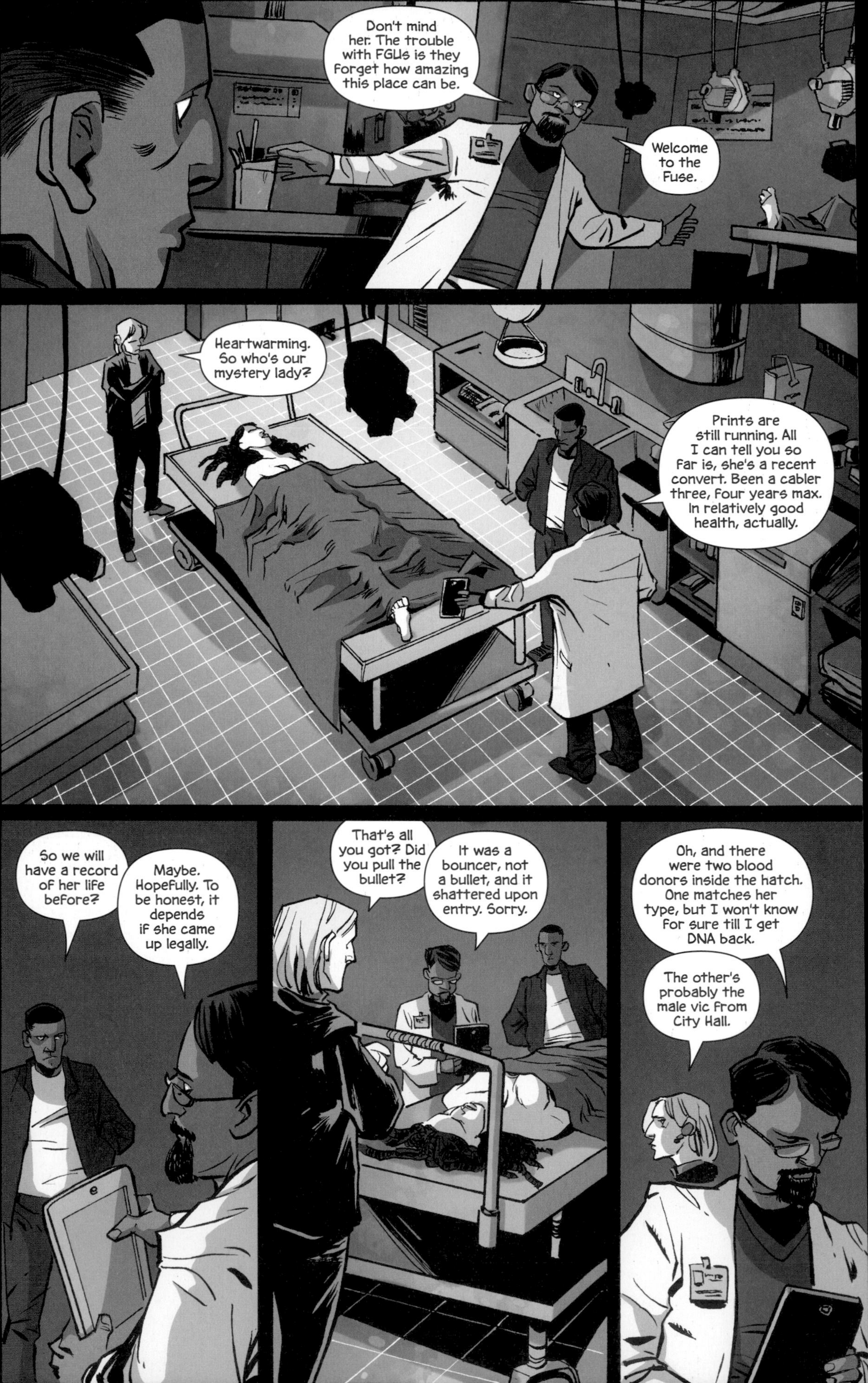
Don't mind her. The trouble with FGUs is they forget how amazing this place can be.
Welcome to the Fuse.
Heartwarming. So who's our mystery lady?
Prints are still running. All I can tell you so far is, she's a recent convert. Been a cabler three, four years max. In relatively good health, actually.
So we will have a record of her life before?
Maybe. Hopefully. To be honest, it depends if she came up legally.
That's all you got? Did you pull the bullet?
It was a bouncer, not a bullet, and it shattered upon entry. Sorry.
Oh, and there were two blood donors inside the hatch. One matches her type, but I won't know for sure till I get DNA back.
The other's probably the male vic from City Hall.

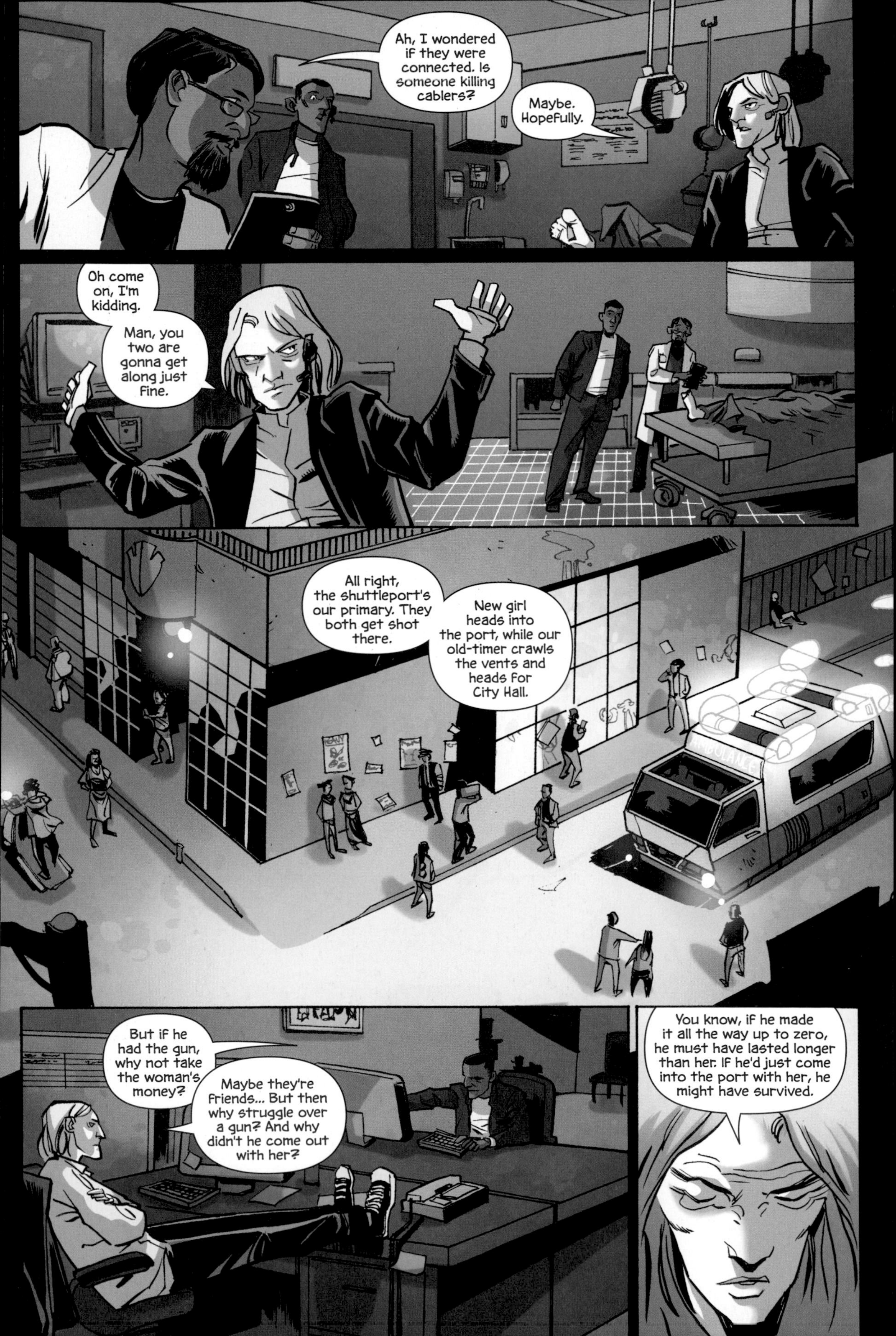
Ah, I wondered if they were connected. Is someone killing cablers?
Maybe. Hopefully.
Oh come on, I'm kidding.
Man, you two are gonna get along just fine.
All right, the shuttleport's our primary. They both get shot there.
New girl heads into the port, while our old-timer crawls the vents and heads for City Hall.
AMBULANCE
But if he had the gun, why not take the woman's money?
Maybe they're friends... But then why struggle over a gun? And why didn't he come out with her?
You know, if he made it all the way up to zero, he must have lasted longer than her. If he'd just come into the port with her, he might have survived.

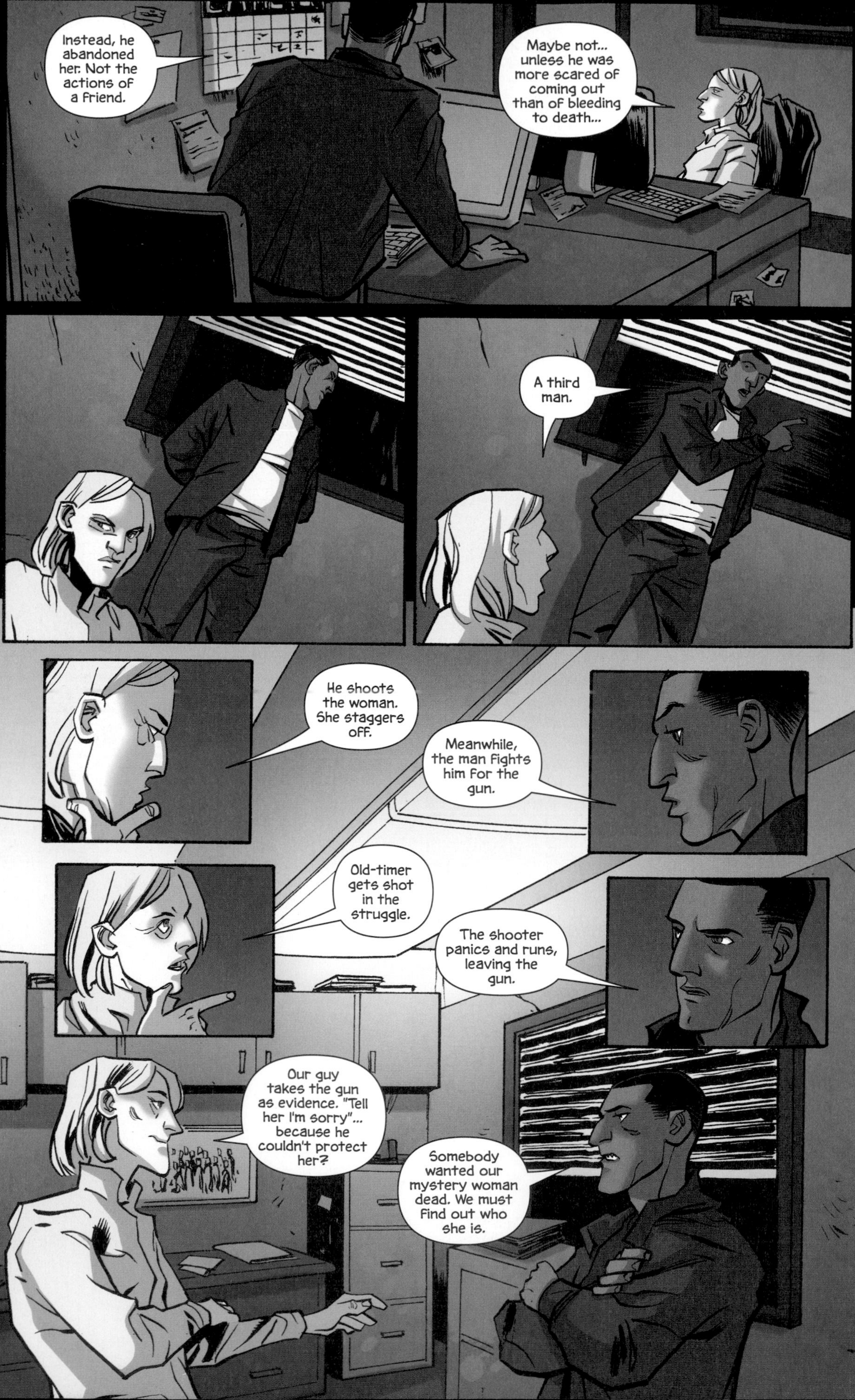
Instead, he abandoned her. Not the actions of a friend.
Maybe not... unless he was more scared of coming out than of bleeding to death...
A third man.
He shoots the woman. She staggers off.
Meanwhile, the man fights him for the gun.
Old-timer gets shot in the struggle.
The shooter panics and runs, leaving the gun.
Our guy takes the gun as evidence. "Tell her I'm sorry"... because he couldn't protect her?
Somebody wanted our mystery woman dead. We must find out who she is.

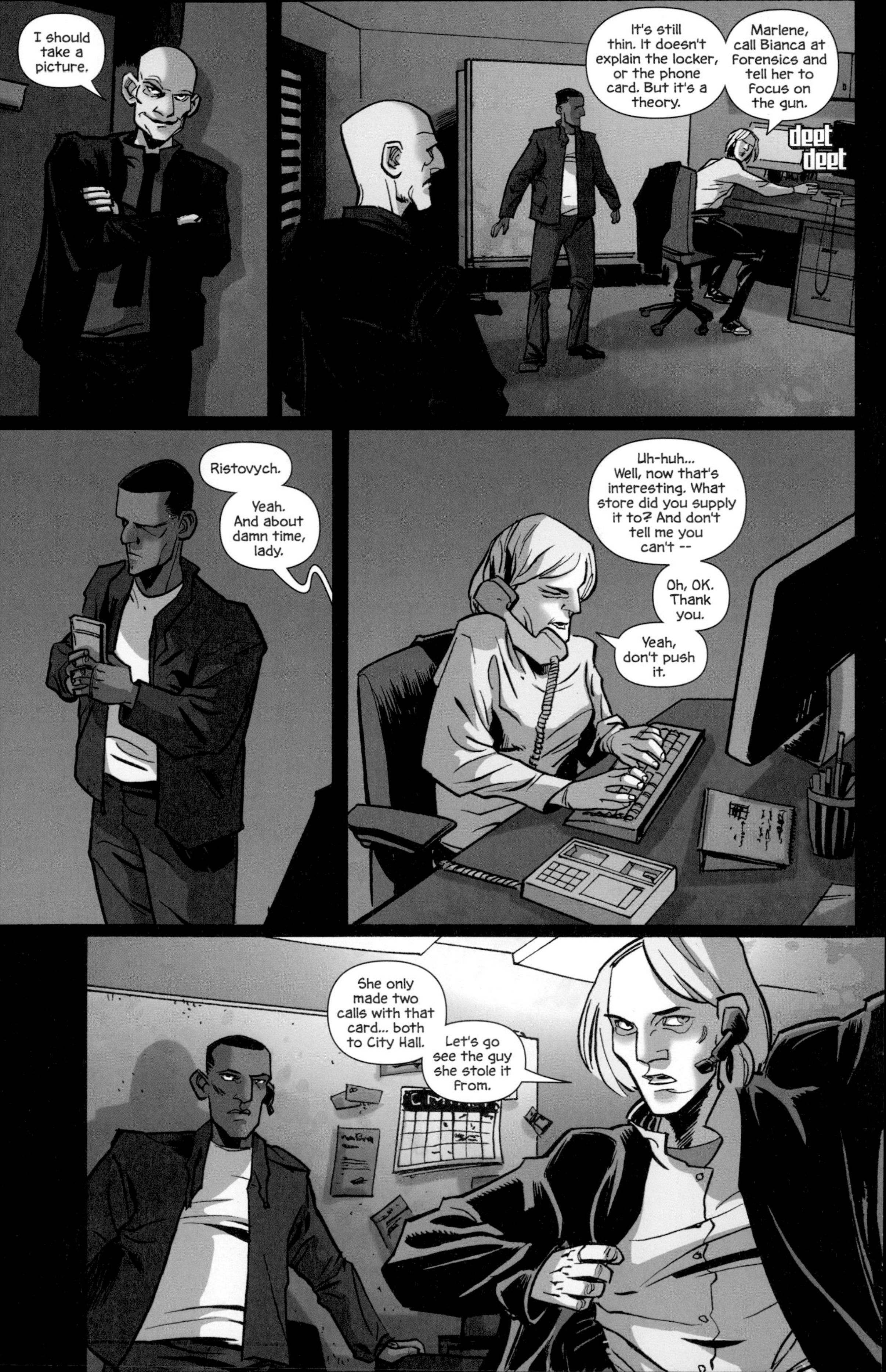

I should take a picture.
It's still thin. It doesn't explain the locker, or the phone card. But it's a theory.
Marlene, call Bianca at Forensics and tell her to focus on the gun.
deet deet
Ristovych.
Yeah. And about damn time, lady.
Uh-huh... Well, now that's interesting. What store did you supply it to? And don't tell me you can't --
Oh, OK. Thank you.
Yeah, don't push it.
She only made two calls with that card... both to City Hall.
Let's go see the guy she stole it from.

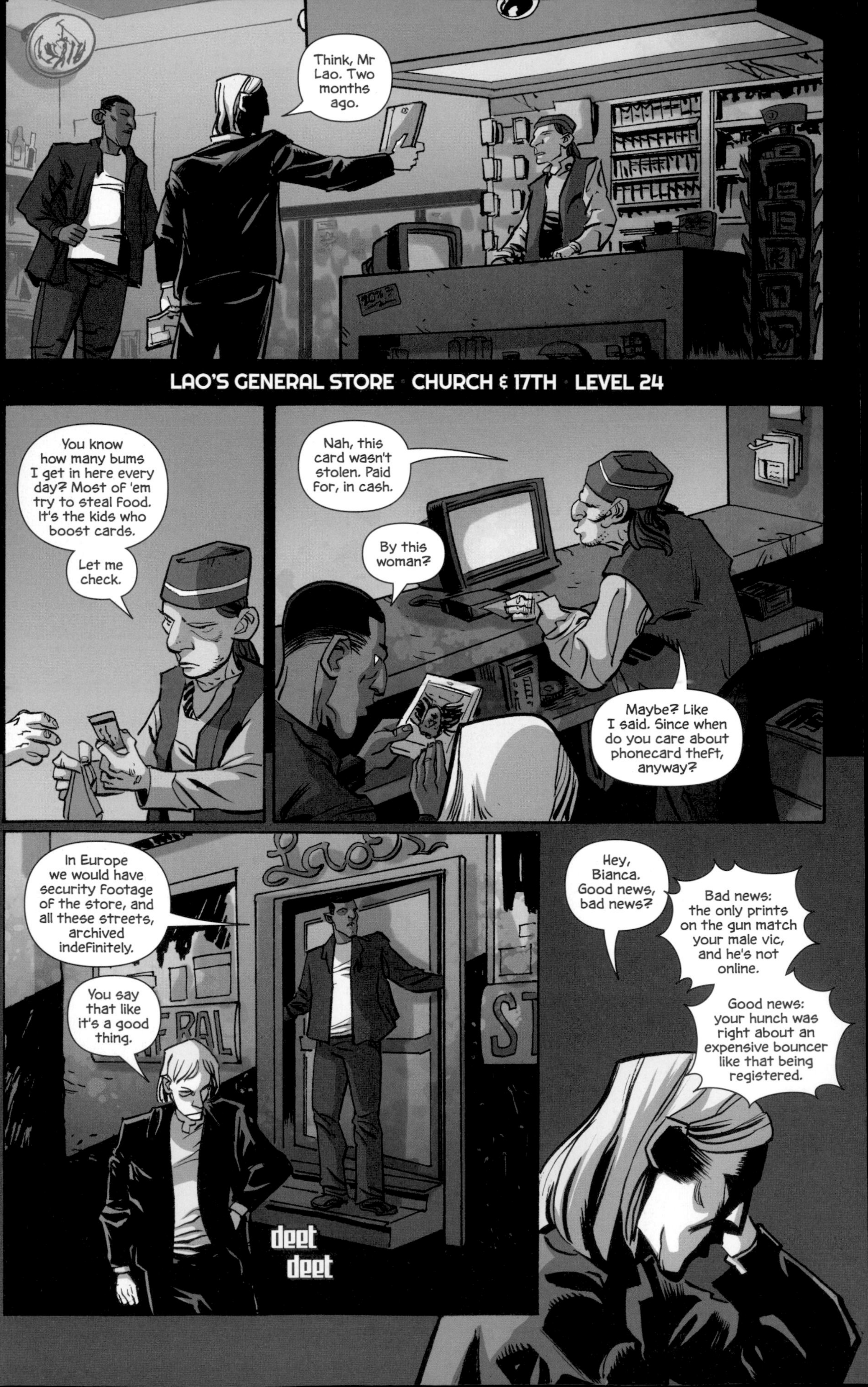
Think, Mr Lao. Two months ago.
LAO'S GENERAL STORE · CHURCH & 17TH · LEVEL 24
You know how many bums I get in here every day? Most of 'em try to steal food. It's the kids who boost cards.
Let me check.
Nah, this card wasn't stolen. Paid for, in cash.
By this woman?
Maybe? Like I said. Since when do you care about phonecard theft, anyway?
In Europe we would have security footage of the store, and all these streets, archived indefinitely.
You say that like it's a good thing.
deet
deet
Hey, Bianca. Good news, bad news?
Bad news: the only prints on the gun match your male vic, and he's not online.
Good news: your hunch was right about an expensive bouncer like that being registered.

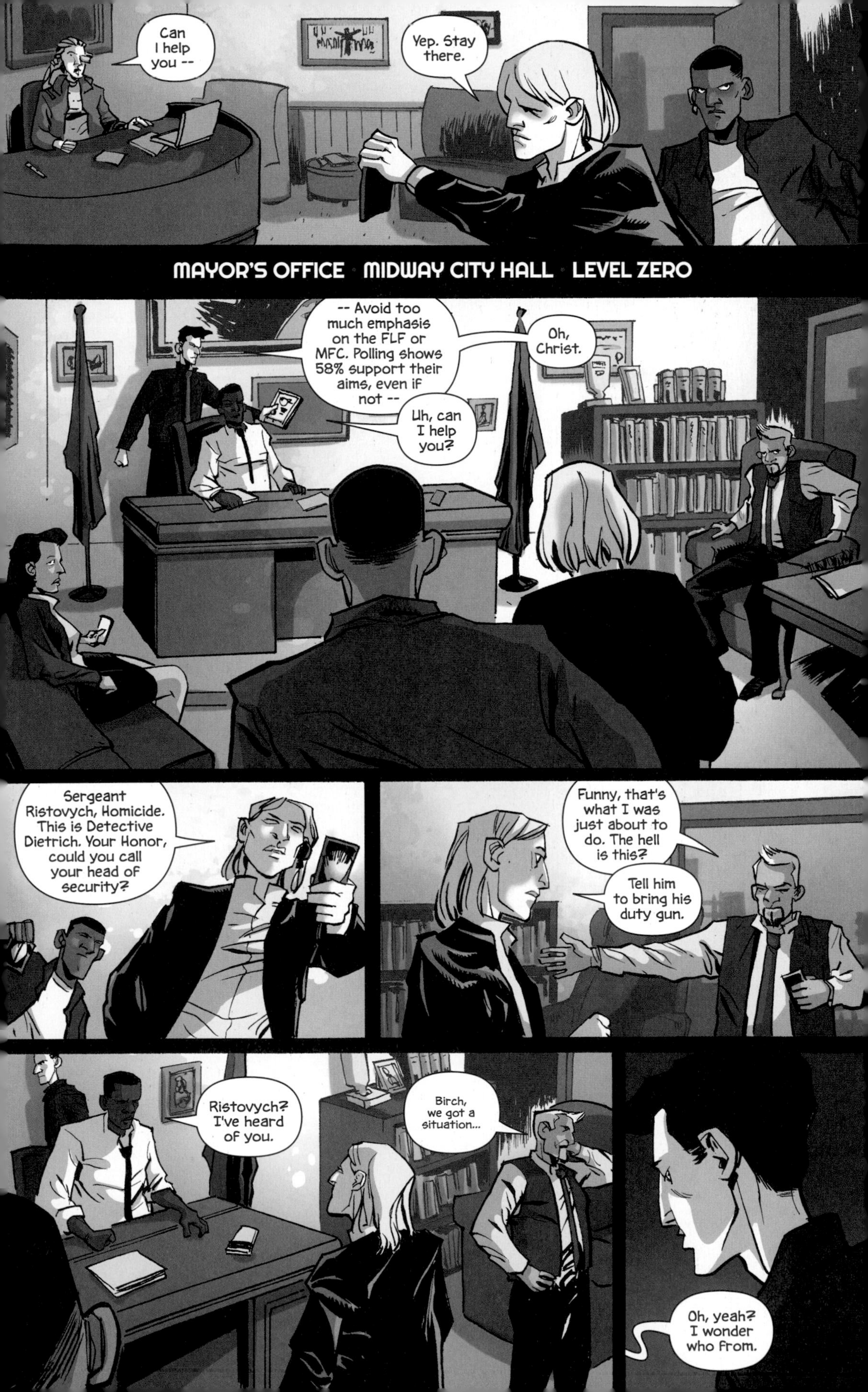
Can I help you --
Yep. Stay there.
MAYOR'S OFFICE · MIDWAY CITY HALL · LEVEL ZERO
-- Avoid too much emphasis on the FLF or MFC. Polling shows 58% support their aims, even if not --
Oh, Christ.
Uh, can I help you?
Sergeant Ristovych, Homicide. This is Detective Dietrich. Your Honor, could you call your head of security?
Funny, that's what I was just about to do. The hell is this?
Tell him to bring his duty gun.
Ristovych? I've heard of you.
Birch, we got a situation...
Oh, yeah? I wonder who from.

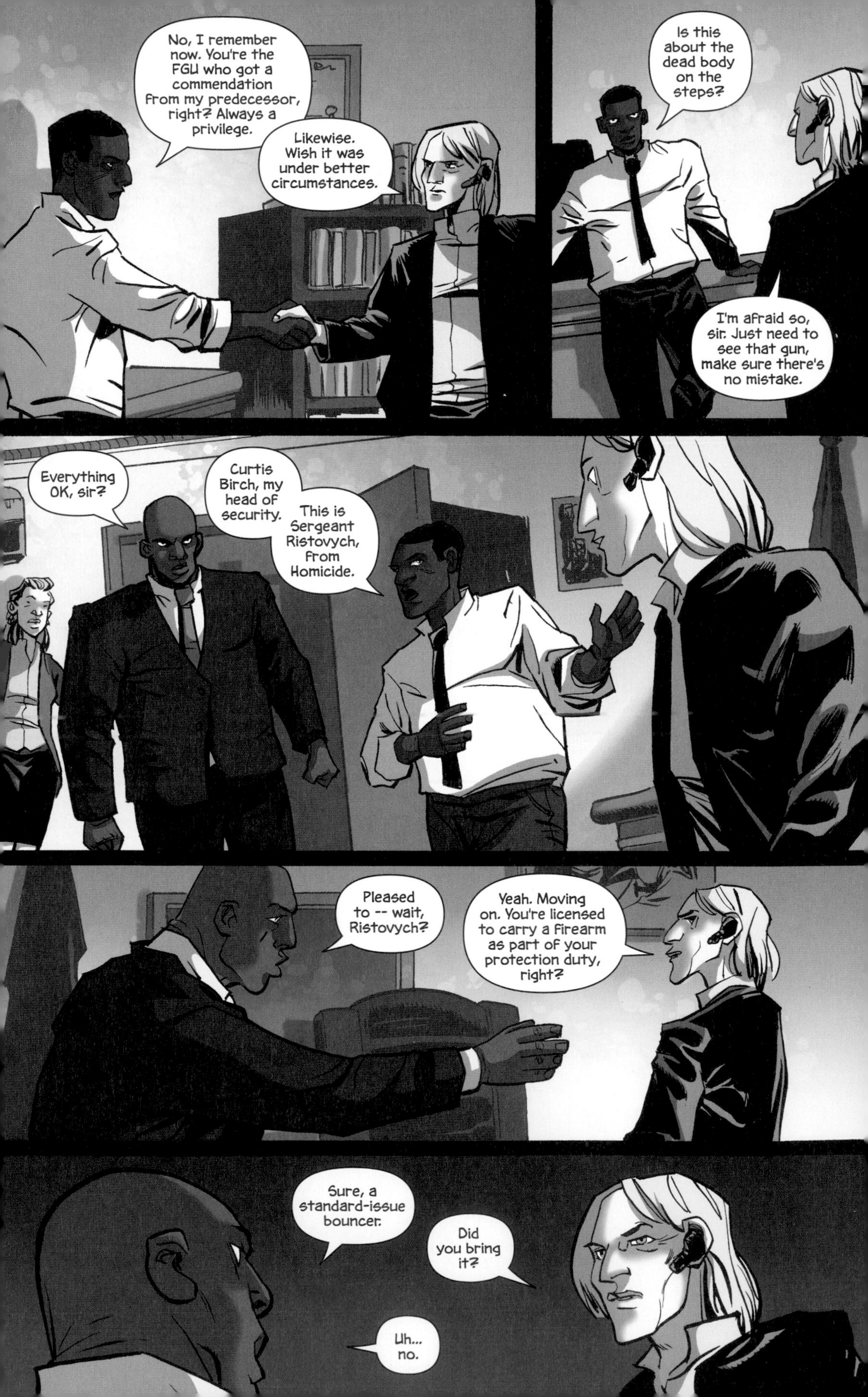

No, I remember now. You're the FGU who got a commendation from my predecessor, right? Always a privilege.
Likewise. Wish it was under better circumstances.
Is this about the dead body on the steps?
I'm afraid so, sir. Just need to see that gun, make sure there's no mistake.
Everything OK, sir?
Curtis Birch, my head of security.
This is Sergeant Ristovych, from Homicide.
Pleased to -- wait, Ristovych?
Yeah. Moving on. You're licensed to carry a firearm as part of your protection duty, right?
Sure, a standard-issue bouncer.
Did you bring it?
Uh... no.

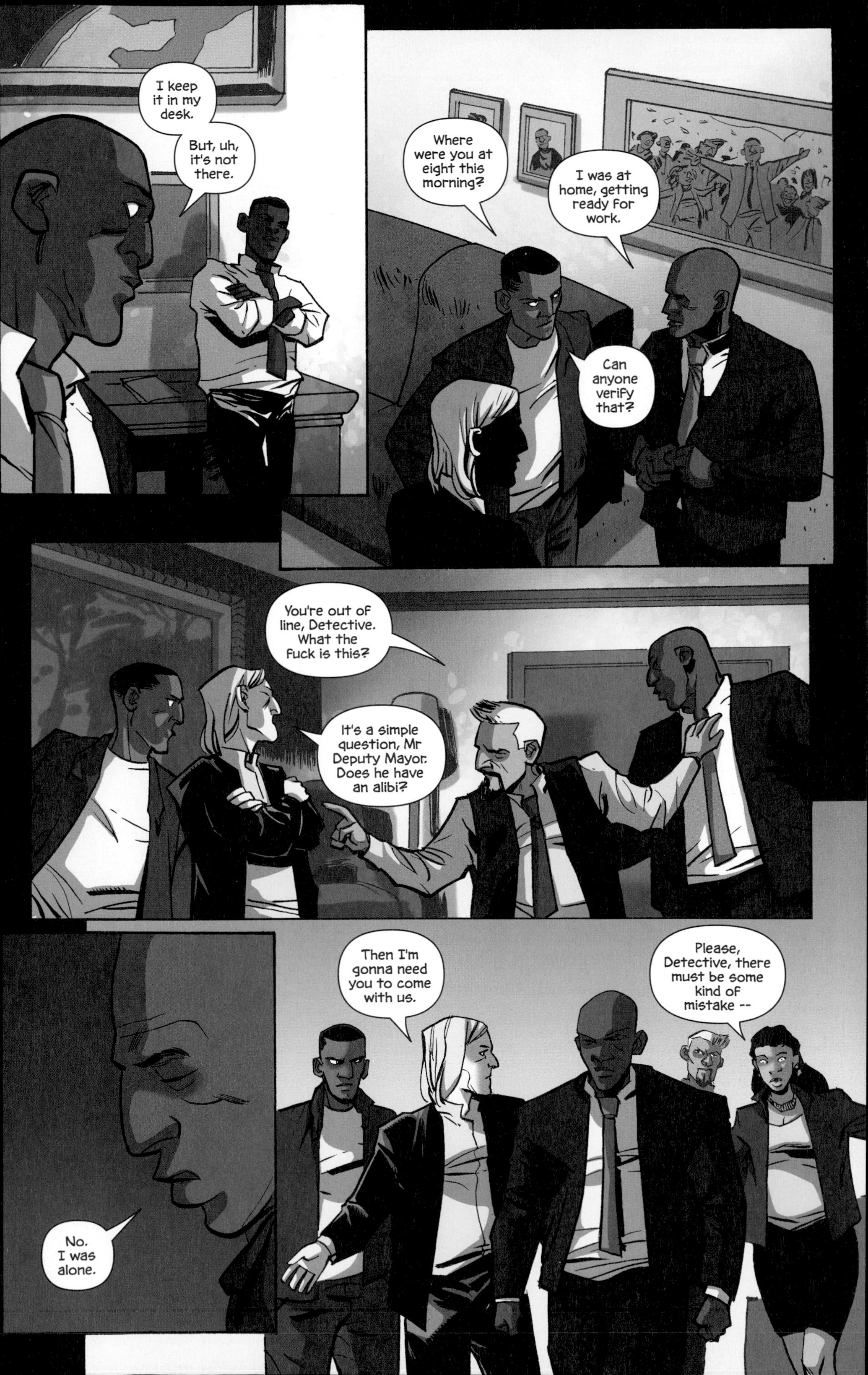
I keep it in my desk.
But, uh, it's not there.
Where were you at eight this morning?
I was at home, getting ready for work.
Can anyone verify that?
You're out of line, Detective. What the fuck is this?
It's a simple question, Mr Deputy Mayor. Does he have an alibi?
No. I was alone.
Then I'm gonna need you to come with us.
Please, Detective, there must be some kind of mistake --

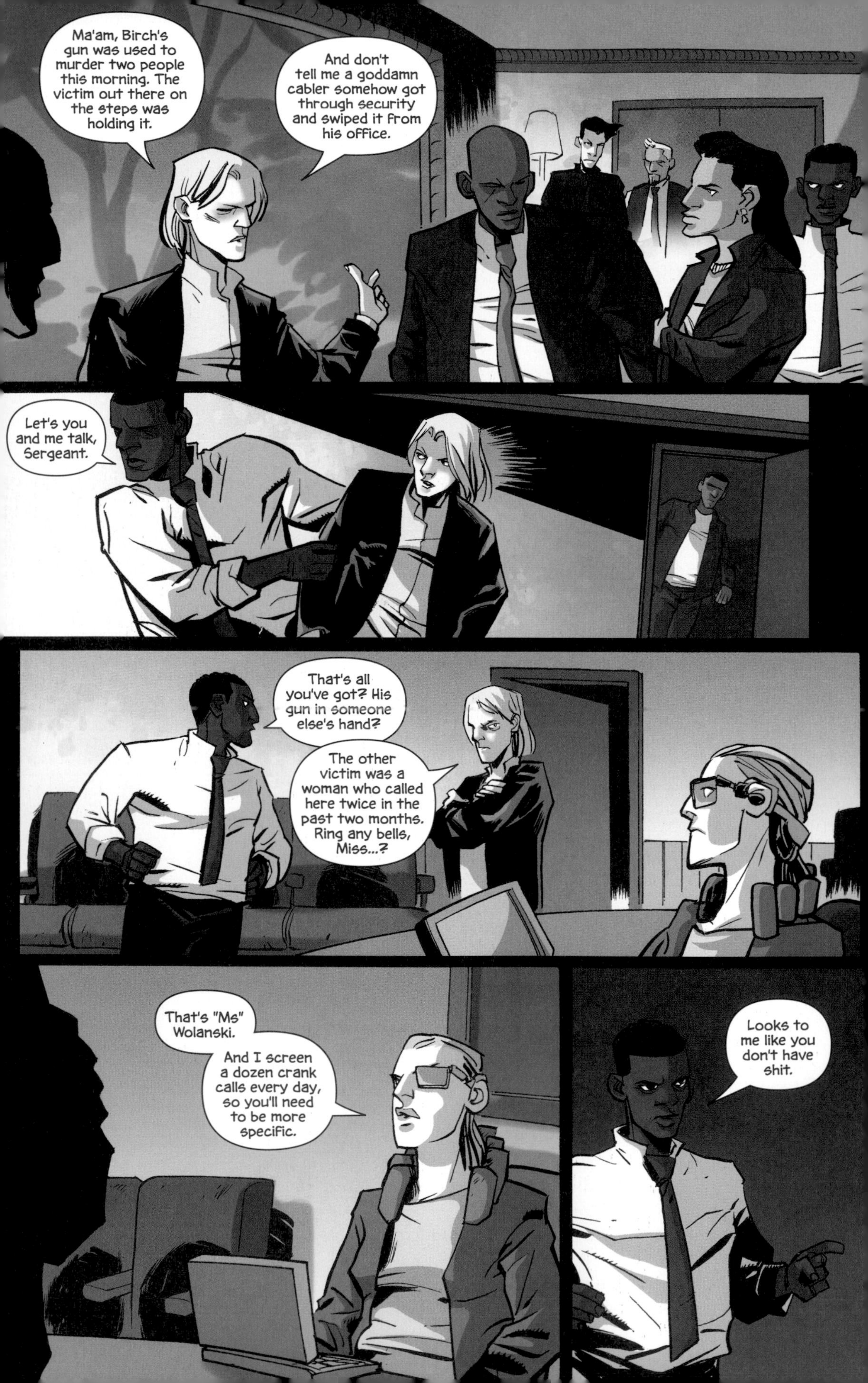
Ma'am, Birch's gun was used to murder two people this morning. The victim out there on the steps was holding it.
And don't tell me a goddamn cabler somehow got through security and swiped it from his office.
Let's you and me talk, Sergeant.
That's all you've got? His gun in someone else's hand?
The other victim was a woman who called here twice in the past two months. Ring any bells, Miss...?
That's "Ms" Wolanski.
And I screen a dozen crank calls every day, so you'll need to be more specific.
Looks to me like you don't have shit.

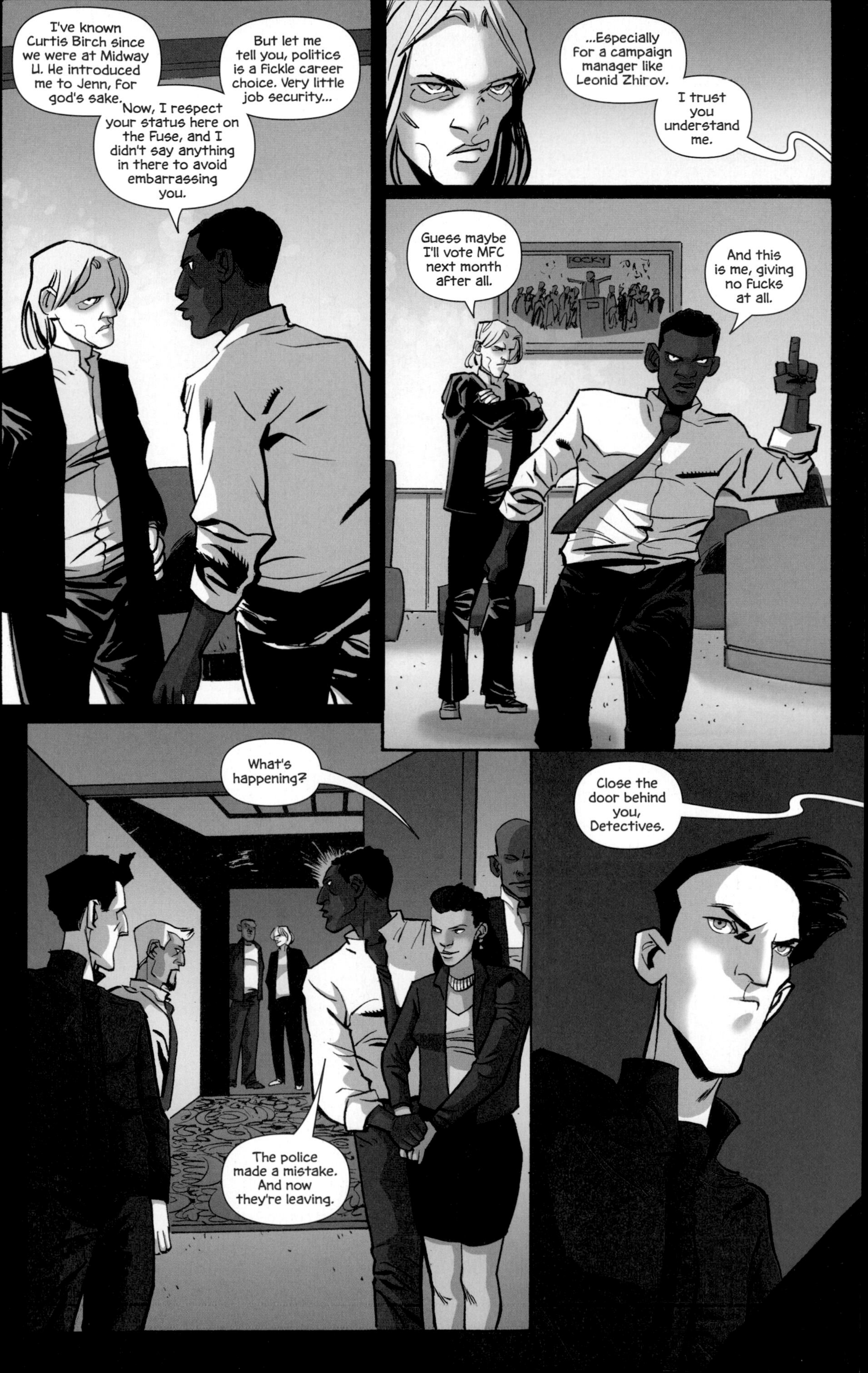
I've known Curtis Birch since we were at Midway U. He introduced me to Jenn, for god's sake.
Now, I respect your status here on the Fuse, and I didn't say anything in there to avoid embarrassing you.
But let me tell you, politics is a fickle career choice. Very little job security...
...Especially for a campaign manager like Leonid Zhirov.
I trust you understand me.
Guess maybe I'll vote MFC next month after all.
And this is me, giving no fucks at all.
What's happening?
The police made a mistake. And now they're leaving.
Close the door behind you, Detectives.

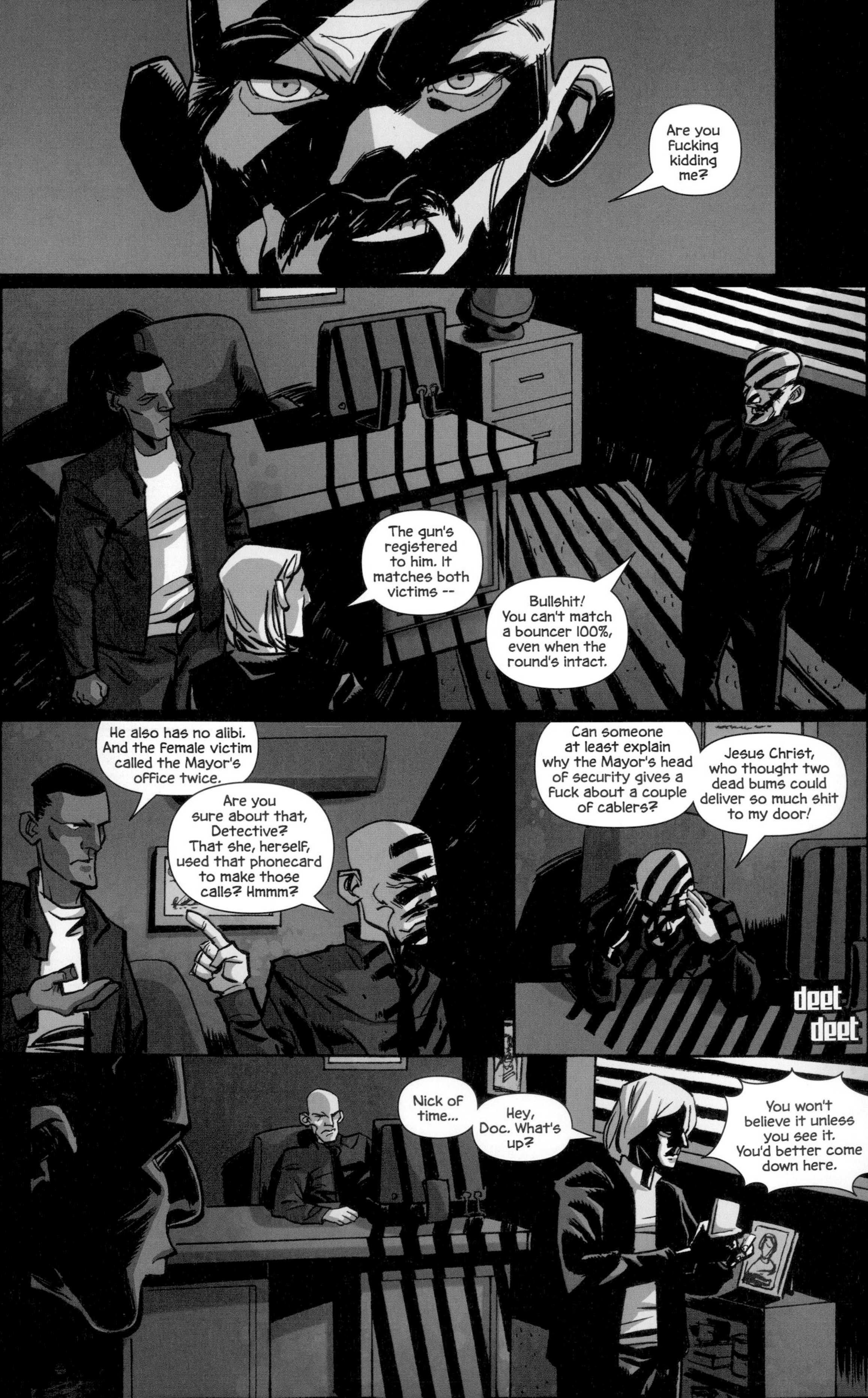

Are you Fucking kidding me?
The gun's registered to him. It matches both victims --
Bullshit! You can't match a bouncer 100%, even when the round's intact.
He also has no alibi. And the female victim called the Mayor's office twice.
Are you sure about that, Detective? That she, herself, used that phonecard to make those calls? Hmmm?
Can someone at least explain why the Mayor's head of security gives a fuck about a couple of cablers?
Jesus Christ, who thought two dead bums could deliver so much shit to my door!
deet deet
Nick of time...
Hey, Doc. What's up?
You won't believe it unless you see it. You'd better come down here.

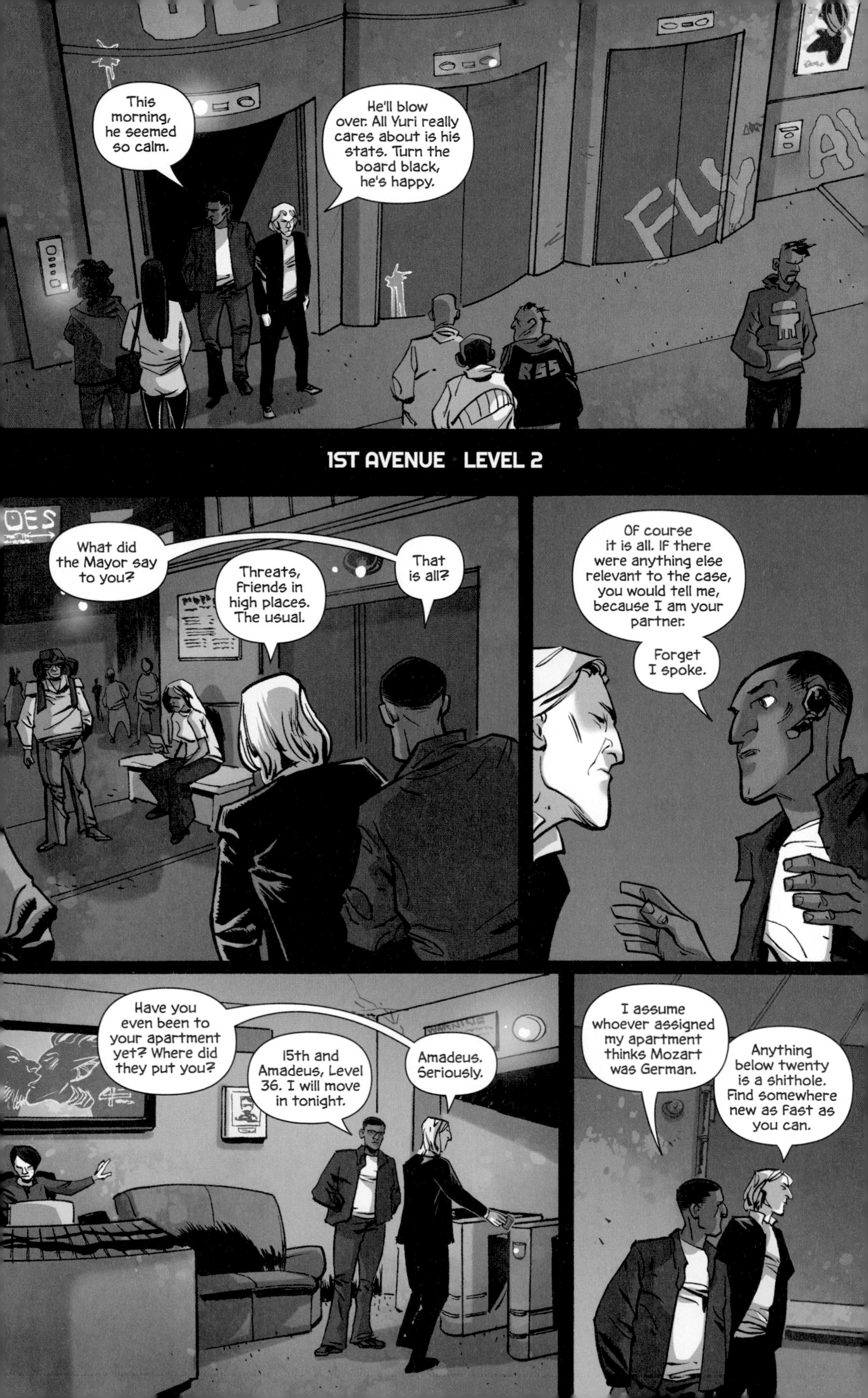
This morning, he seemed so calm.
He'll blow over. All Yuri really cares about is his stats. Turn the board black, he's happy.
FLY
1ST AVENUE LEVEL 2
What did the Mayor say to you?
Threats, friends in high places. The usual.
That is all?
Of course it is all. If there were anything else relevant to the case, you would tell me, because I am your partner.
Forget I spoke.
Have you even been to your apartment yet? Where did they put you?
15th and Amadeus, Level 36. I will move in tonight.
Amadeus. Seriously.
I assume whoever assigned my apartment thinks Mozart was German.
Anything below twenty is a shithole. Find somewhere new as fast as you can.

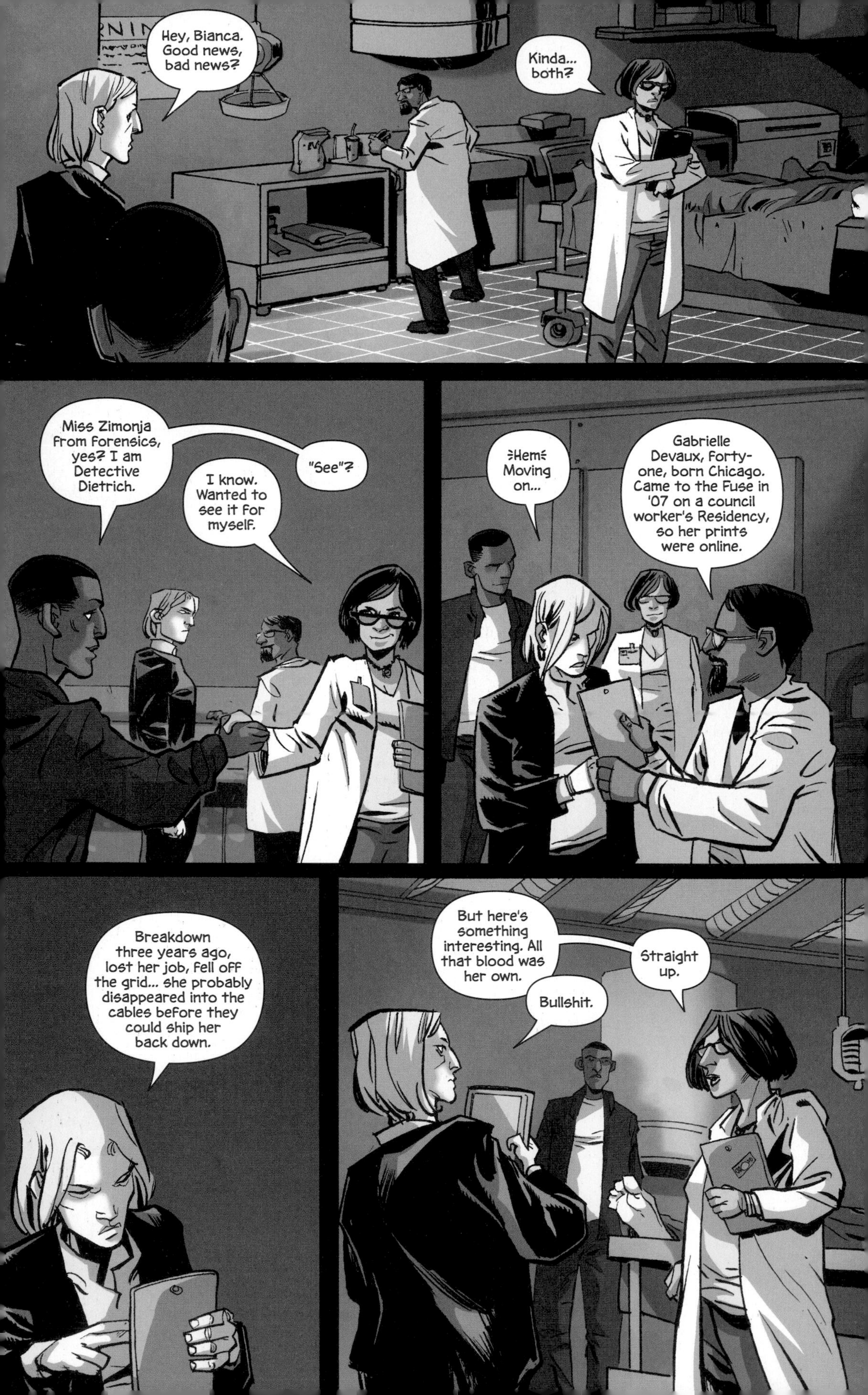
Hey, Bianca. Good news, bad news?
Kinda... both?
Miss Zimonja from Forensics, yes? I am Detective Dietrich.
"See"?
I know. Wanted to see it for myself.
=Hem= Moving on...
Gabrielle Devaux, Forty-one, born Chicago. Came to the Fuse in '07 on a council worker's Residency, so her prints were online.
Breakdown three years ago, lost her job, fell off the grid... she probably disappeared into the cables before they could ship her back down.
But here's something interesting. All that blood was her own.
Straight up.
Bullshit.

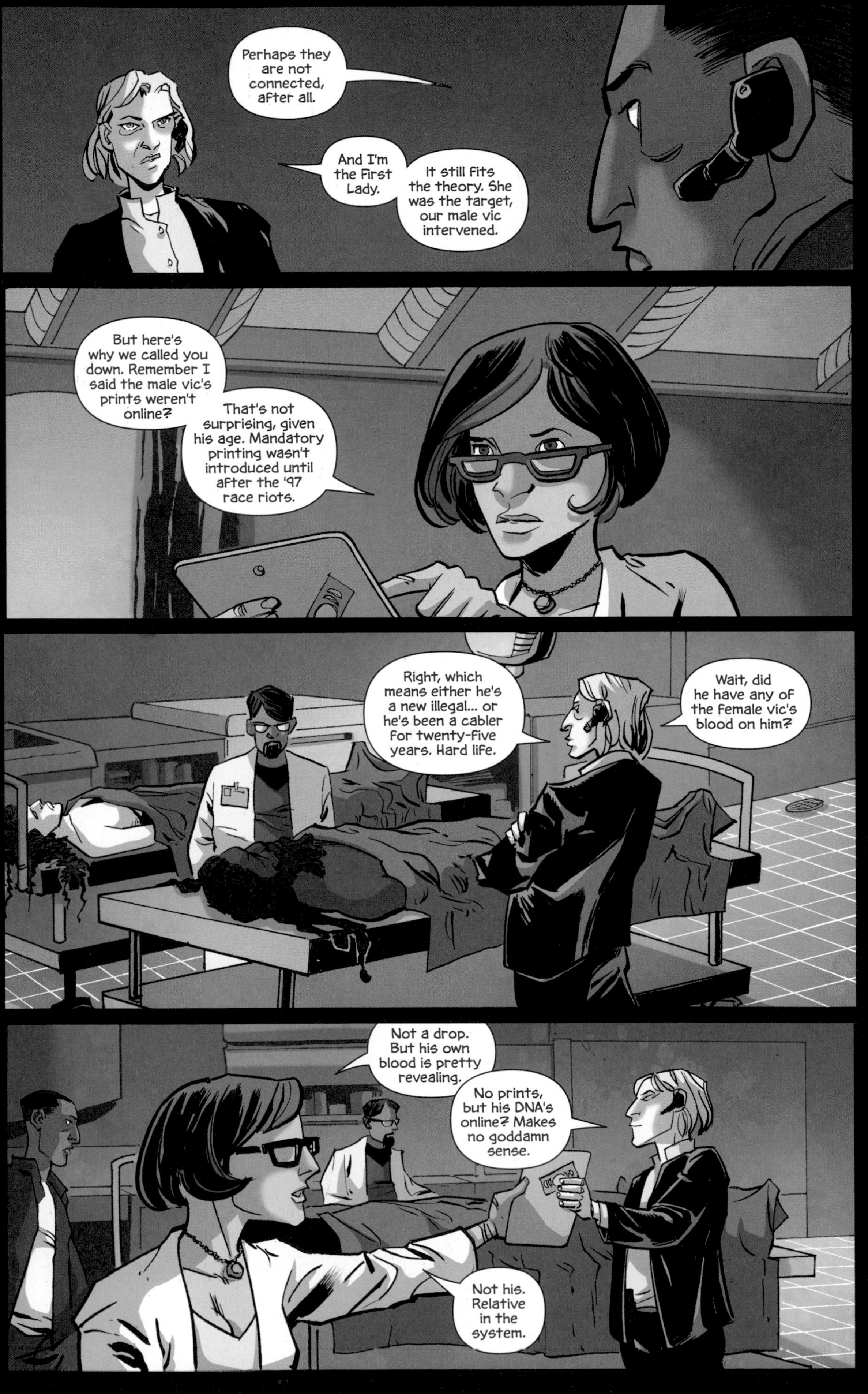
Perhaps they are not connected, after all.
And I'm the First Lady.
It still fits the theory. She was the target, our male vic intervened.
But here's why we called you down. Remember I said the male vic's prints weren't online?
That's not surprising, given his age. Mandatory printing wasn't introduced until after the '97 race riots.
Right, which means either he's a new illegal... or he's been a cabler for twenty-five years. Hard life.
Wait, did he have any of the female vic's blood on him?
Not a drop. But his own blood is pretty revealing.
No prints, but his DNA's online? Makes no goddamn sense.
Not his. Relative in the system.

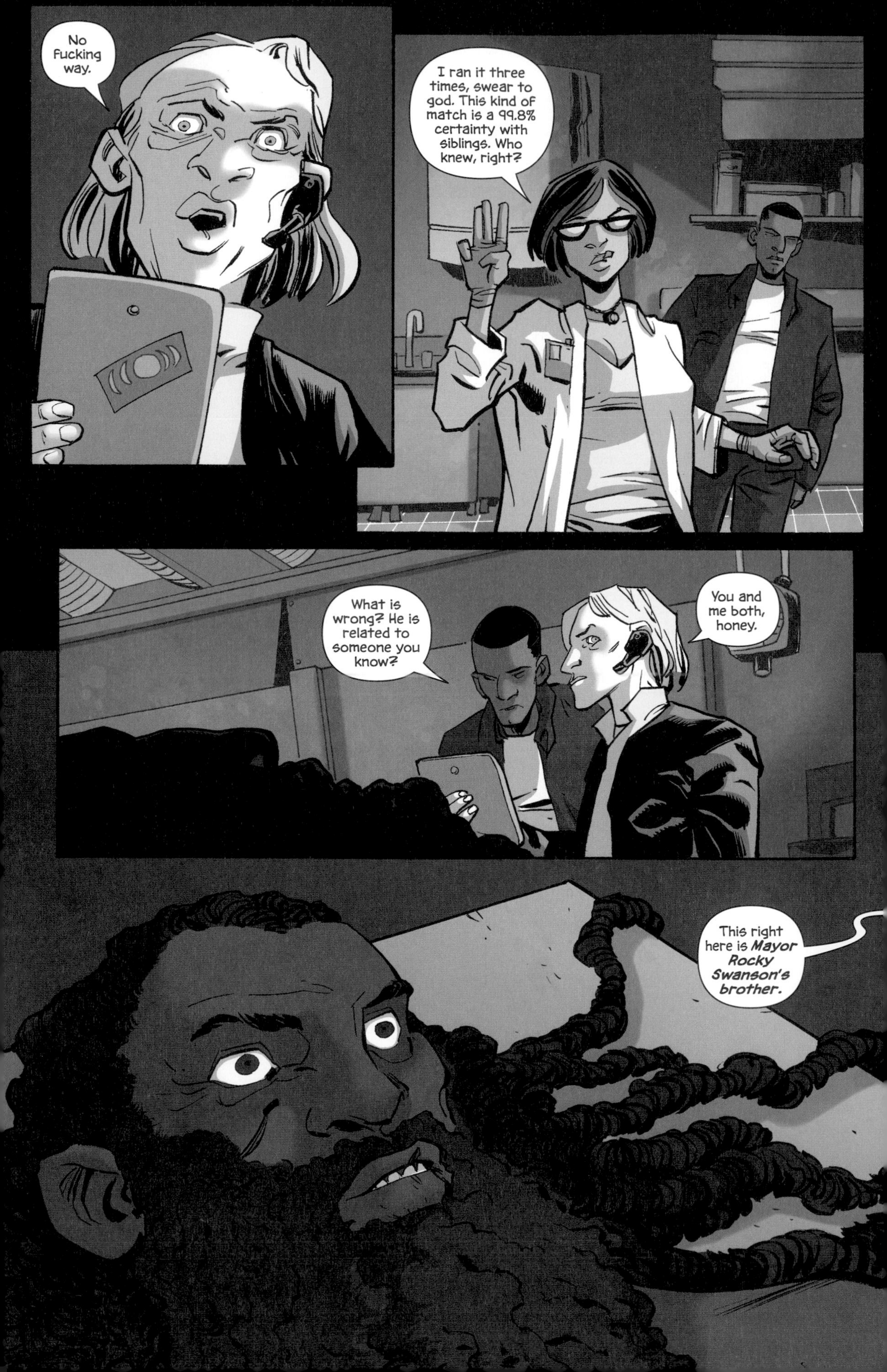
No Fucking way.
I ran it three times, swear to god. This kind of match is a 99.8% certainty with siblings. Who knew, right?
What is wrong? He is related to someone you know?
You and me both, honey.
This right here is *Mayor Rocky Swanson's brother.*

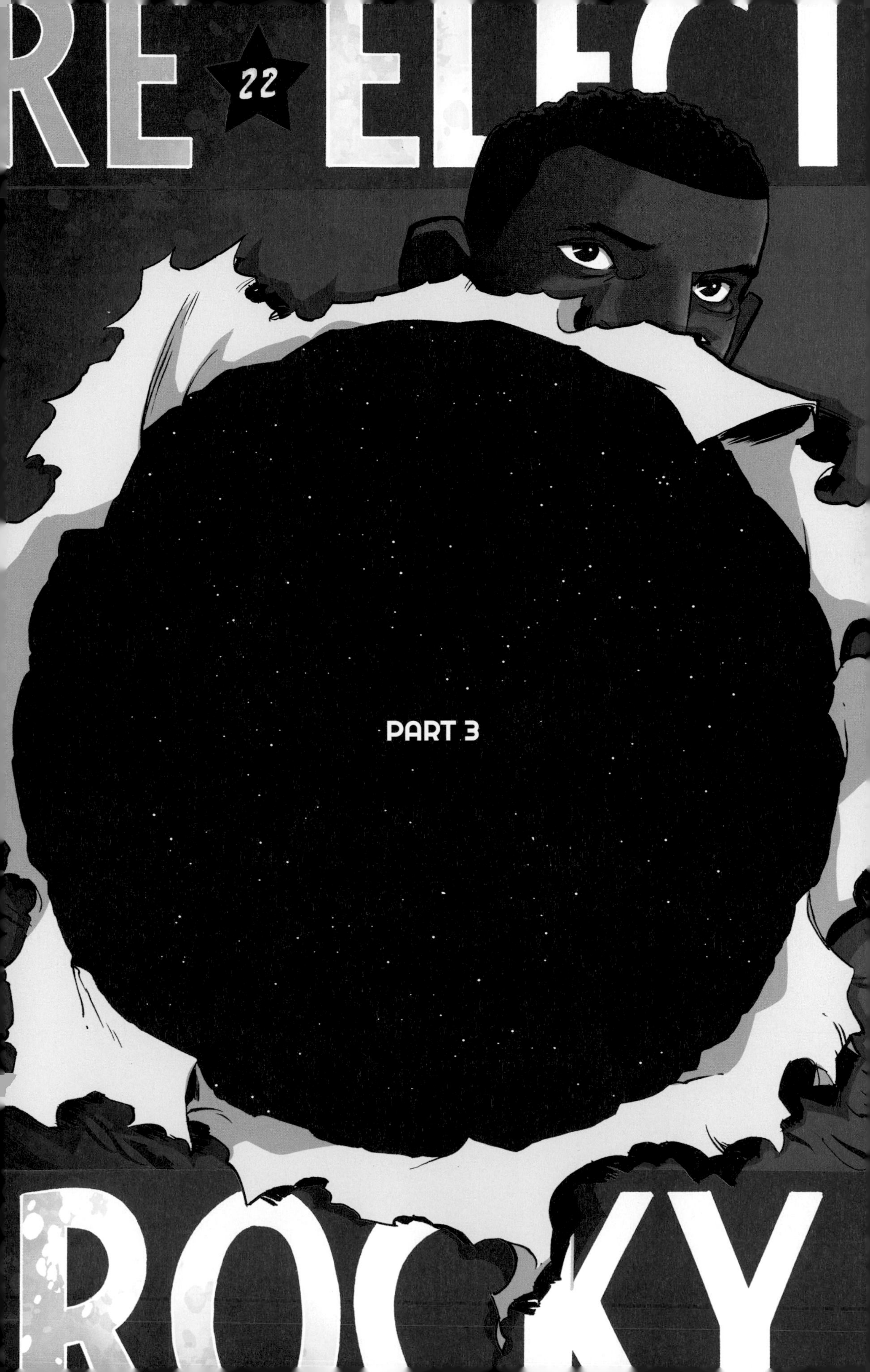
RE ELECT
22
PART 3
ROCKY

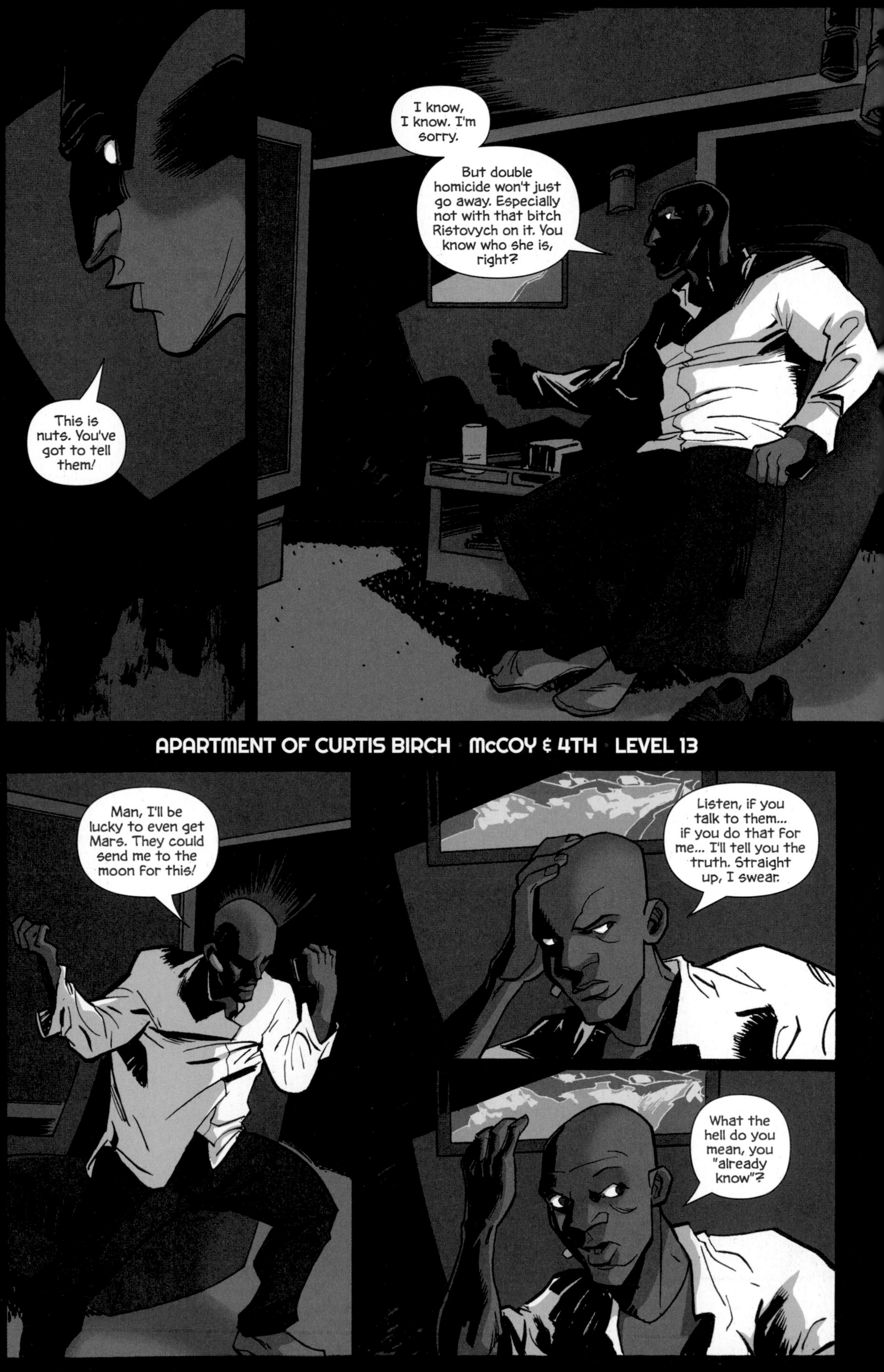
I know, I know. I'm sorry.
But double homicide won't just go away. Especially not with that bitch Ristovych on it. You know who she is, right?
This is nuts. You've got to tell them!
APARTMENT OF CURTIS BIRCH · McCOY & 4TH · LEVEL 13
Man, I'll be lucky to even get Mars. They could send me to the moon for this!
Listen, if you talk to them... if you do that for me... I'll tell you the truth. Straight up, I swear.
What the hell do you mean, you "already know"?

APARTMENT OF RALPH DIETRICH · AMADEUS & 15TH · LEVEL 36

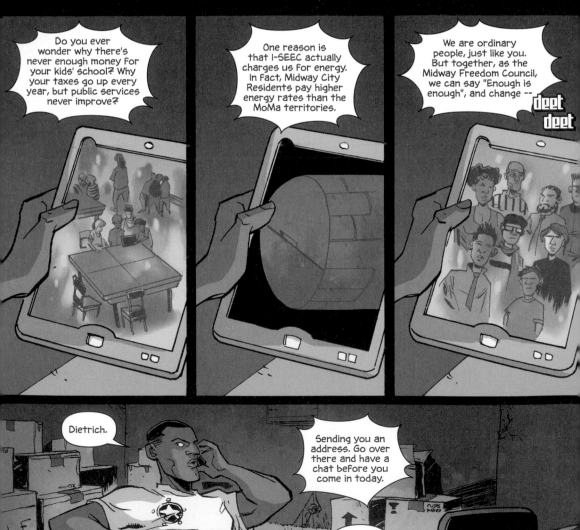

Do you ever wonder why there's never enough money for your kids' school? Why your taxes go up every year, but public services never improve?

One reason is that I-SEEC actually charges us for energy. In fact, Midway City Residents pay higher energy rates than the MoMa territories.

We are ordinary people, just like you. But together, as the Midway Freedom Council, we can say "Enough is enough", and change --

deet
deet

Dietrich.

Sending you an address. Go over there and have a chat before you come in today.

Guten morgen to you too, Sergeant.

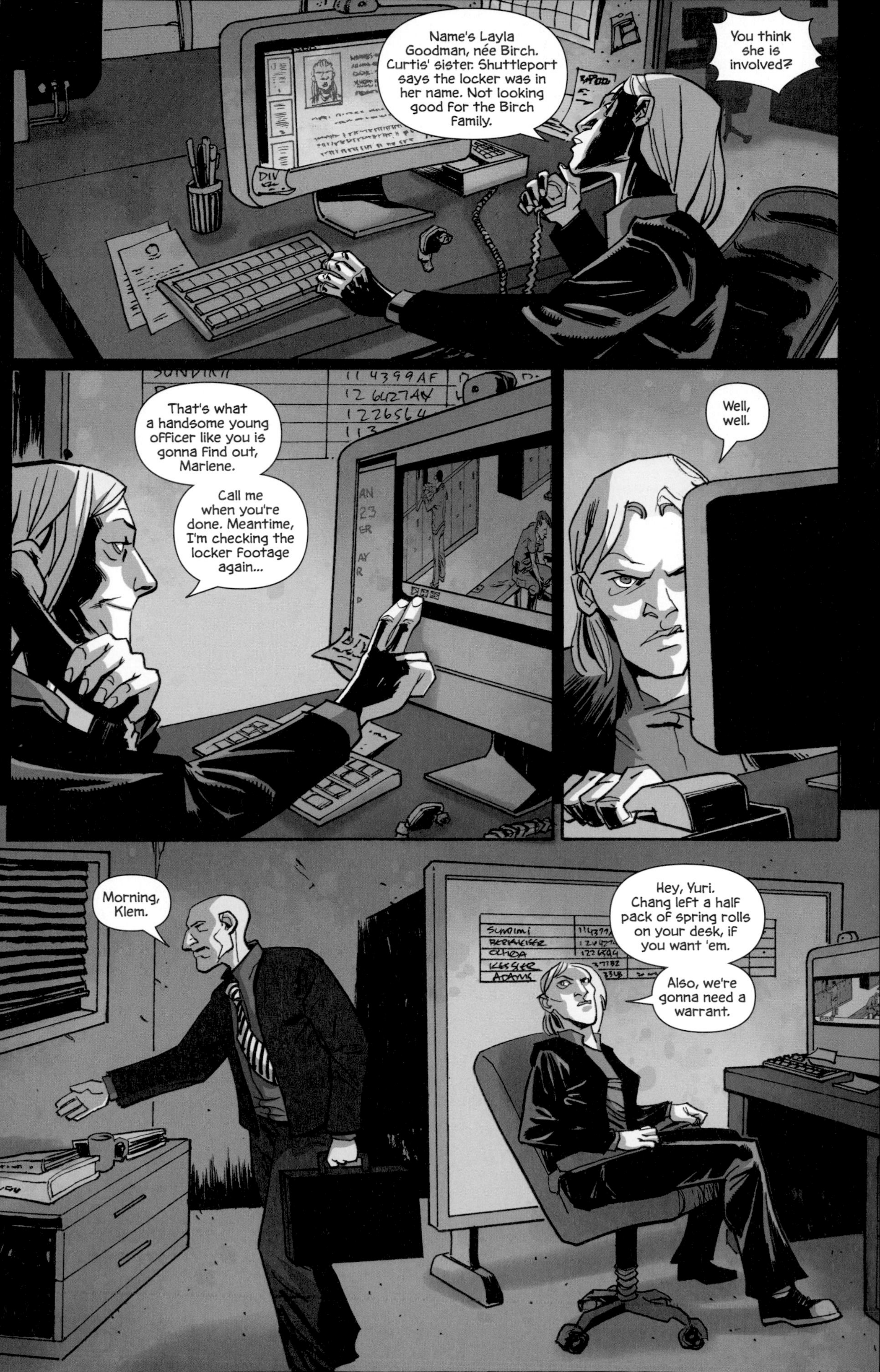

Name's Layla Goodman, née Birch. Curtis' sister. Shuttleport says the locker was in her name. Not looking good for the Birch Family.
You think she is involved?
That's what a handsome young officer like you is gonna find out, Marlene.
Call me when you're done. Meantime, I'm checking the locker footage again...
Well, well.
Morning, Klem.
Hey, Yuri. Chang left a half pack of spring rolls on your desk, if you want 'em.
Also, we're gonna need a warrant.

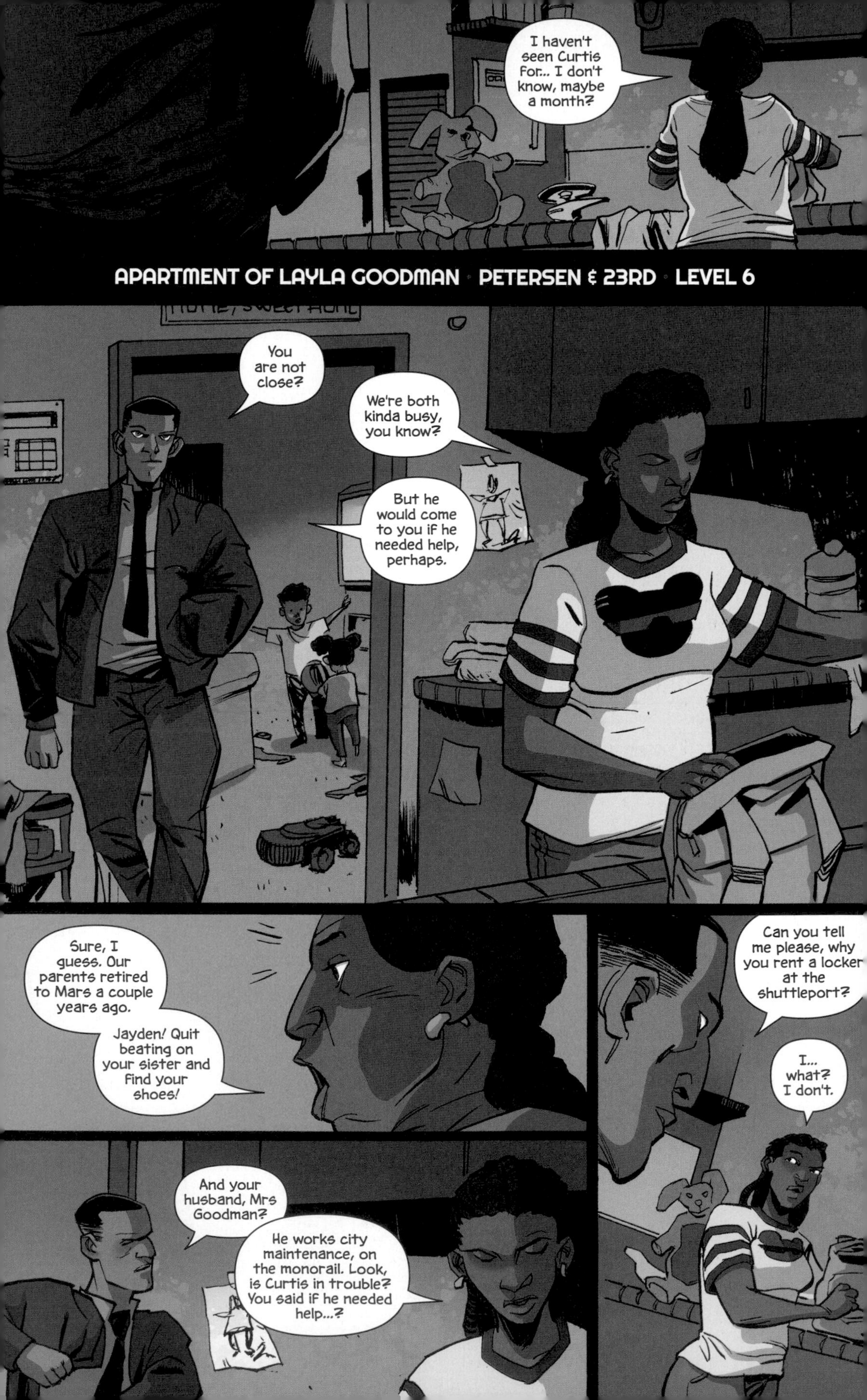
I haven't seen Curtis for... I don't know, maybe a month?
APARTMENT OF LAYLA GOODMAN · PETERSEN & 23RD · LEVEL 6
You are not close?
We're both kinda busy, you know?
But he would come to you if he needed help, perhaps.
Sure, I guess. Our parents retired to Mars a couple years ago.
Jayden! Quit beating on your sister and find your shoes!
And your husband, Mrs Goodman?
He works city maintenance, on the monorail. Look, is Curtis in trouble? You said if he needed help...?
Can you tell me please, why you rent a locker at the shuttleport?
I... what? I don't.

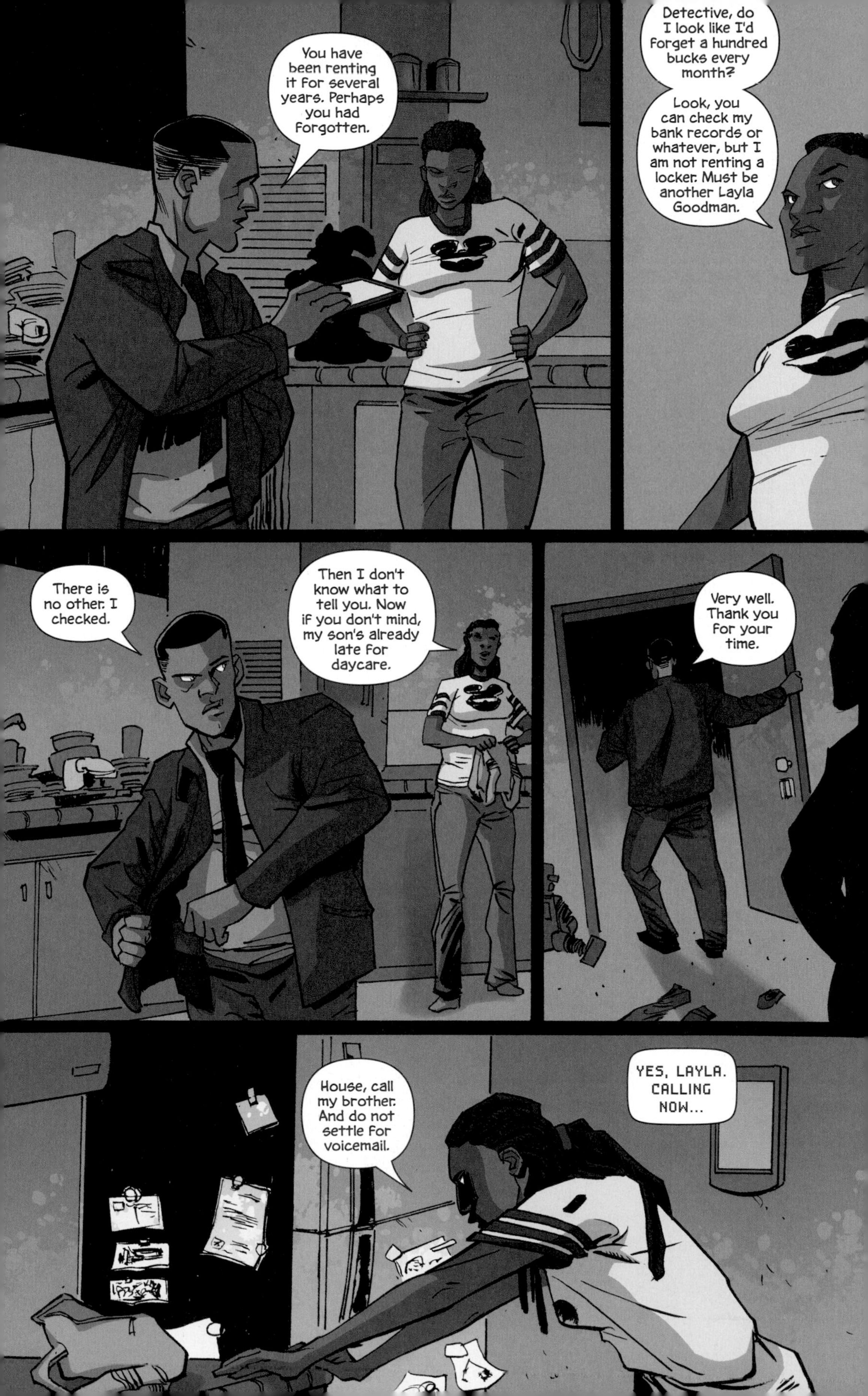
You have been renting it for several years. Perhaps you had forgotten.
Detective, do I look like I'd forget a hundred bucks every month?
Look, you can check my bank records or whatever, but I am not renting a locker. Must be another Layla Goodman.
There is no other. I checked.
Then I don't know what to tell you. Now if you don't mind, my son's already late for daycare.
Very well. Thank you for your time.
House, call my brother. And do not settle for voicemail.
YES, LAYLA. CALLING NOW...

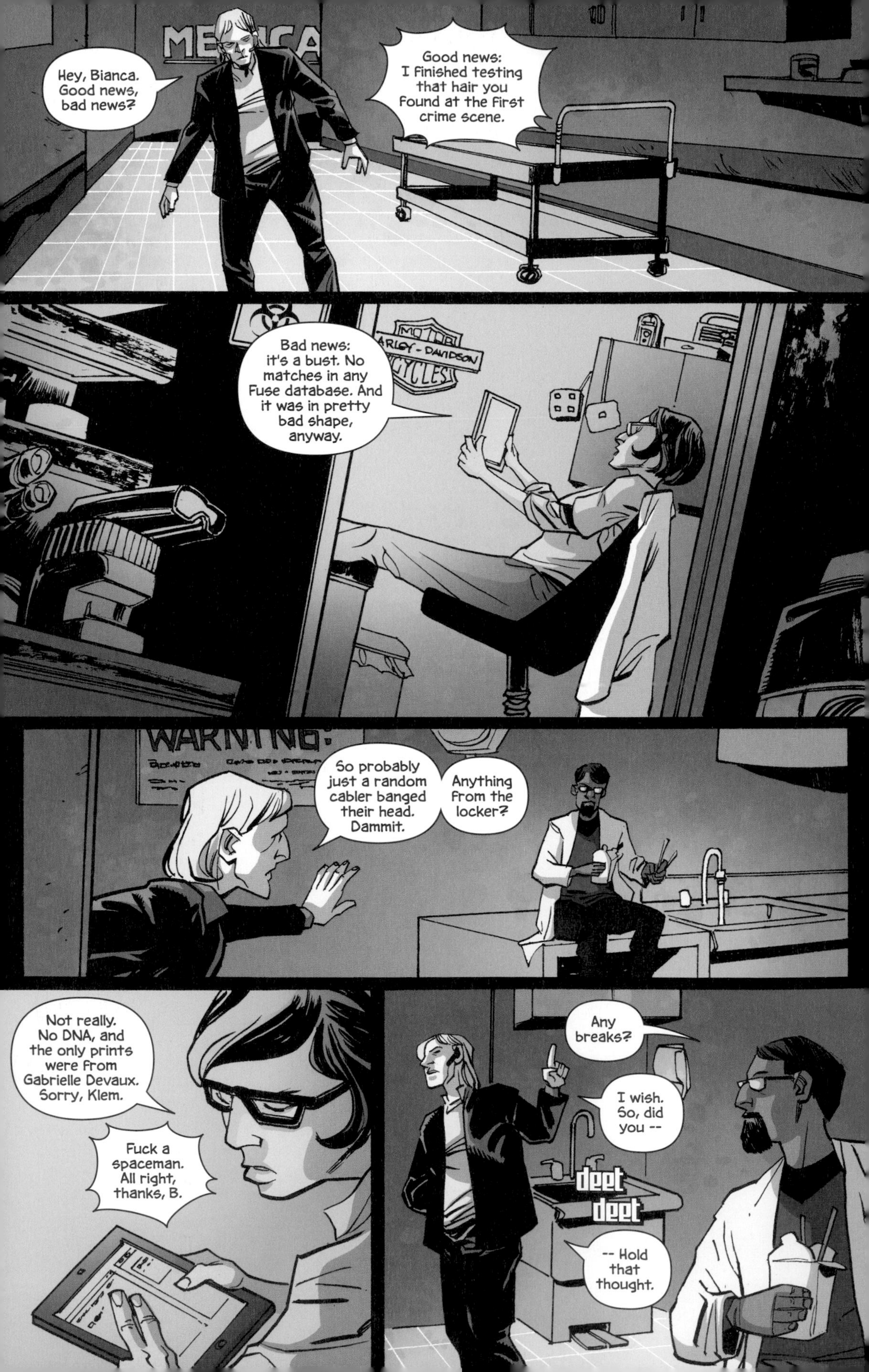

Hey, Bianca. Good news, bad news?
Good news: I finished testing that hair you found at the first crime scene.
Bad news: it's a bust. No matches in any Fuse database. And it was in pretty bad shape, anyway.
WARNING:
So probably just a random cabler banged their head. Dammit.
Anything from the locker?
Not really. No DNA, and the only prints were from Gabrielle Devaux. Sorry, Klem.
Fuck a spaceman. All right, thanks, B.
Any breaks?
I wish. So, did you --
deet
deet
-- Hold that thought.

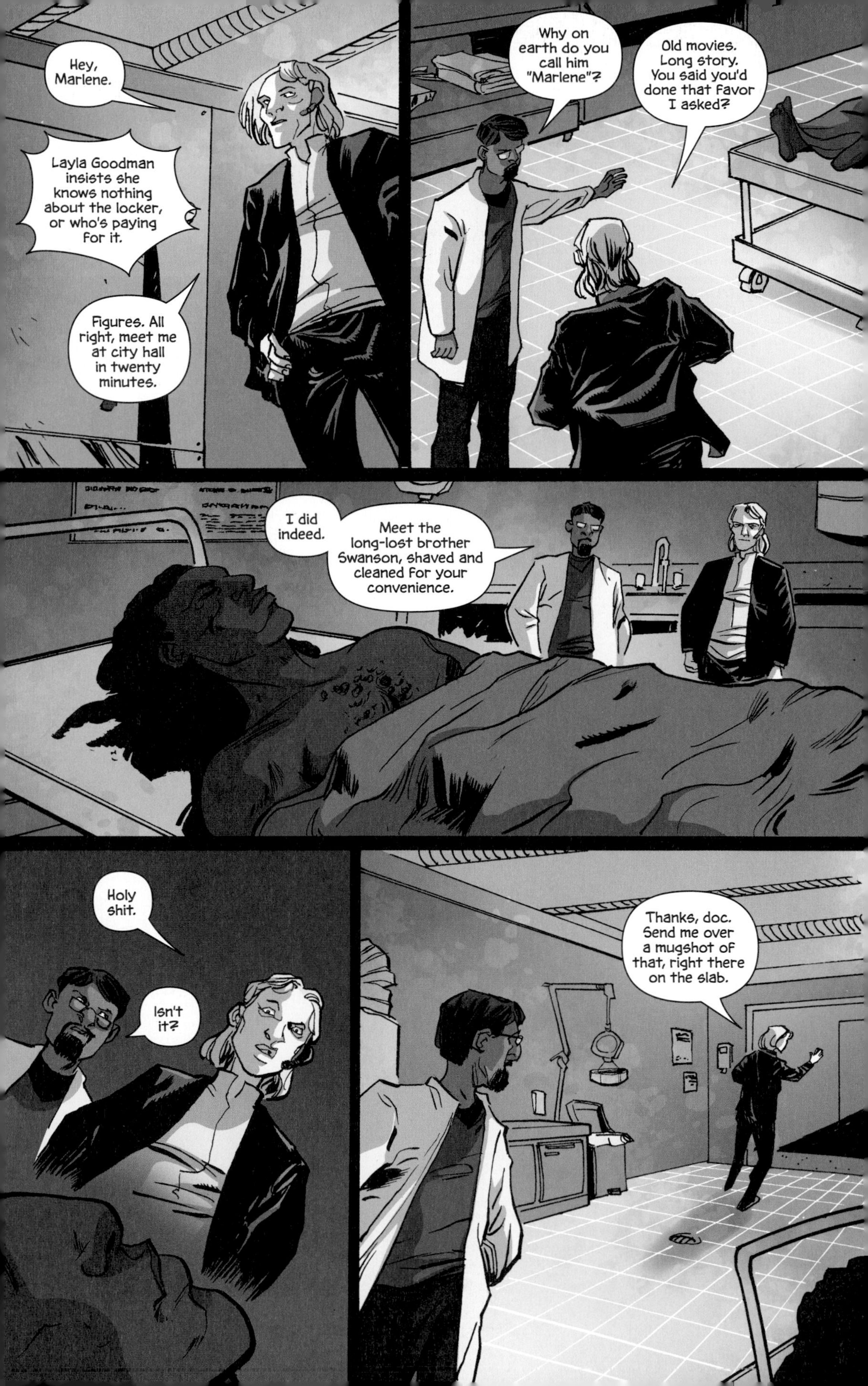
Hey, Marlene.
Layla Goodman insists she knows nothing about the locker, or who's paying for it.
Figures. All right, meet me at city hall in twenty minutes.
Why on earth do you call him "Marlene"?
Old movies. Long story. You said you'd done that favor I asked?
I did indeed.
Meet the long-lost brother Swanson, shaved and cleaned for your convenience.
Holy shit.
Isn't it?
Thanks, doc. Send me over a mugshot of that, right there on the slab.

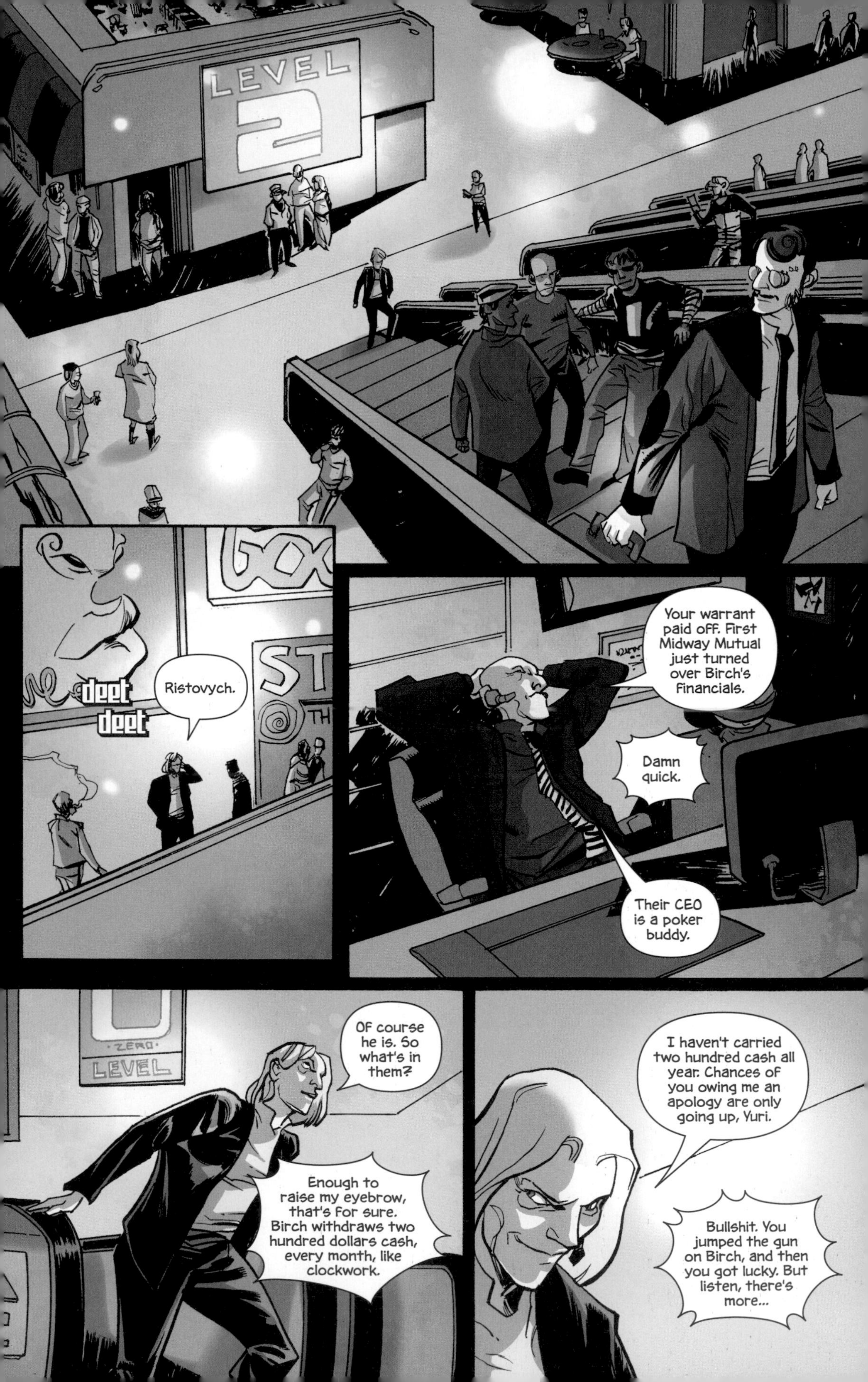
LEVEL
2
deet
deet
Ristovych.
Your warrant paid off. First Midway Mutual just turned over Birch's financials.
Damn quick.
Their CEO is a poker buddy.
ZERO
LEVEL
Of course he is. So what's in them?
Enough to raise my eyebrow, that's for sure. Birch withdraws two hundred dollars cash, every month, like clockwork.
I haven't carried two hundred cash all year. Chances of you owing me an apology are only going up, Yuri.
Bullshit. You jumped the gun on Birch, and then you got lucky. But listen, there's more...

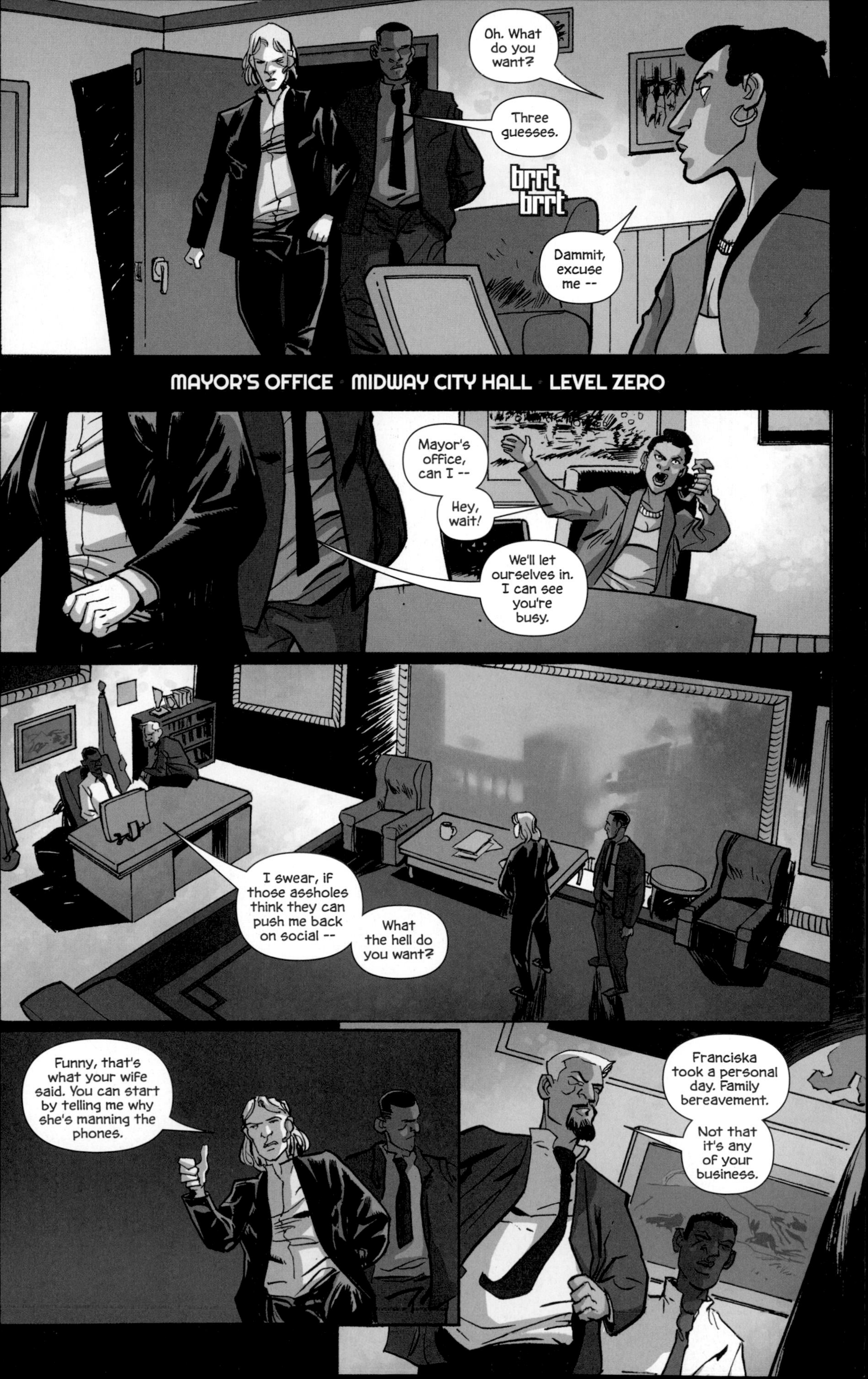
Oh. What do you want?
Three guesses.
brrt brrt
Dammit, excuse me --
MAYOR'S OFFICE · MIDWAY CITY HALL · LEVEL ZERO
Mayor's office, can I --
Hey, wait!
We'll let ourselves in. I can see you're busy.
I swear, if those assholes think they can push me back on social --
What the hell do you want?
Funny, that's what your wife said. You can start by telling me why she's manning the phones.
Franciska took a personal day. Family bereavement.
Not that it's any of your business.

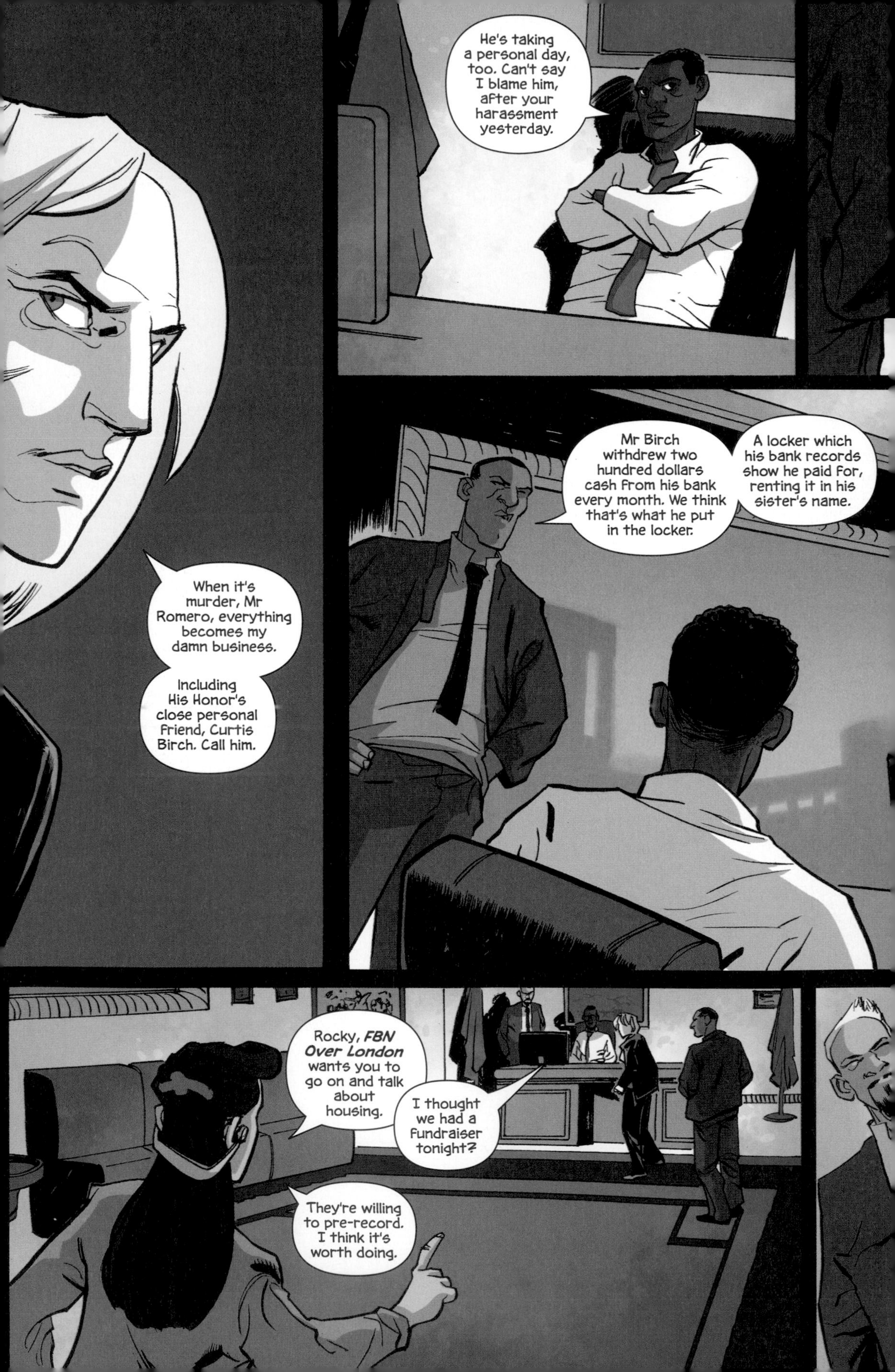
He's taking a personal day, too. Can't say I blame him, after your harassment yesterday.
When it's murder, Mr Romero, everything becomes my damn business.
Including His Honor's close personal friend, Curtis Birch. Call him.
Mr Birch withdrew two hundred dollars cash from his bank every month. We think that's what he put in the locker.
A locker which his bank records show he paid for, renting it in his sister's name.
Rocky, ***FBN Over London*** wants you to go on and talk about housing.
I thought we had a fundraiser tonight?
They're willing to pre-record. I think it's worth doing.

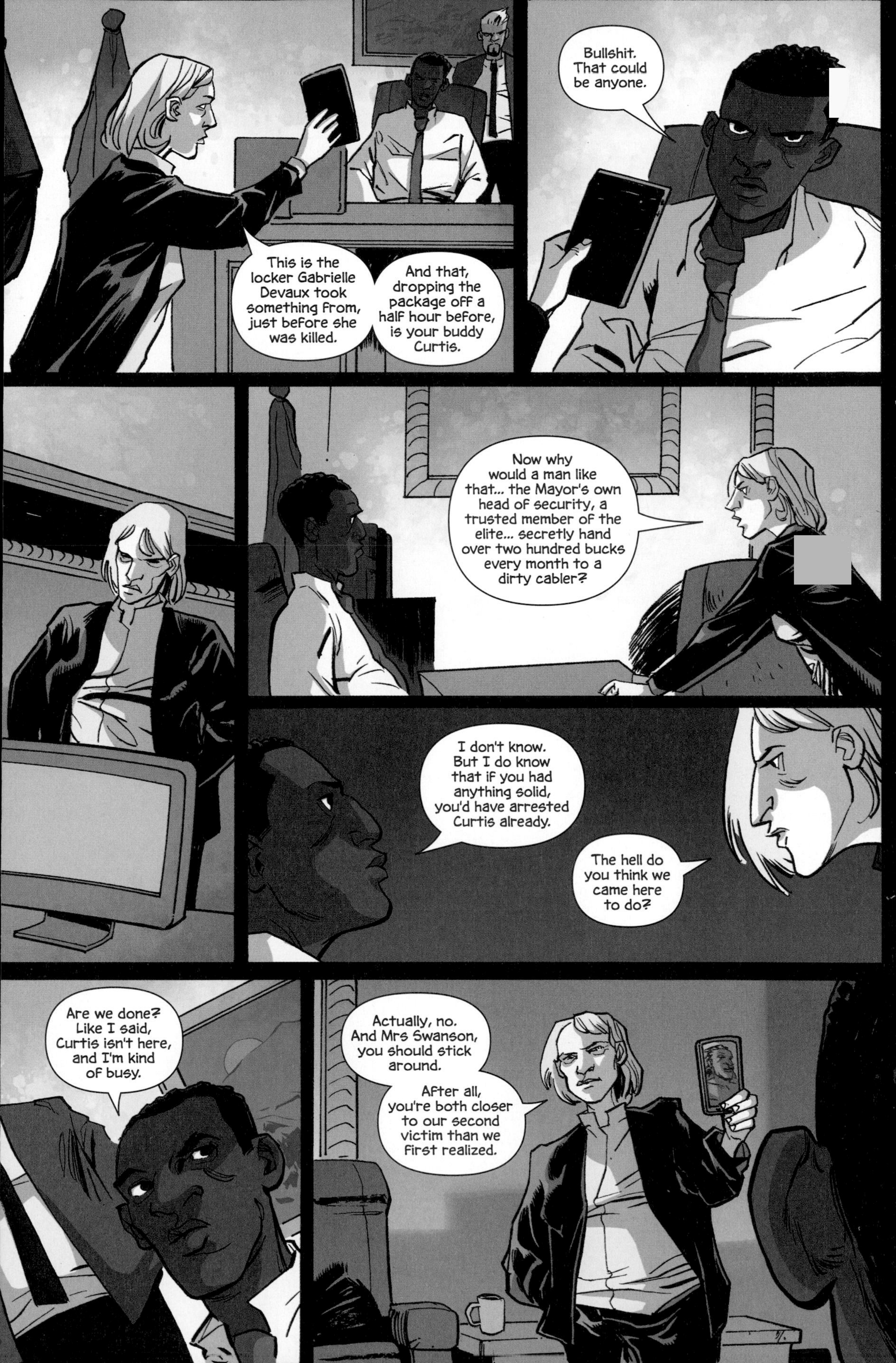
This is the locker Gabrielle Devaux took something from, just before she was killed.
And that, dropping the package off a half hour before, is your buddy Curtis.
Bullshit. That could be anyone.
Now why would a man like that... the Mayor's own head of security, a trusted member of the elite... secretly hand over two hundred bucks every month to a dirty cabler?
I don't know. But I do know that if you had anything solid, you'd have arrested Curtis already.
The hell do you think we came here to do?
Are we done? Like I said, Curtis isn't here, and I'm kind of busy.
Actually, no. And Mrs Swanson, you should stick around.
After all, you're both closer to our second victim than we first realized.

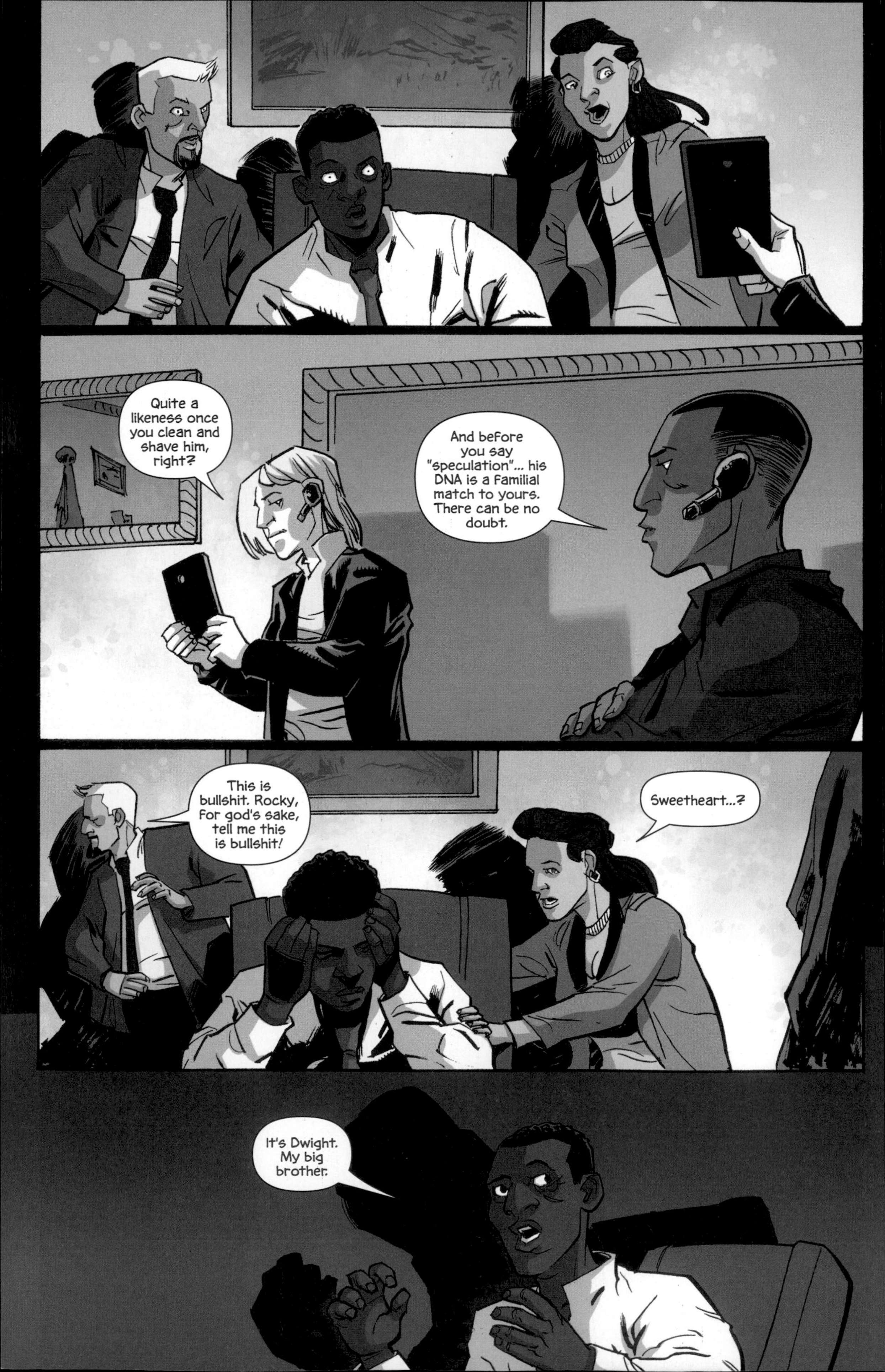
Quite a likeness once you clean and shave him, right?
And before you say "speculation"... his DNA is a familial match to yours. There can be no doubt.
This is bullshit. Rocky, for god's sake, tell me this is bullshit!
Sweetheart...?
It's Dwight. My big brother.

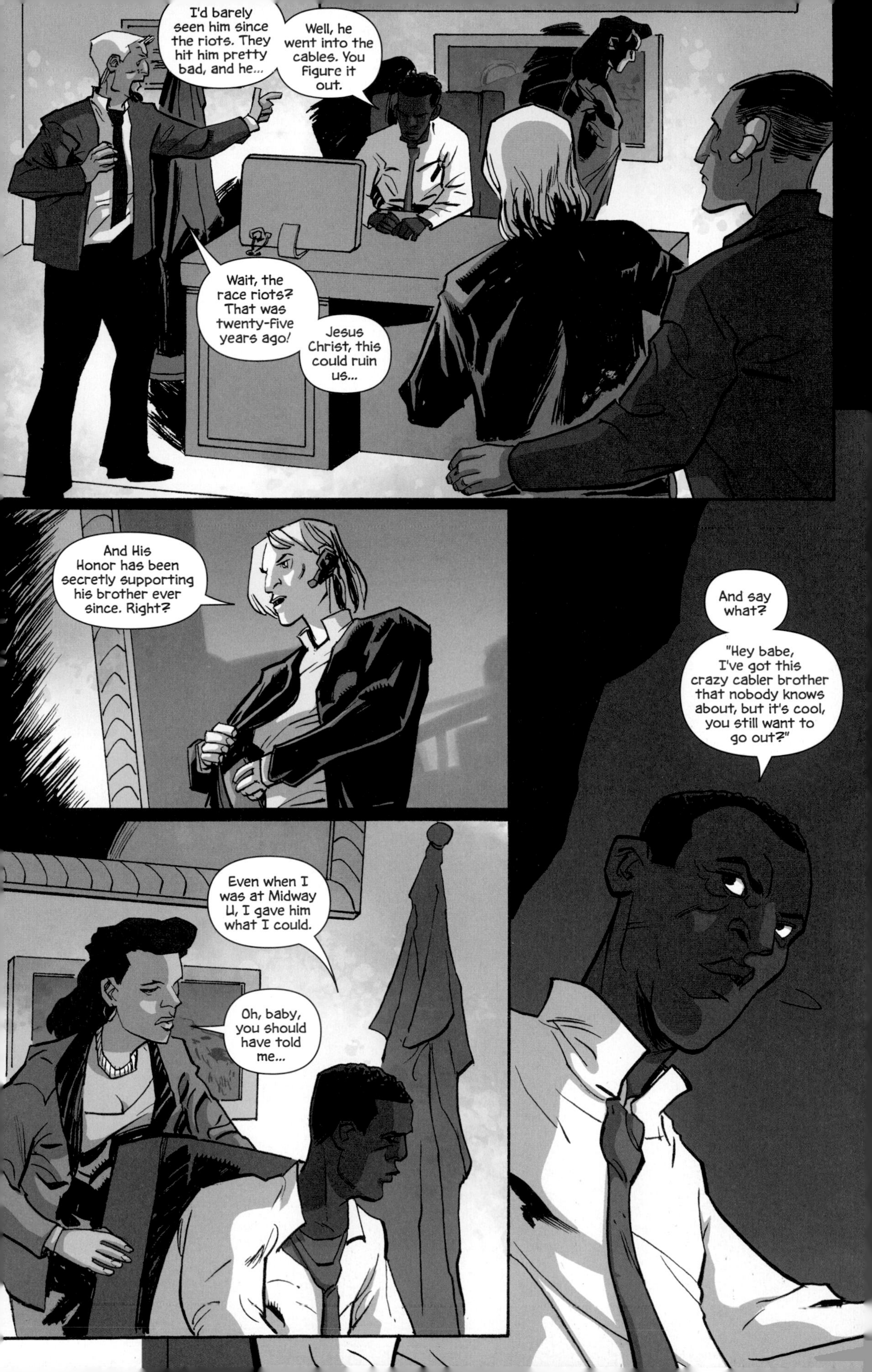
I'd barely seen him since the riots. They hit him pretty bad, and he...
Well, he went into the cables. You figure it out.
Wait, the race riots? That was twenty-five years ago!
Jesus Christ, this could ruin us...
And His Honor has been secretly supporting his brother ever since. Right?
Even when I was at Midway U, I gave him what I could.
Oh, baby, you should have told me...
And say what?
"Hey babe, I've got this crazy cabler brother that nobody knows about, but it's cool, you still want to go out?"

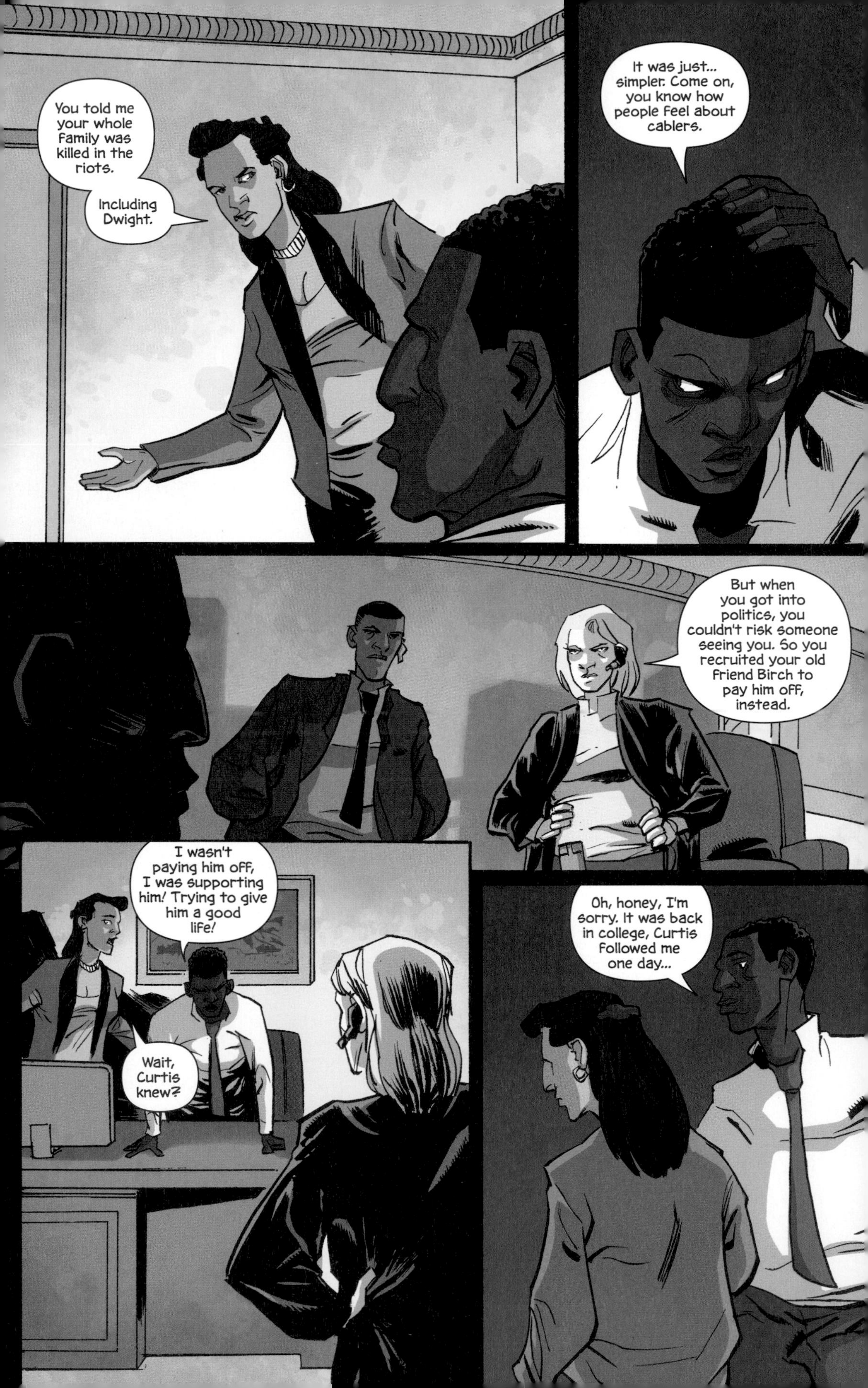
You told me your whole family was killed in the riots.
Including Dwight.
It was just... simpler. Come on, you know how people feel about cablers.
But when you got into politics, you couldn't risk someone seeing you. So you recruited your old friend Birch to pay him off, instead.
I wasn't paying him off, I was supporting him! Trying to give him a good life!
Wait, Curtis knew?
Oh, honey, I'm sorry. It was back in college, Curtis followed me one day...

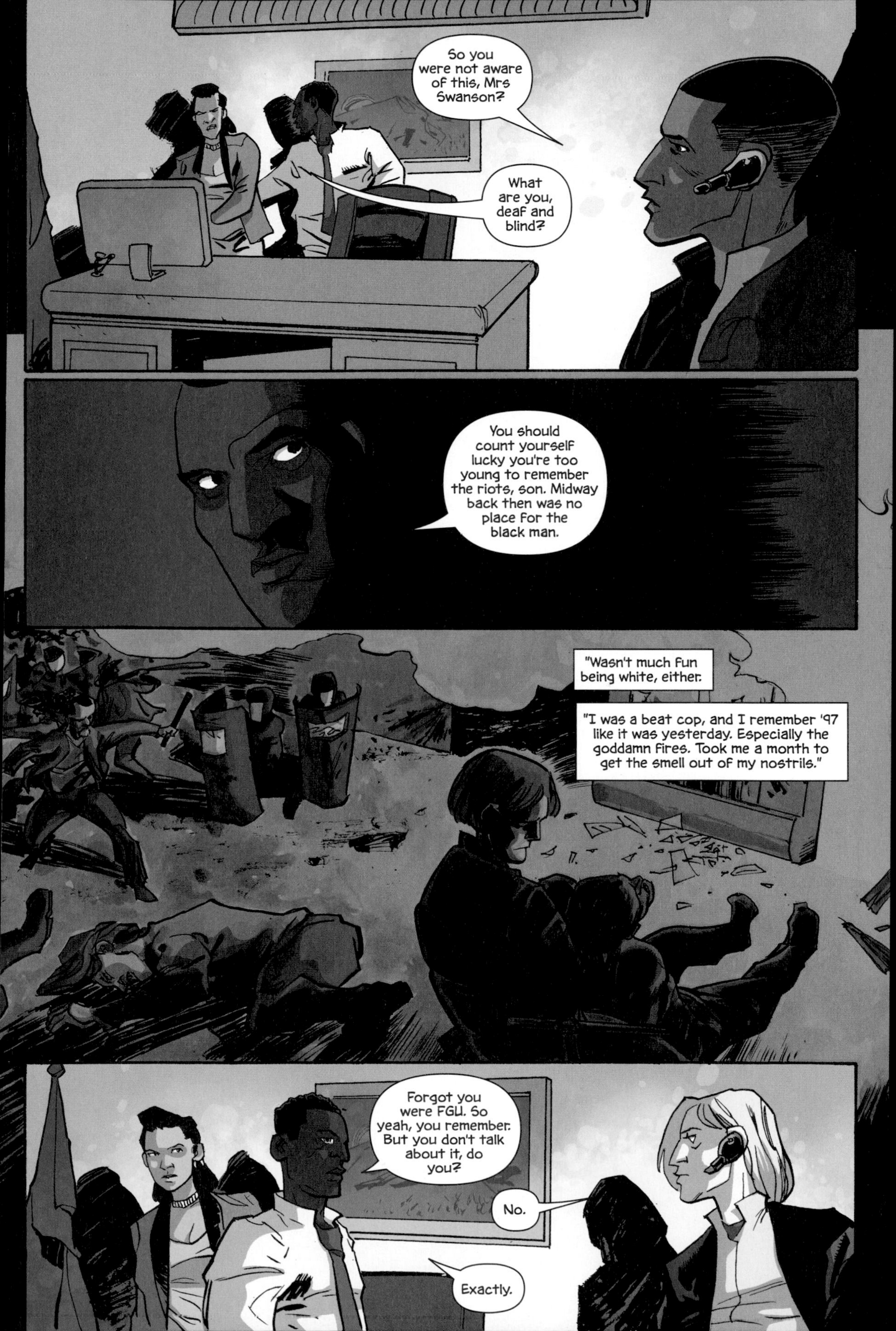
So you were not aware of this, Mrs Swanson?
What are you, deaf and blind?
You should count yourself lucky you're too young to remember the riots, son. Midway back then was no place for the black man.
"Wasn't much fun being white, either.
"I was a beat cop, and I remember '97 like it was yesterday. Especially the goddamn fires. Took me a month to get the smell out of my nostrils."
Forgot you were FGU. So yeah, you remember. But you don't talk about it, do you?
No.
Exactly.

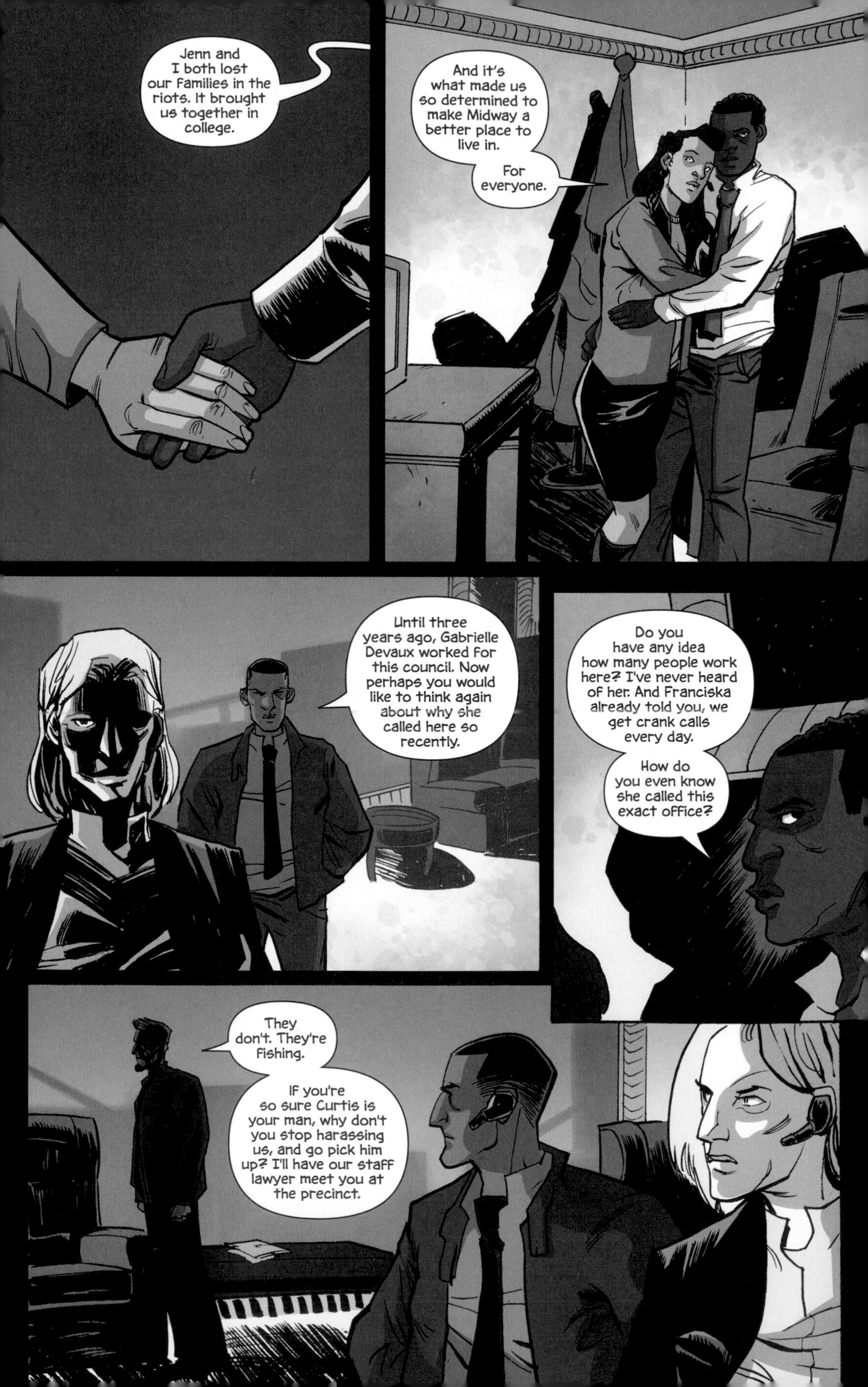

Jenn and I both lost our families in the riots. It brought us together in college.
And it's what made us so determined to make Midway a better place to live in.
For everyone.
Until three years ago, Gabrielle Devaux worked for this council. Now perhaps you would like to think again about why she called here so recently.
Do you have any idea how many people work here? I've never heard of her. And Franciska already told you, we get crank calls every day.
How do you even know she called this exact office?
They don't. They're fishing.
If you're so sure Curtis is your man, why don't you stop harassing us, and go pick him up? I'll have our staff lawyer meet you at the precinct.

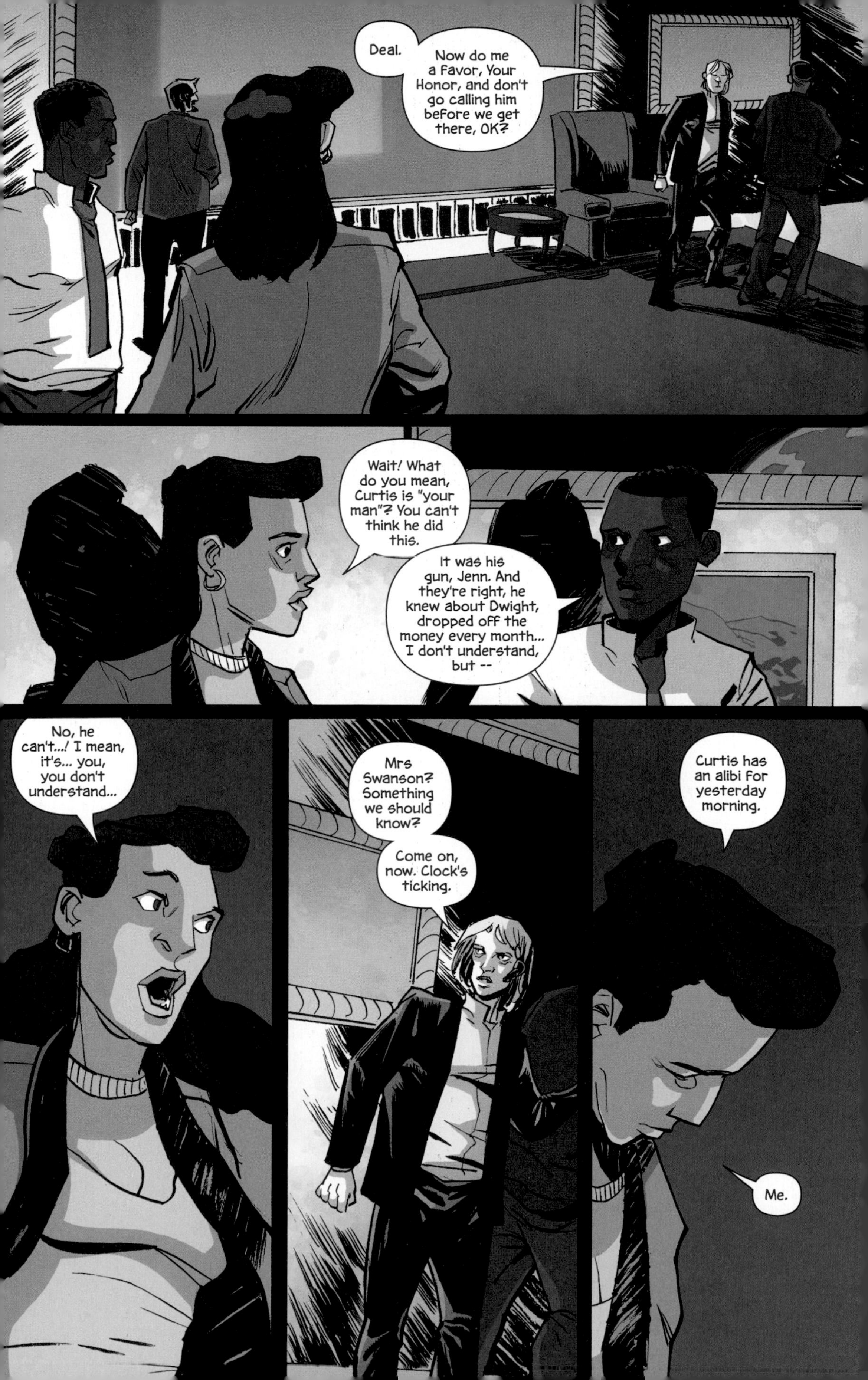
Deal.
Now do me a favor, Your Honor, and don't go calling him before we get there, OK?
Wait! What do you mean, Curtis is "your man"? You can't think he did this.
It was his gun, Jenn. And they're right, he knew about Dwight, dropped off the money every month... I don't understand, but --
No, he can't...! I mean, it's... you, you don't understand...
Mrs Swanson? Something we should know?
Come on, now. Clock's ticking.
Curtis has an alibi for yesterday morning.
Me.

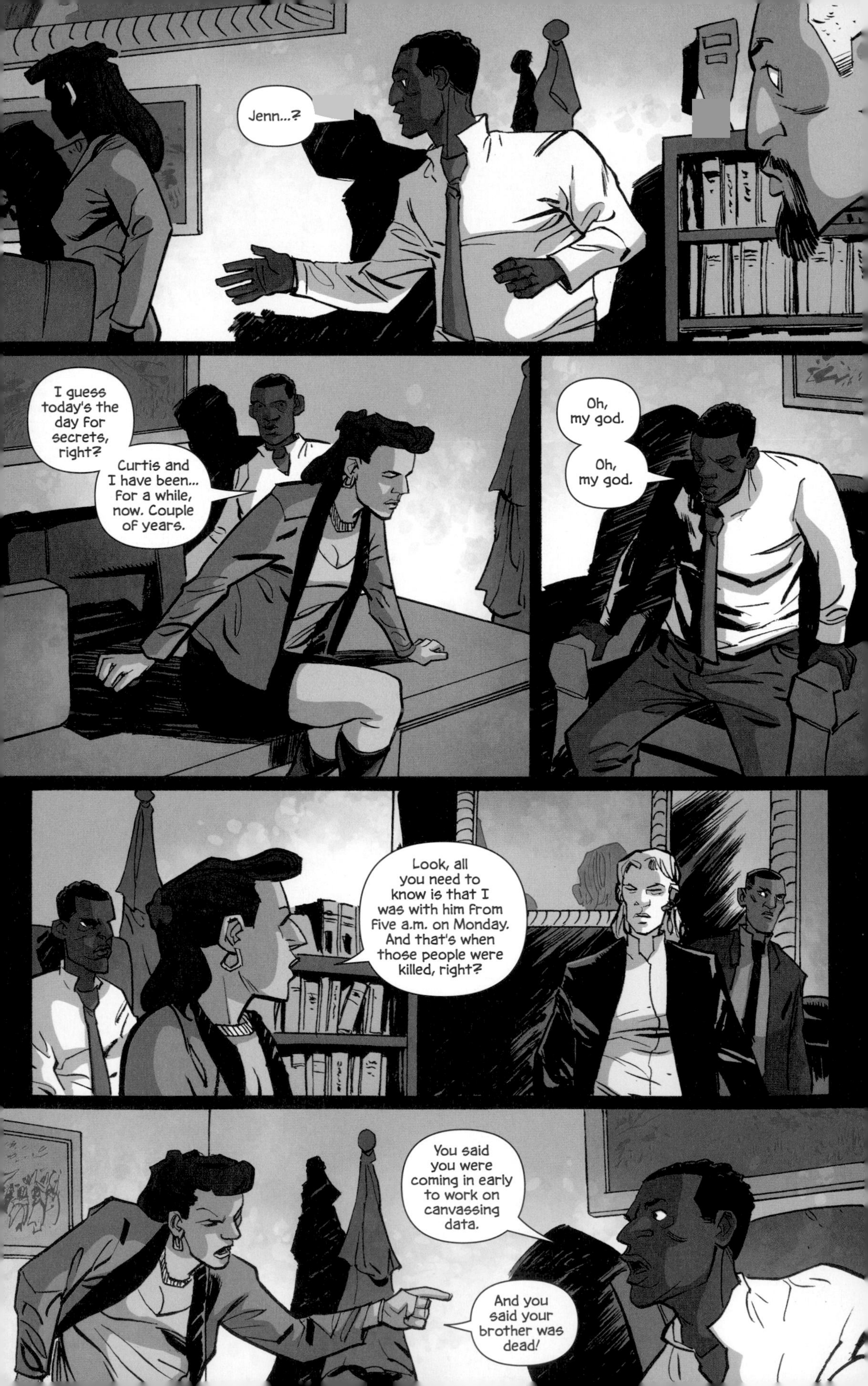
Jenn...?
I guess today's the day for secrets, right?
Curtis and I have been... for a while, now. Couple of years.
Oh, my god.
Oh, my god.
Look, all you need to know is that I was with him from five a.m. on Monday. And that's when those people were killed, right?
You said you were coming in early to work on canvassing data.
And you said your brother was dead!

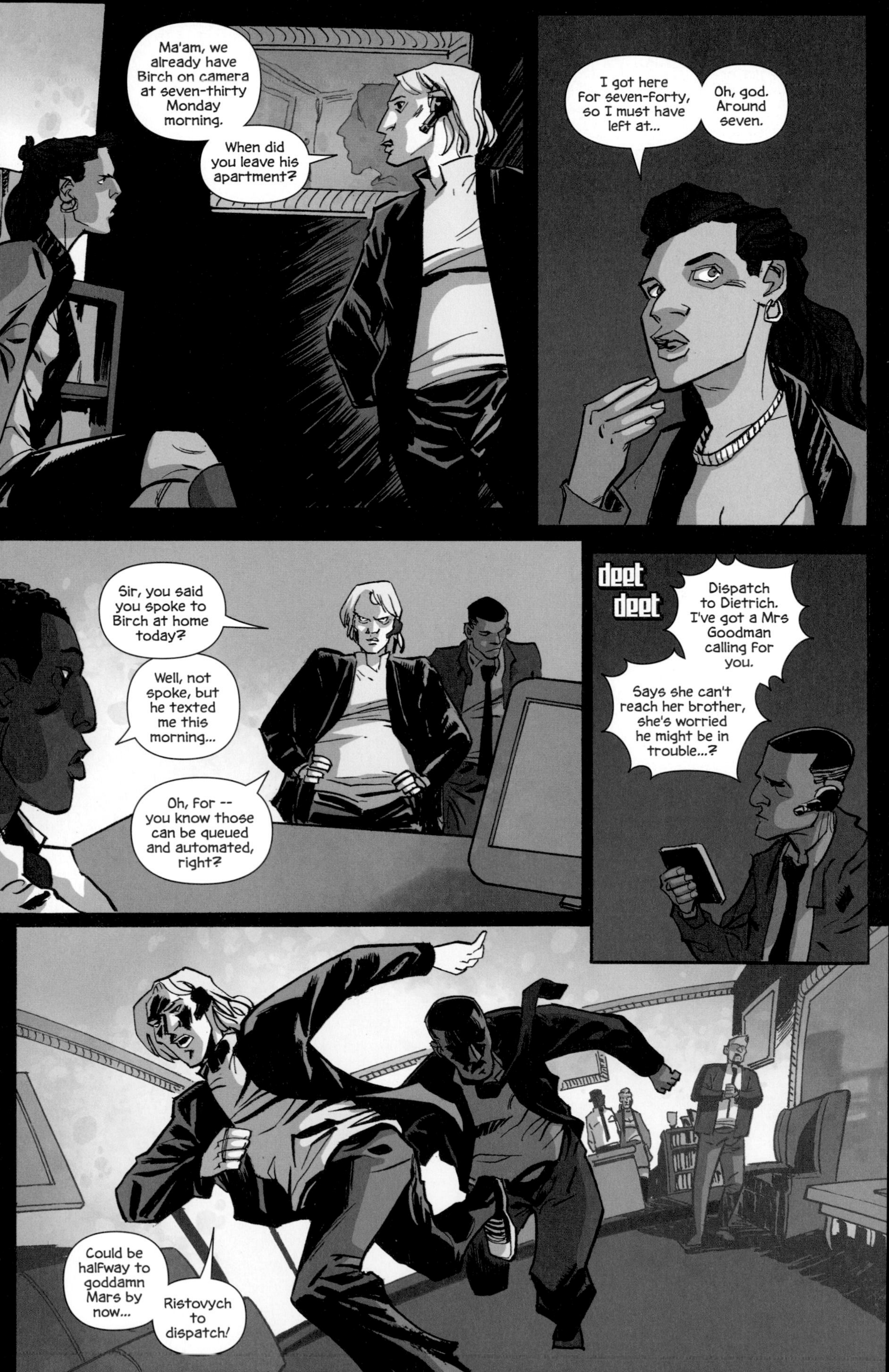
Ma'am, we already have Birch on camera at seven-thirty Monday morning.
When did you leave his apartment?
I got here for seven-forty, so I must have left at...
Oh, god. Around seven.
Sir, you said you spoke to Birch at home today?
Well, not spoke, but he texted me this morning...
Oh, for -- you know those can be queued and automated, right?
deet
deet
Dispatch to Dietrich. I've got a Mrs Goodman calling for you.
Says she can't reach her brother, she's worried he might be in trouble...?
Could be halfway to goddamn Mars by now...
Ristovych to dispatch!

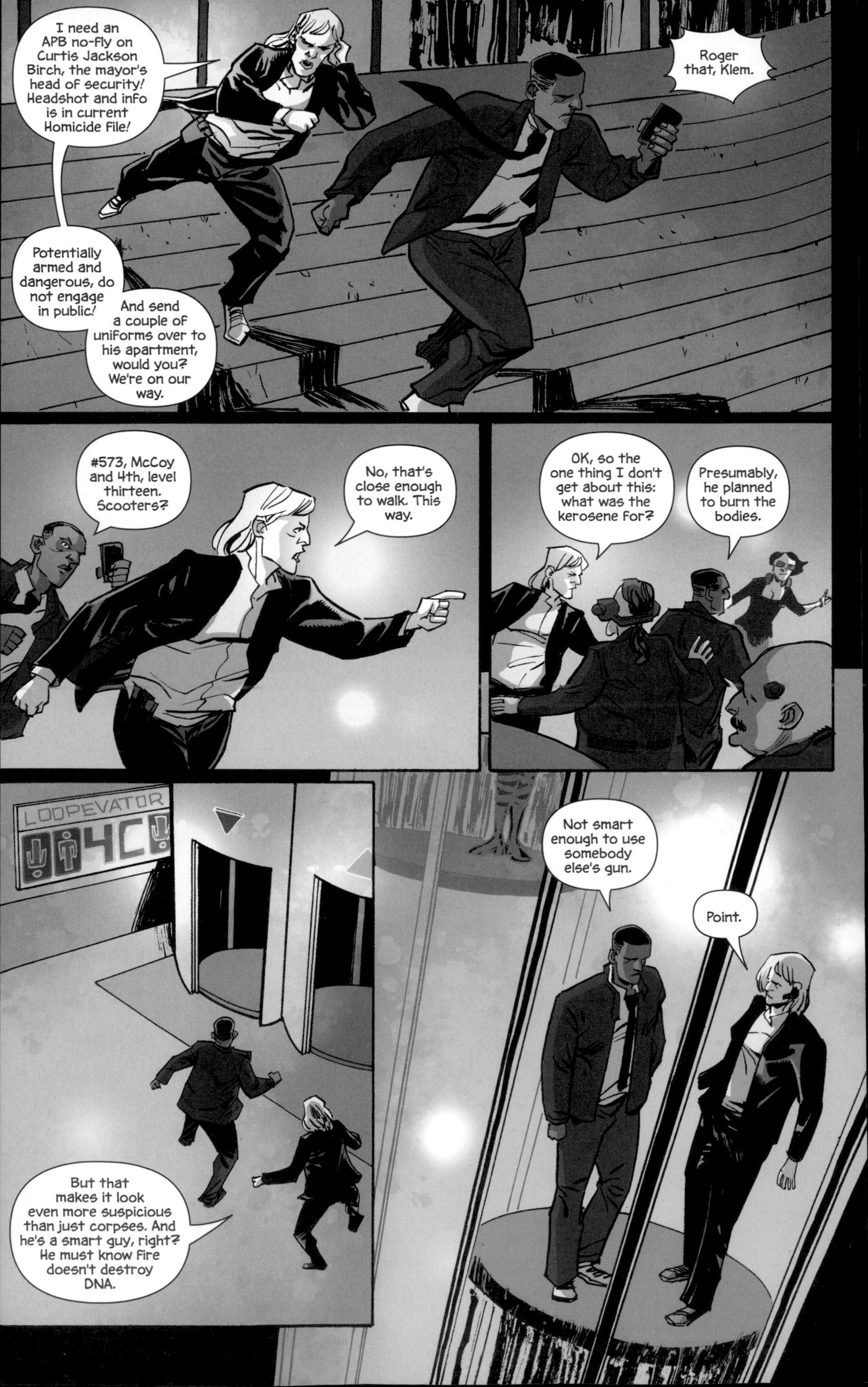
I need an APB no-fly on Curtis Jackson Birch, the mayor's head of security! Headshot and info is in current Homicide File!
Potentially armed and dangerous, do not engage in public!
And send a couple of uniforms over to his apartment, would you? We're on our way.
Roger that, Klem.
#573, McCoy and 4th, level thirteen. Scooters?
No, that's close enough to walk. This way.
OK, so the one thing I don't get about this: what was the kerosene for?
Presumably, he planned to burn the bodies.
LOOPEVATOR
4C
But that makes it look even more suspicious than just corpses. And he's a smart guy, right? He must know fire doesn't destroy DNA.
Not smart enough to use somebody else's gun.
Point.

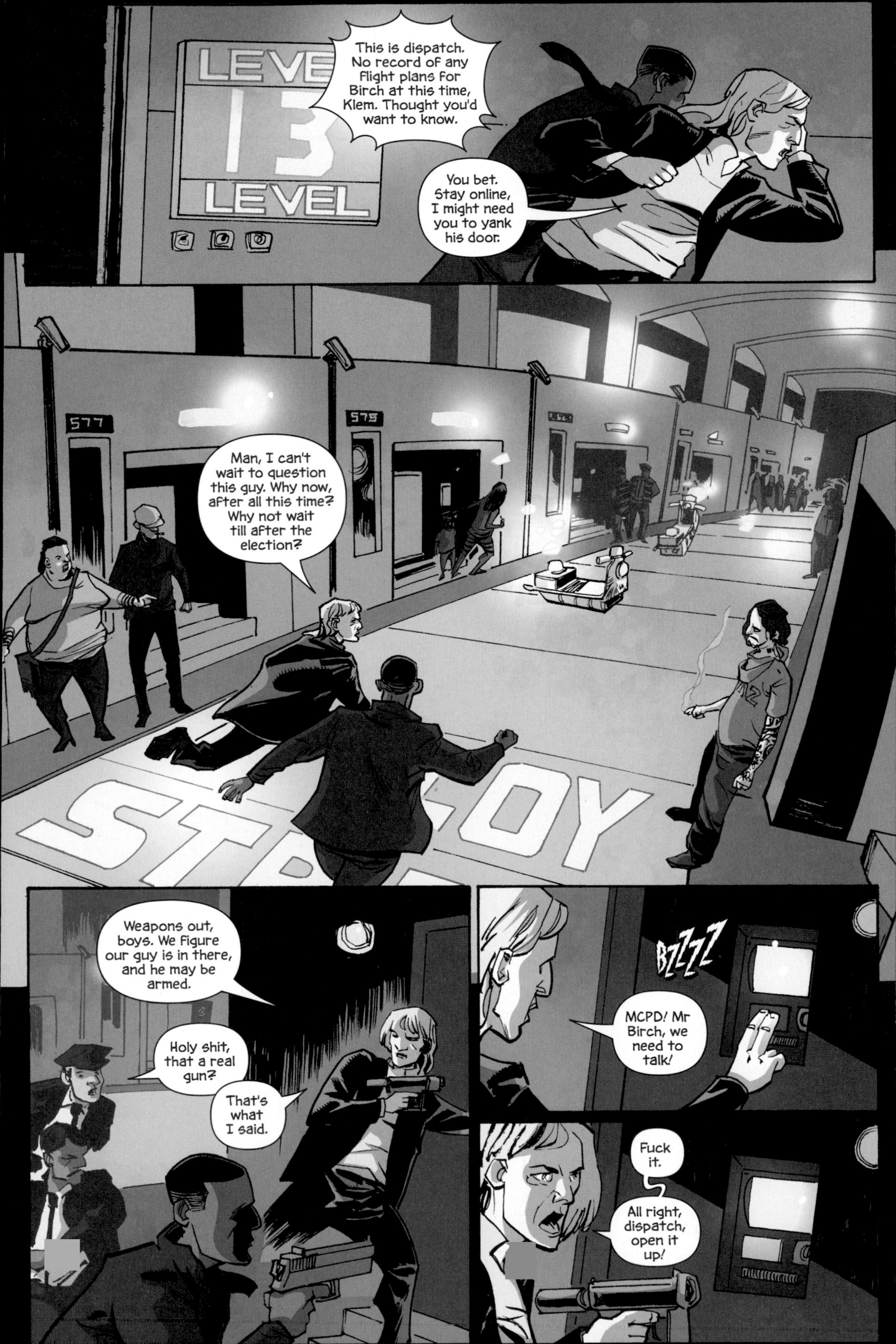
LEVEL
13
LEVEL
This is dispatch. No record of any flight plans for Birch at this time, Klem. Thought you'd want to know.
You bet. Stay online, I might need you to yank his door.
577
575
Man, I can't wait to question this guy. Why now, after all this time? Why not wait till after the election?
Weapons out, boys. We figure our guy is in there, and he may be armed.
Holy shit, that a real gun?
That's what I said.
BZZZZ
MCPD! Mr Birch, we need to talk!
Fuck it.
All right, dispatch, open it up!

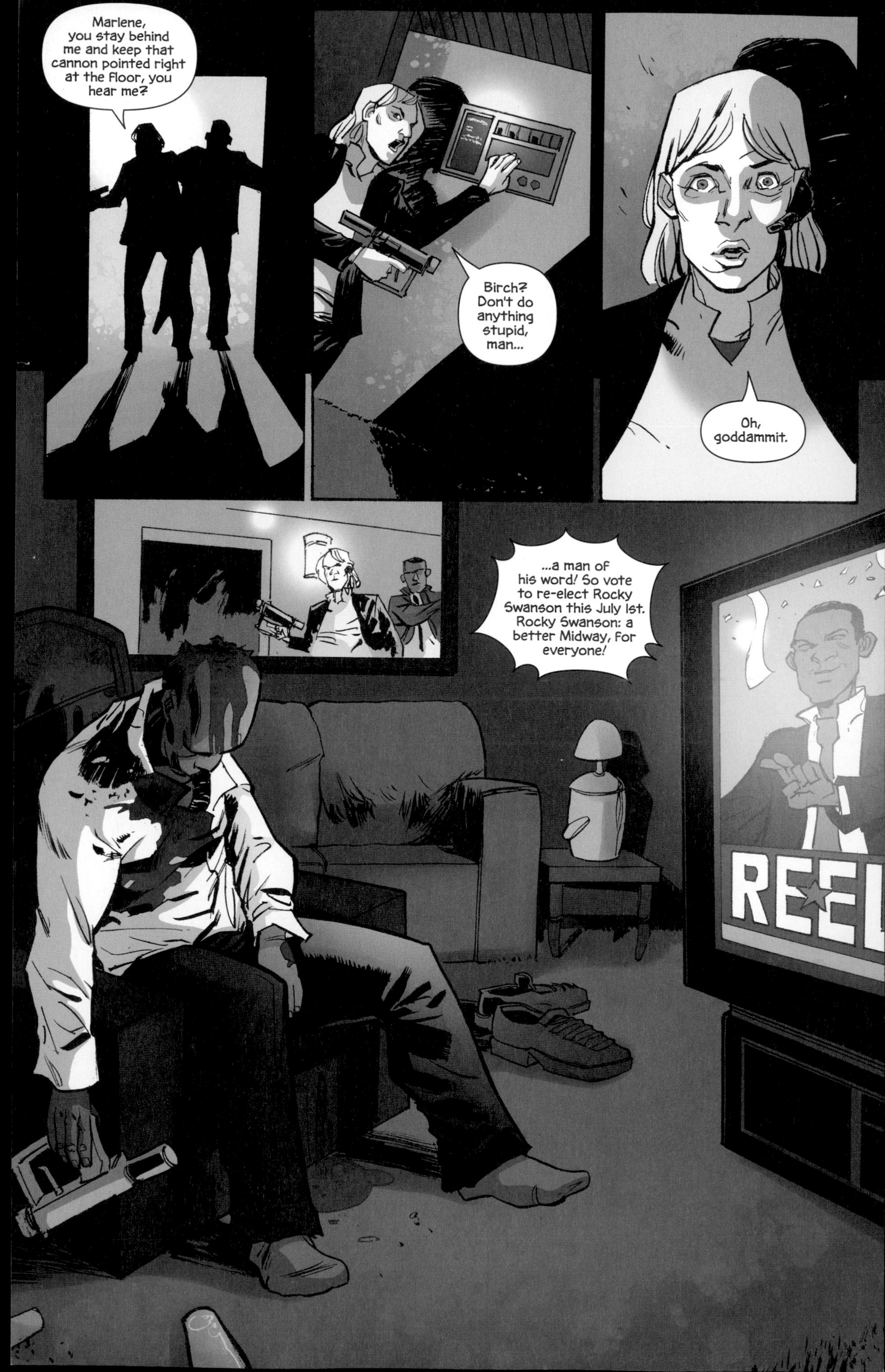
Marlene, you stay behind me and keep that cannon pointed right at the floor, you hear me?
Birch? Don't do anything stupid, man...
Oh, goddammit.
...a man of his word! So vote to re-elect Rocky Swanson this July 1st. Rocky Swanson: a better Midway, for everyone!
REEL

PART 4

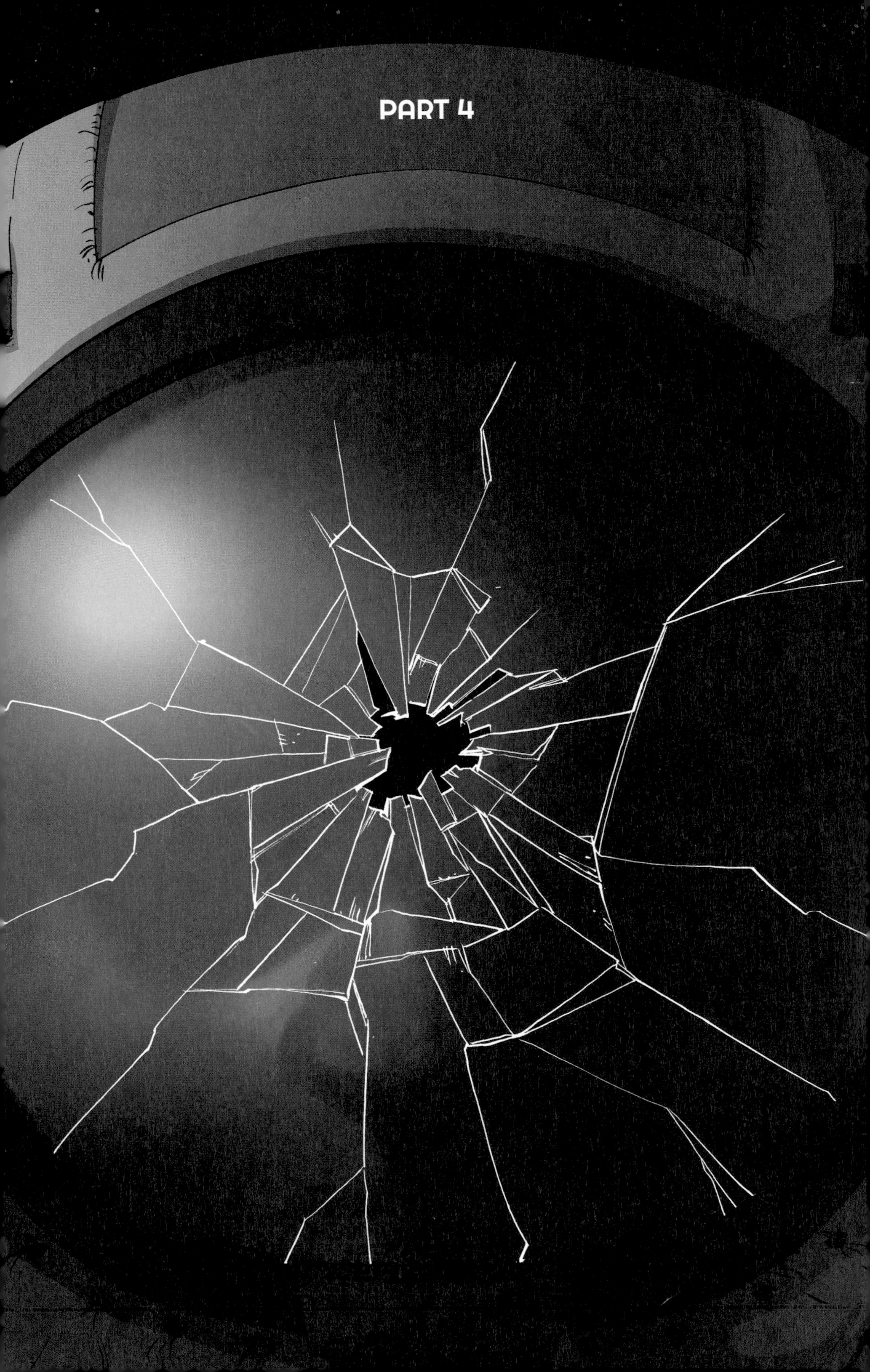

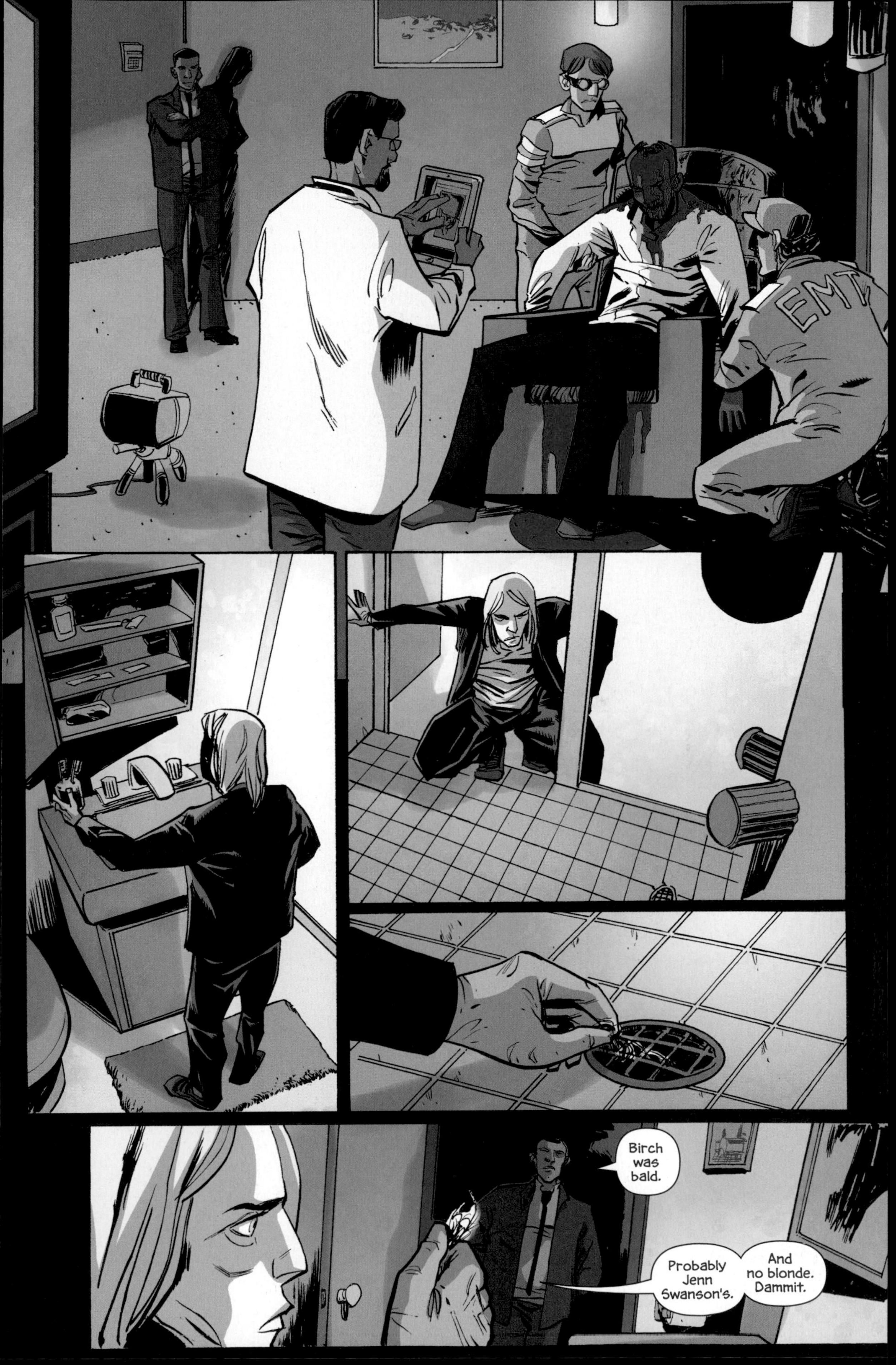
EMT
Birch was bald.
Probably Jenn Swanson's.
And no blonde. Dammit.

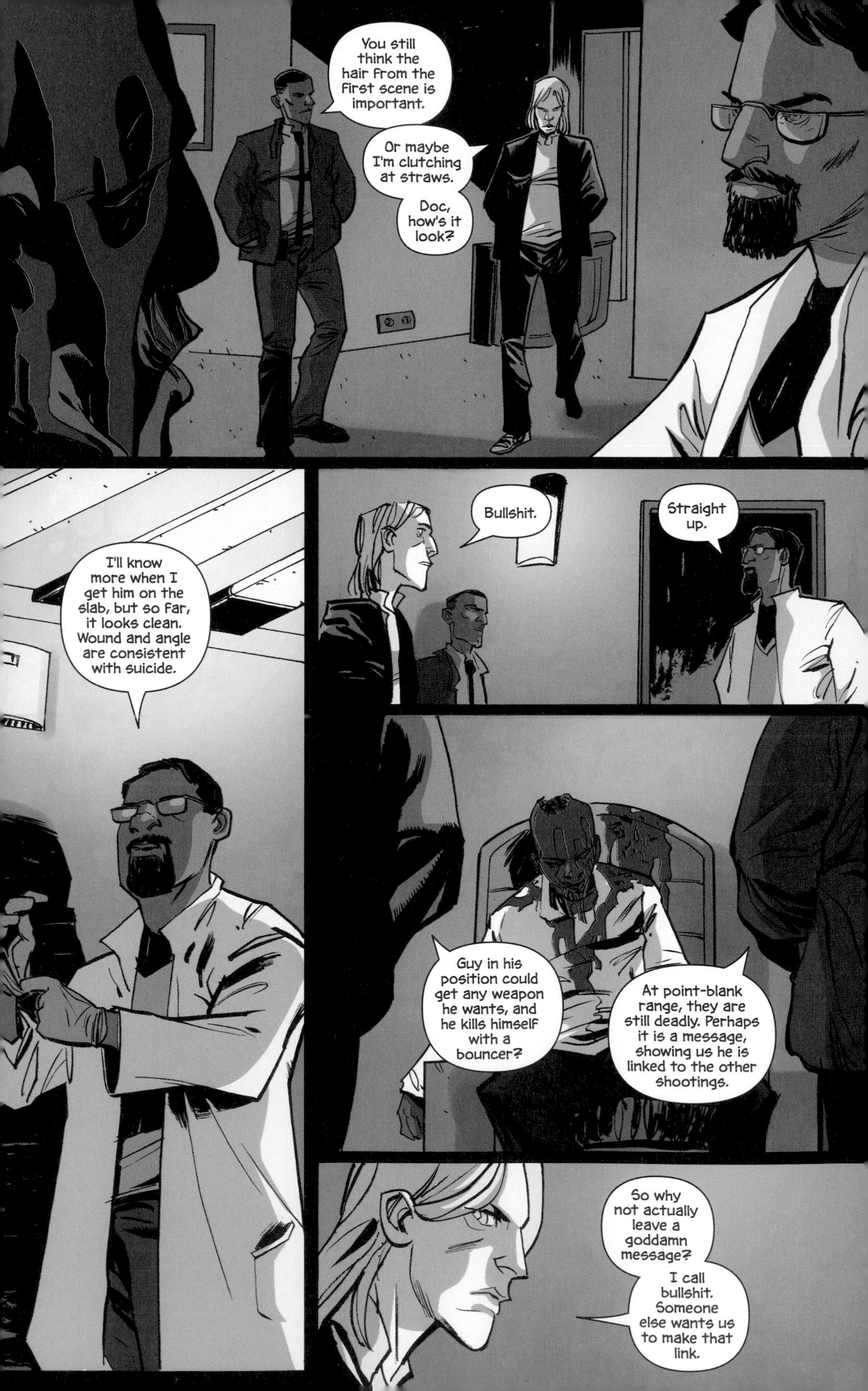
You still think the hair from the first scene is important.
Or maybe I'm clutching at straws.
Doc, how's it look?
I'll know more when I get him on the slab, but so far, it looks clean. Wound and angle are consistent with suicide.
Bullshit.
Straight up.
Guy in his position could get any weapon he wants, and he kills himself with a bouncer?
At point-blank range, they are still deadly. Perhaps it is a message, showing us he is linked to the other shootings.
So why not actually leave a goddamn message?
I call bullshit. Someone else wants us to make that link.

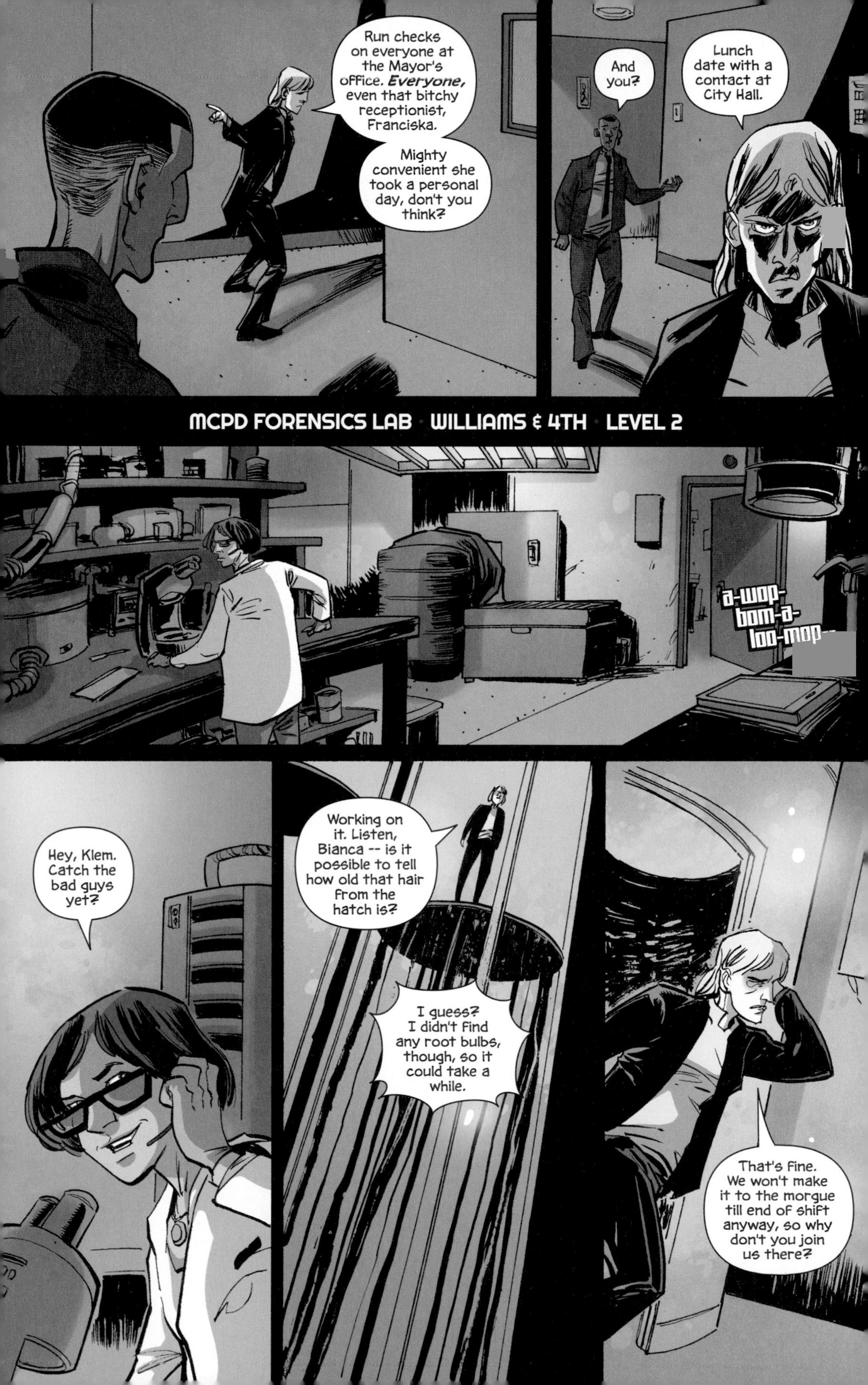
Run checks on everyone at the Mayor's office. *Everyone,* even that bitchy receptionist, Franciska.
Mighty convenient she took a personal day, don't you think?
And you?
Lunch date with a contact at City Hall.
MCPD FORENSICS LAB · WILLIAMS & 4TH · LEVEL 2
a-wop-bom-a-loo-mop--
Hey, Klem. Catch the bad guys yet?
Working on it. Listen, Bianca -- is it possible to tell how old that hair from the hatch is?
I guess? I didn't find any root bulbs, though, so it could take a while.
That's fine. We won't make it to the morgue till end of shift anyway, so why don't you join us there?

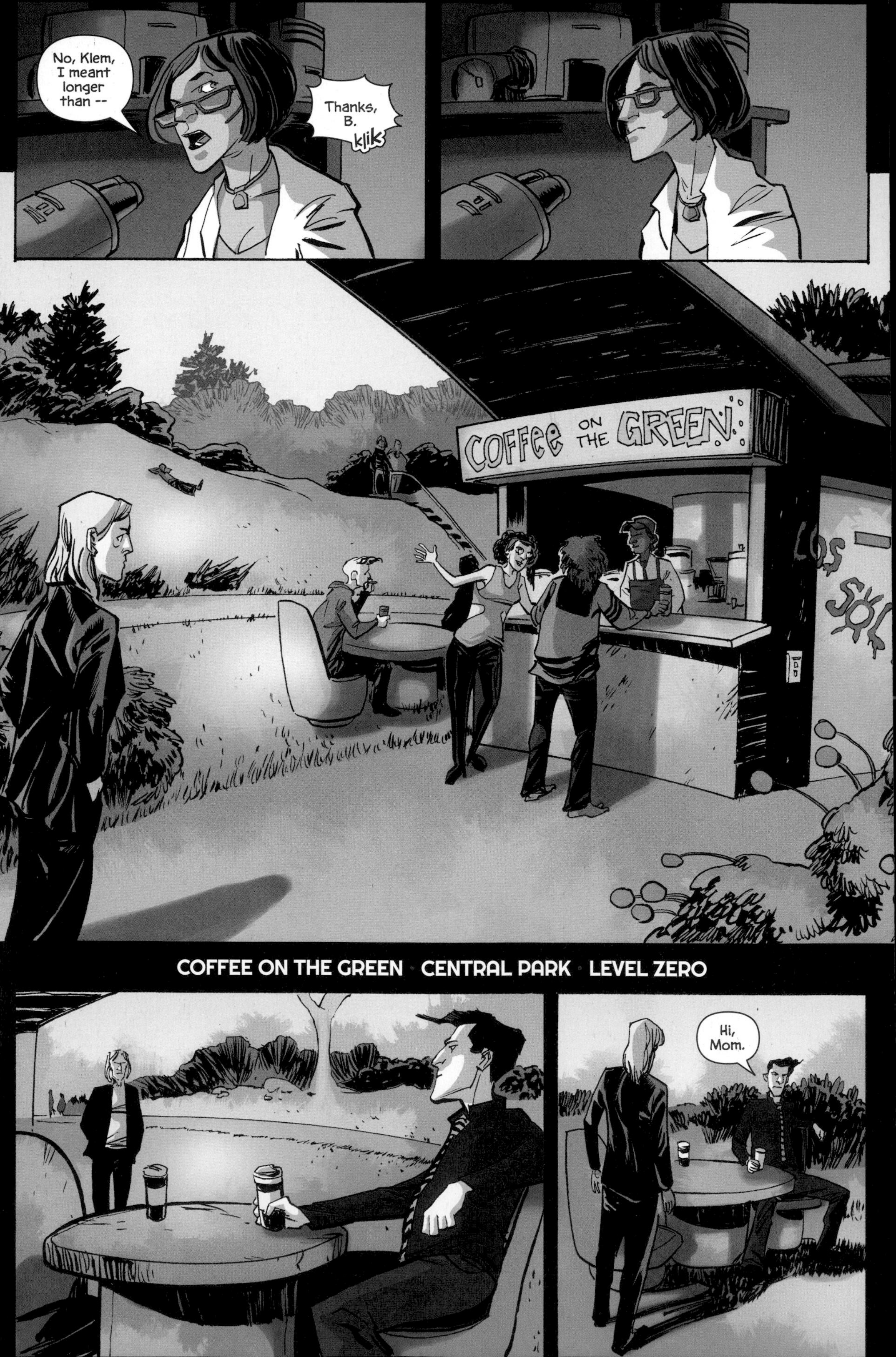
No, Klem, I meant longer than --
Thanks, B.
klik
COFFEE ON THE GREEN
LOS
SOL
COFFEE ON THE GREEN · CENTRAL PARK · LEVEL ZERO
Hi, Mom.

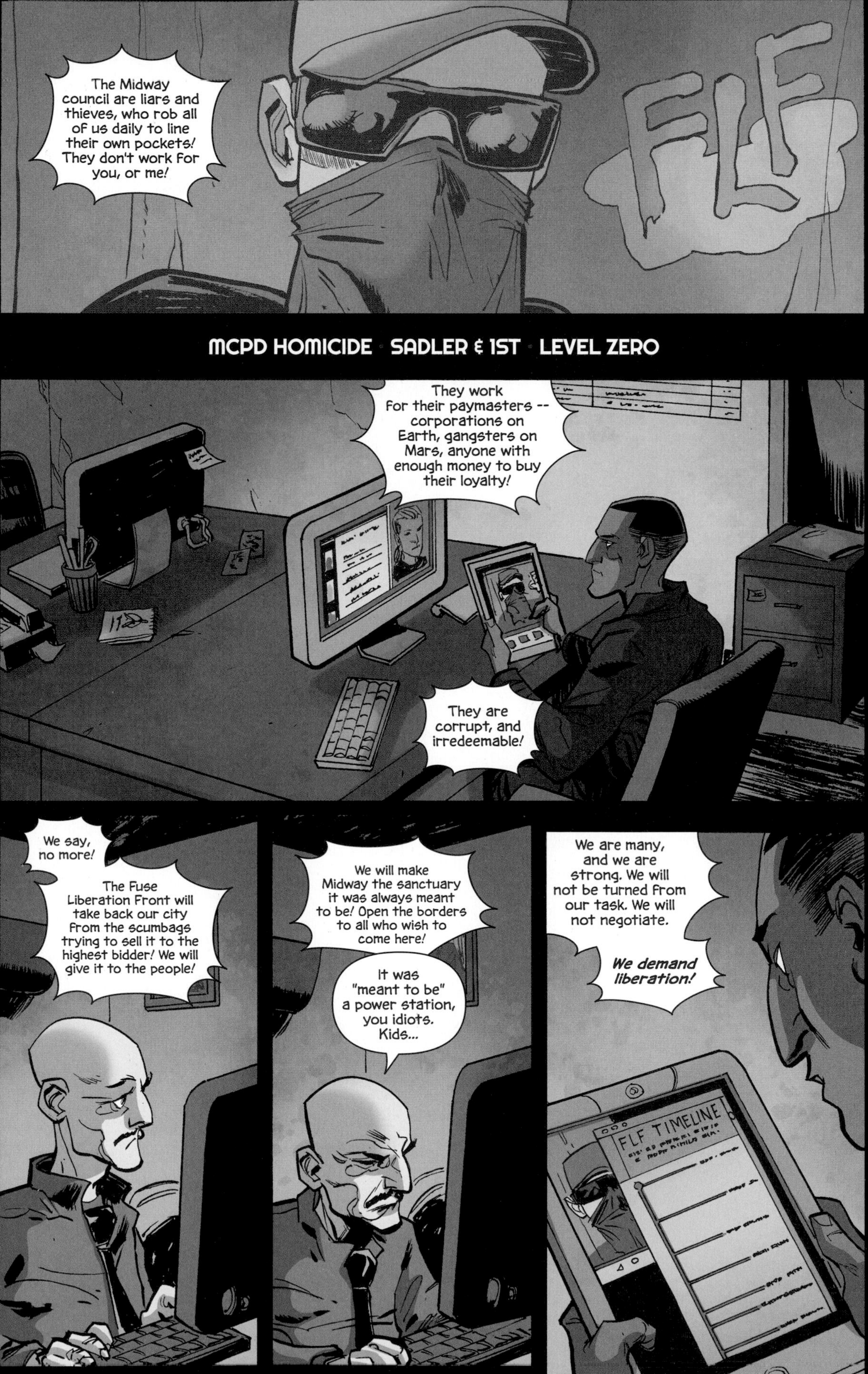
The Midway council are liars and thieves, who rob all of us daily to line their own pockets! They don't work for you, or me!
FLF
MCPD HOMICIDE · SADLER & 1ST · LEVEL ZERO
They work for their paymasters -- corporations on Earth, gangsters on Mars, anyone with enough money to buy their loyalty!
They are corrupt, and irredeemable!
We say, no more!
The Fuse Liberation Front will take back our city from the scumbags trying to sell it to the highest bidder! We will give it to the people!
We will make Midway the sanctuary it was always meant to be! Open the borders to all who wish to come here!
It was "meant to be" a power station, you idiots. Kids...
We are many, and we are strong. We will not be turned from our task. We will not negotiate.
We demand liberation!
FLF TIMELINE

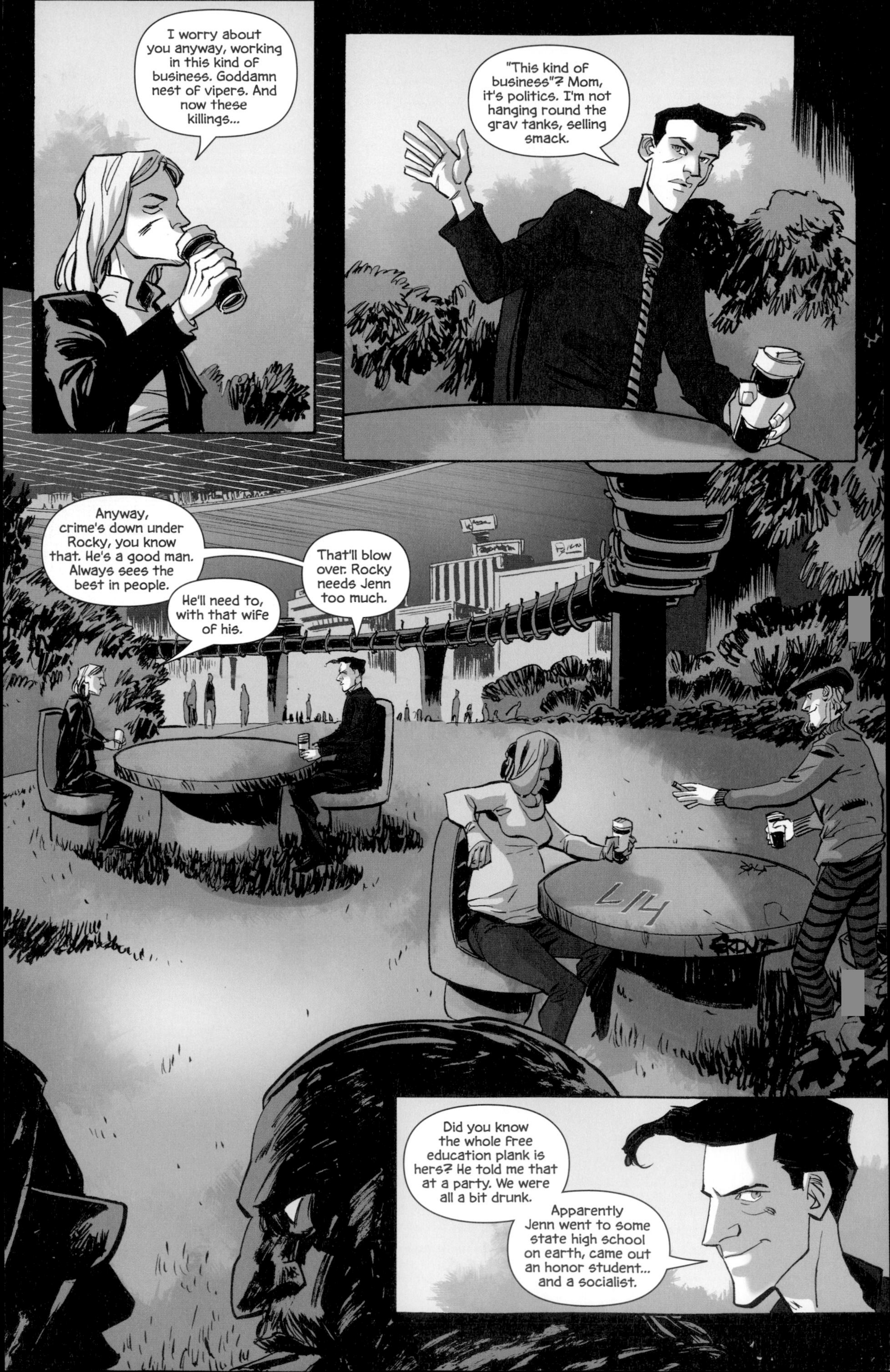
I worry about you anyway, working in this kind of business. Goddamn nest of vipers. And now these killings...
"This kind of business"? Mom, it's politics. I'm not hanging round the grav tanks, selling smack.
Anyway, crime's down under Rocky, you know that. He's a good man. Always sees the best in people.
He'll need to, with that wife of his.
That'll blow over. Rocky needs Jenn too much.
L14
Did you know the whole free education plank is hers? He told me that at a party. We were all a bit drunk.
Apparently Jenn went to some state high school on earth, came out an honor student... and a socialist.

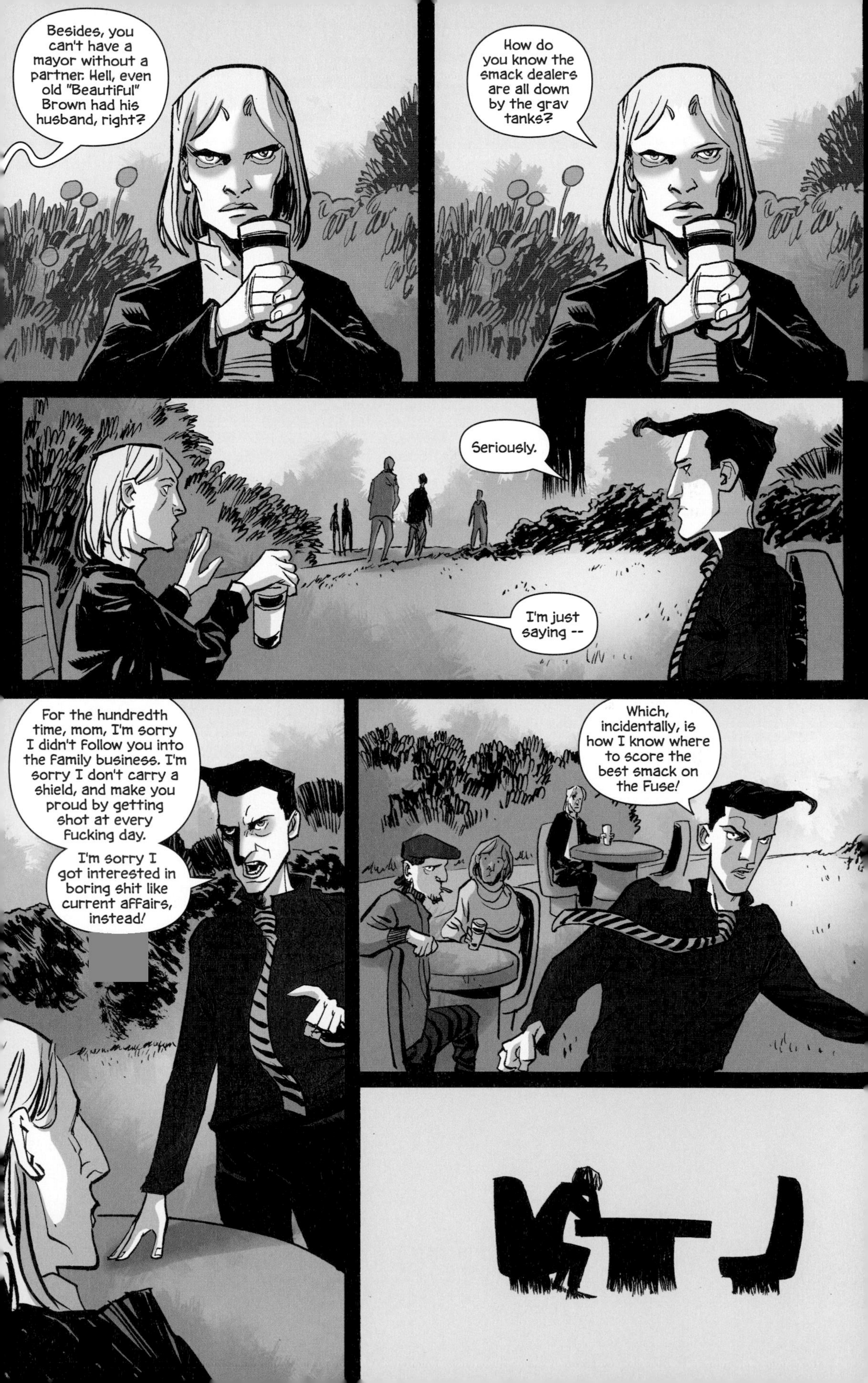

Besides, you can't have a mayor without a partner. Hell, even old "Beautiful" Brown had his husband, right?
How do you know the smack dealers are all down by the grav tanks?
Seriously.
I'm just saying --
For the hundredth time, mom, I'm sorry I didn't follow you into the family business. I'm sorry I don't carry a shield, and make you proud by getting shot at every fucking day.
I'm sorry I got interested in boring shit like current affairs, instead!
Which, incidentally, is how I know where to score the best smack on the Fuse!

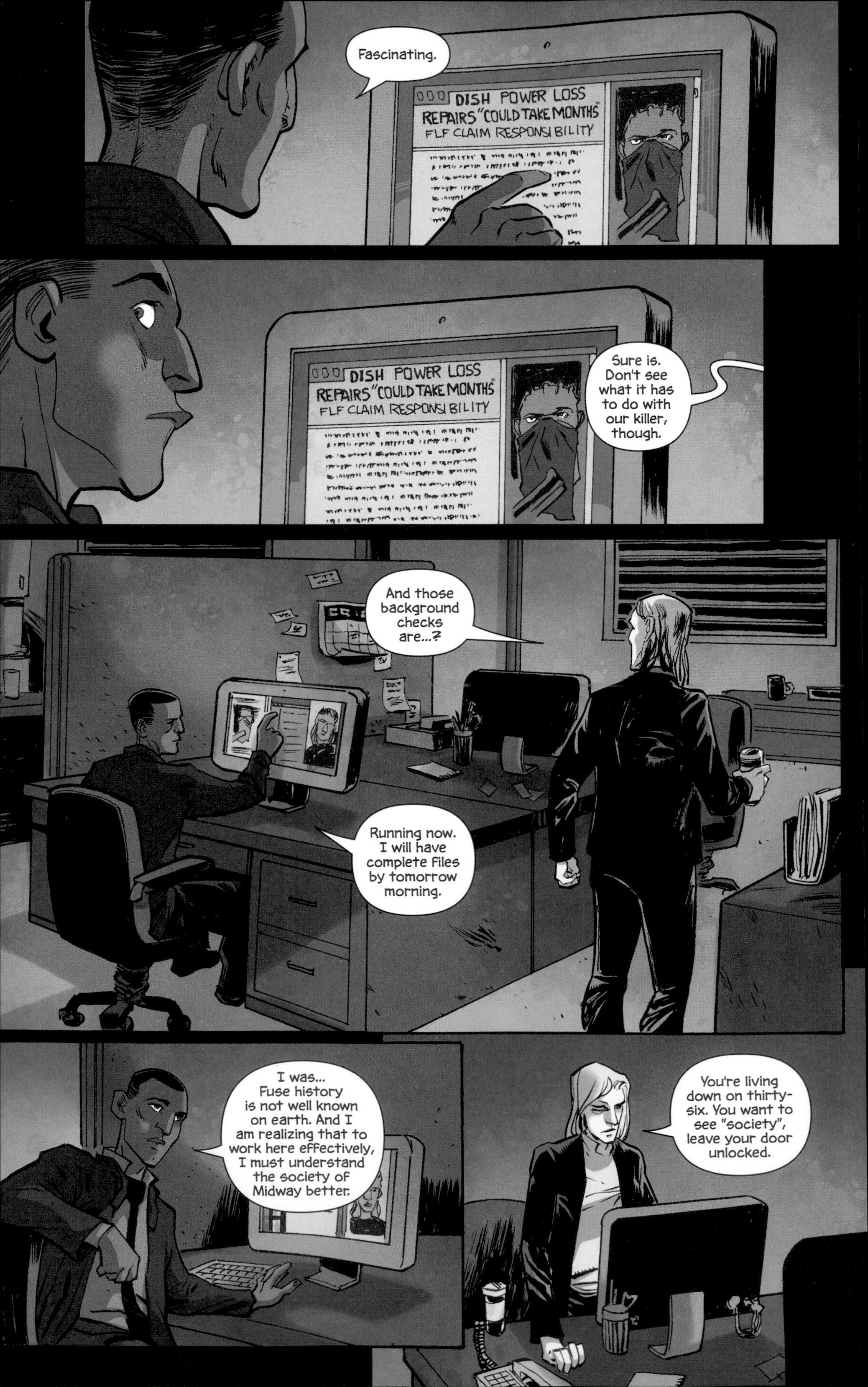
Fascinating.
DISH POWER LOSS
REPAIRS "COULD TAKE MONTHS"
FLF CLAIM RESPONSIBILITY
DISH POWER LOSS
REPAIRS "COULD TAKE MONTHS"
FLF CLAIM RESPONSIBILITY
Sure is. Don't see what it has to do with our killer, though.
And those background checks are...?
Running now. I will have complete files by tomorrow morning.
I was... Fuse history is not well known on earth. And I am realizing that to work here effectively, I must understand the society of Midway better.
You're living down on thirty-six. You want to see "society", leave your door unlocked.

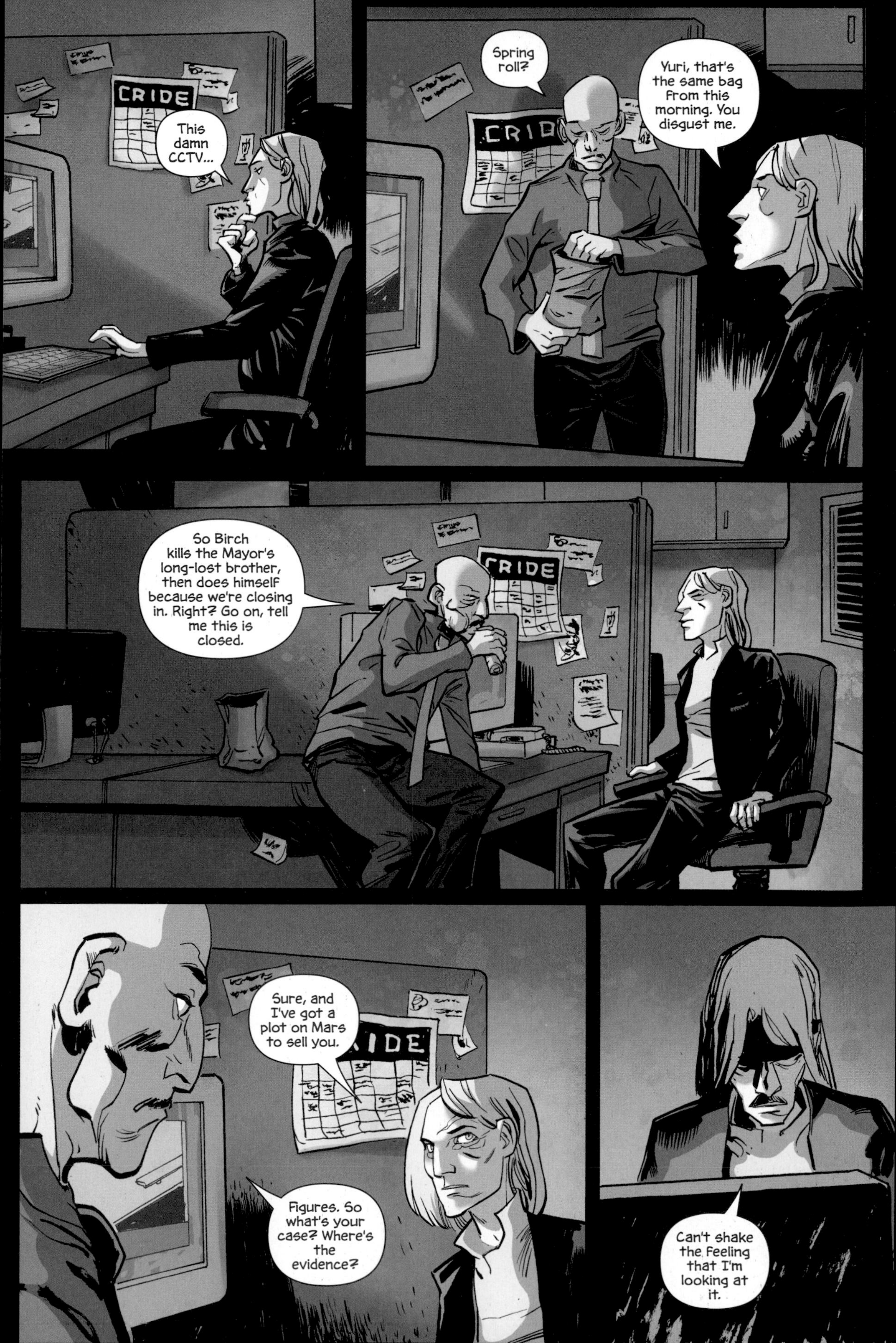
CRIDE
This damn CCTV...
Spring roll?
Yuri, that's the same bag from this morning. You disgust me.
So Birch kills the Mayor's long-lost brother, then does himself because we're closing in. Right? Go on, tell me this is closed.
Sure, and I've got a plot on Mars to sell you.
Figures. So what's your case? Where's the evidence?
Can't shake the feeling that I'm looking at it.

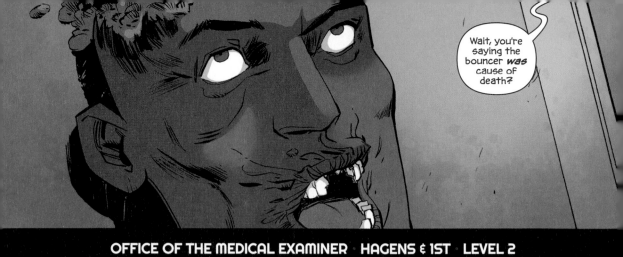

Wait, you're saying the bouncer *was* cause of death?

OFFICE OF THE MEDICAL EXAMINER · HAGENS & 1ST · LEVEL 2

Yep. Until the bouncer entered his brain, he was still alive.

I told you. The damage, angle of entry, distance from shot... it's all consistent with suicide.

There were no signs of struggle at his apartment. Maybe it is true.

Sorry, Klem. Barring new evidence, I'm ruling this one as self-inflicted.

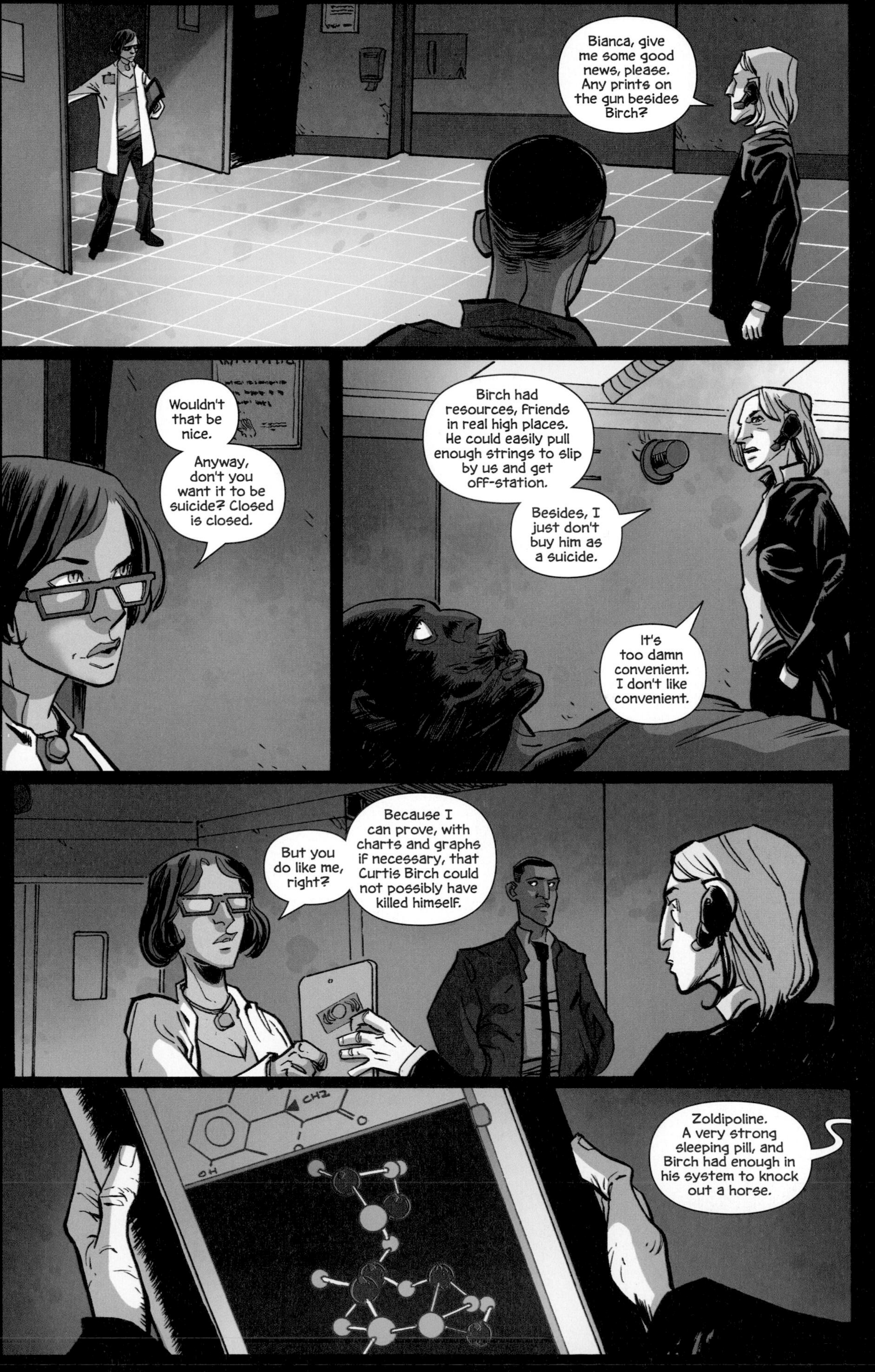
Bianca, give me some good news, please. Any prints on the gun besides Birch?
Wouldn't that be nice.
Anyway, don't you want it to be suicide? Closed is closed.
Birch had resources, friends in real high places. He could easily pull enough strings to slip by us and get off-station.
Besides, I just don't buy him as a suicide.
It's too damn convenient. I don't like convenient.
But you do like me, right?
Because I can prove, with charts and graphs if necessary, that Curtis Birch could not possibly have killed himself.
Zoldipoline. A very strong sleeping pill, and Birch had enough in his system to knock out a horse.

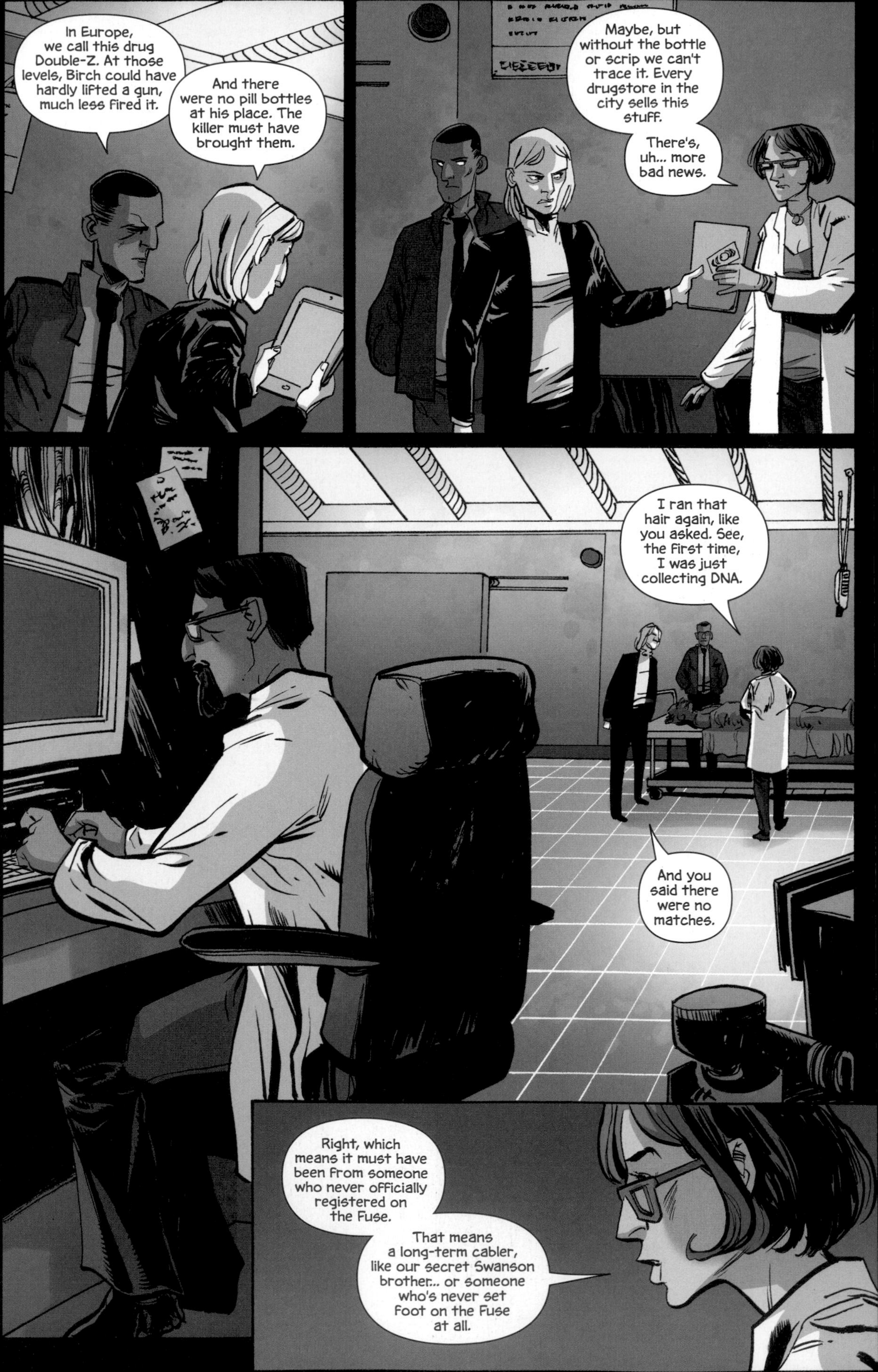
In Europe, we call this drug Double-Z. At those levels, Birch could have hardly lifted a gun, much less fired it.
And there were no pill bottles at his place. The killer must have brought them.
Maybe, but without the bottle or scrip we can't trace it. Every drugstore in the city sells this stuff.
There's, uh... more bad news.
I ran that hair again, like you asked. See, the first time, I was just collecting DNA.
And you said there were no matches.
Right, which means it must have been from someone who never officially registered on the Fuse.
That means a long-term cabler, like our secret Swanson brother... or someone who's never set foot on the Fuse at all.

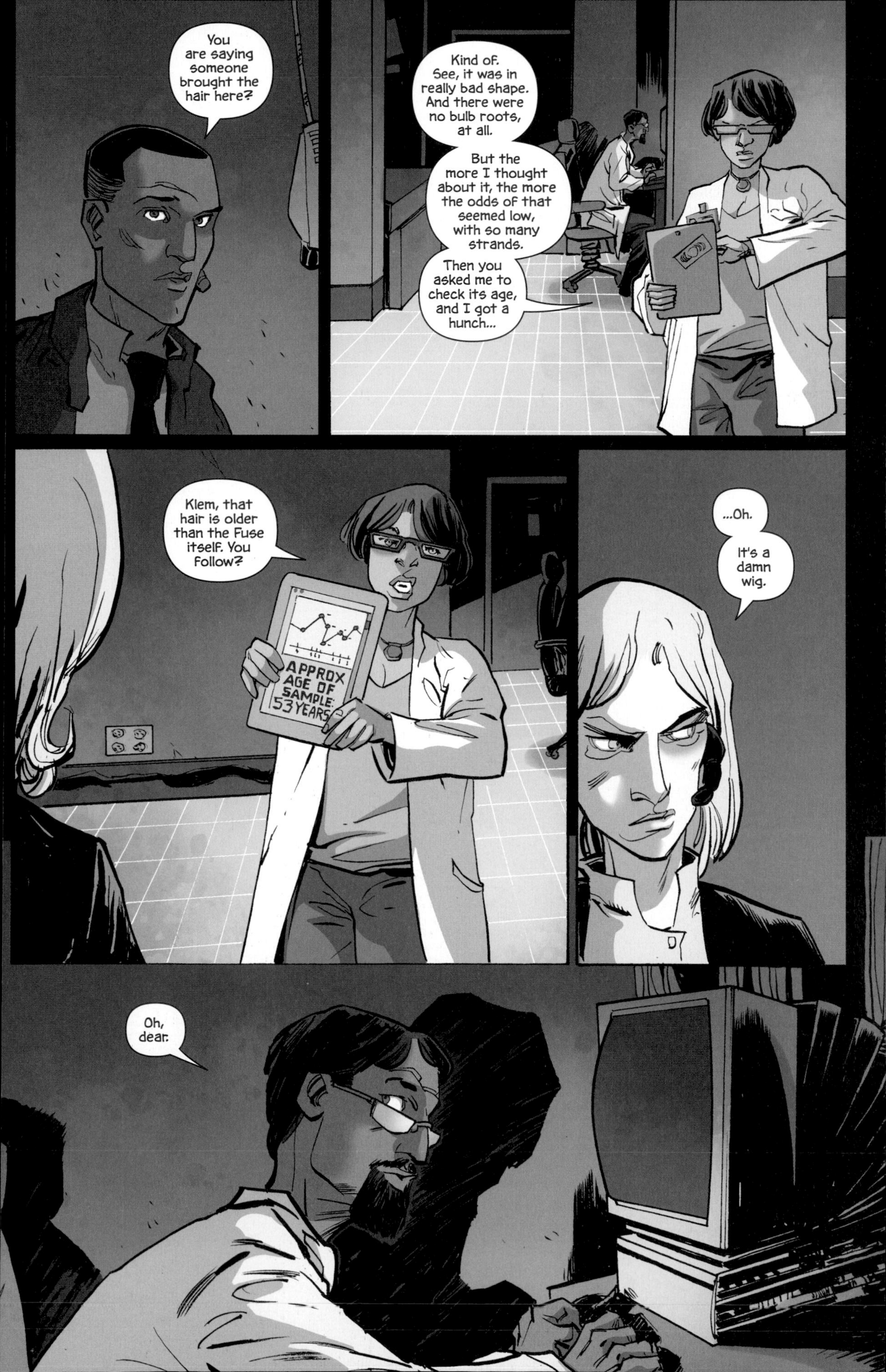
You are saying someone brought the hair here?
Kind of. See, it was in really bad shape. And there were no bulb roots, at all.
But the more I thought about it, the more the odds of that seemed low, with so many strands.
Then you asked me to check its age, and I got a hunch...
Klem, that hair is older than the Fuse itself. You follow?
APPROX AGE OF SAMPLE: 53 YEARS
...Oh.
It's a damn wig.
Oh, dear.

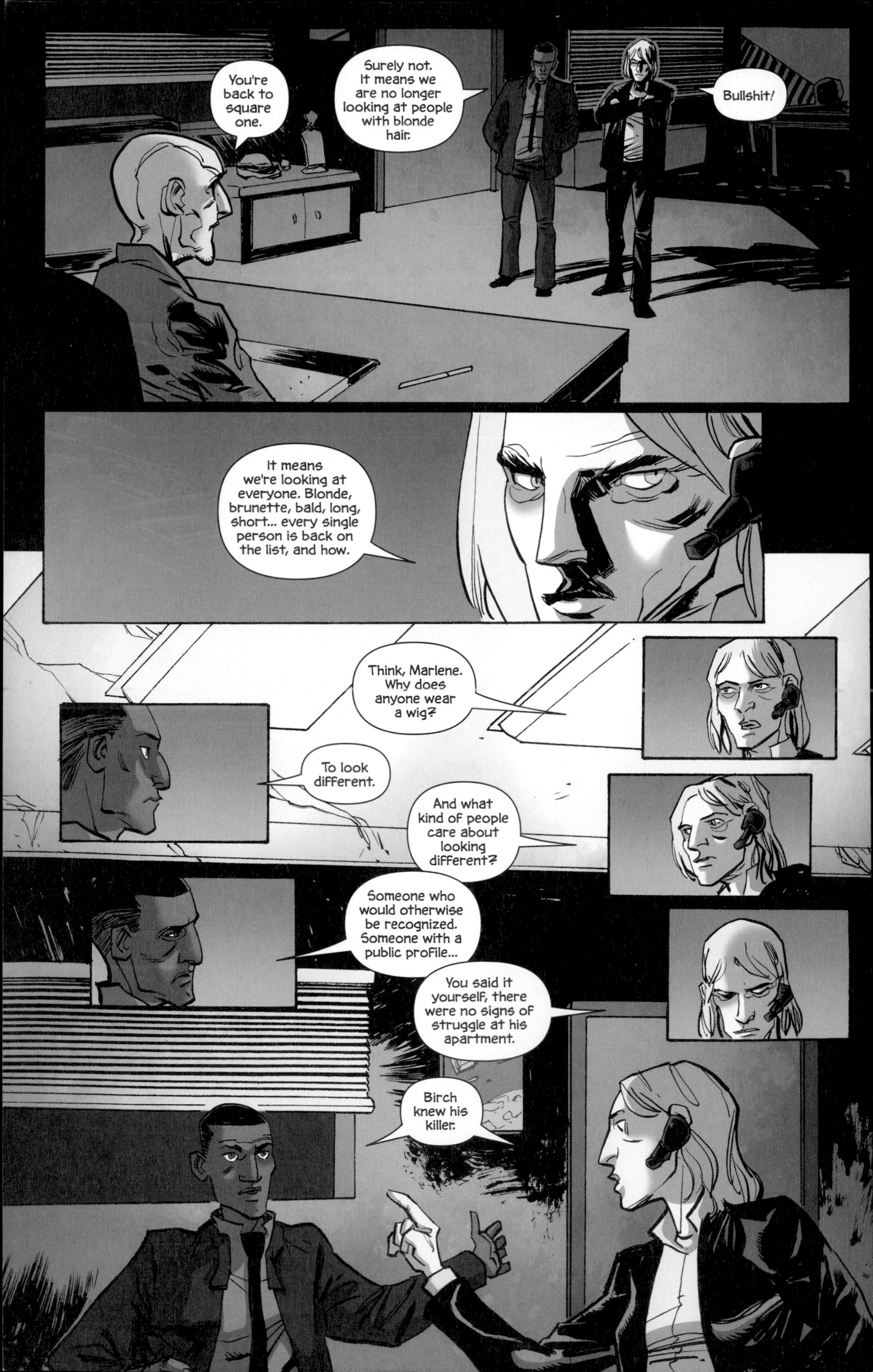
You're back to square one.
Surely not. It means we are no longer looking at people with blonde hair.
Bullshit!
It means we're looking at everyone. Blonde, brunette, bald, long, short... every single person is back on the list, and how.
Think, Marlene. Why does anyone wear a wig?
To look different.
And what kind of people care about looking different?
Someone who would otherwise be recognized. Someone with a public profile...
You said it yourself, there were no signs of struggle at his apartment.
Birch knew his killer.

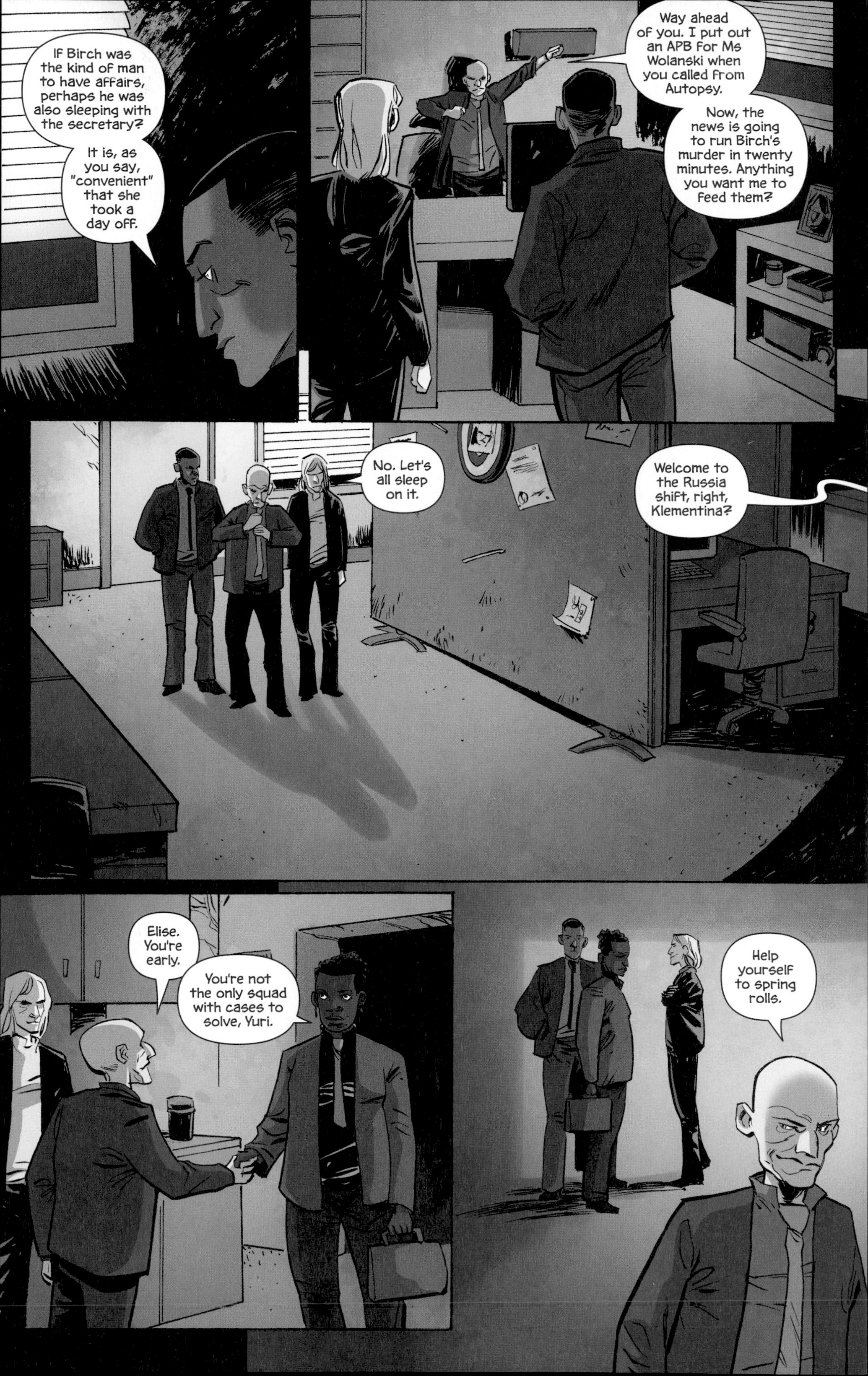
If Birch was the kind of man to have affairs, perhaps he was also sleeping with the secretary?
It is, as you say, "convenient" that she took a day off.
Way ahead of you. I put out an APB for Ms Wolanski when you called from Autopsy.
Now, the news is going to run Birch's murder in twenty minutes. Anything you want me to feed them?
No. Let's all sleep on it.
Welcome to the Russia shift, right, Klementina?
Elise. You're early.
You're not the only squad with cases to solve, Yuri.
Help yourself to spring rolls.

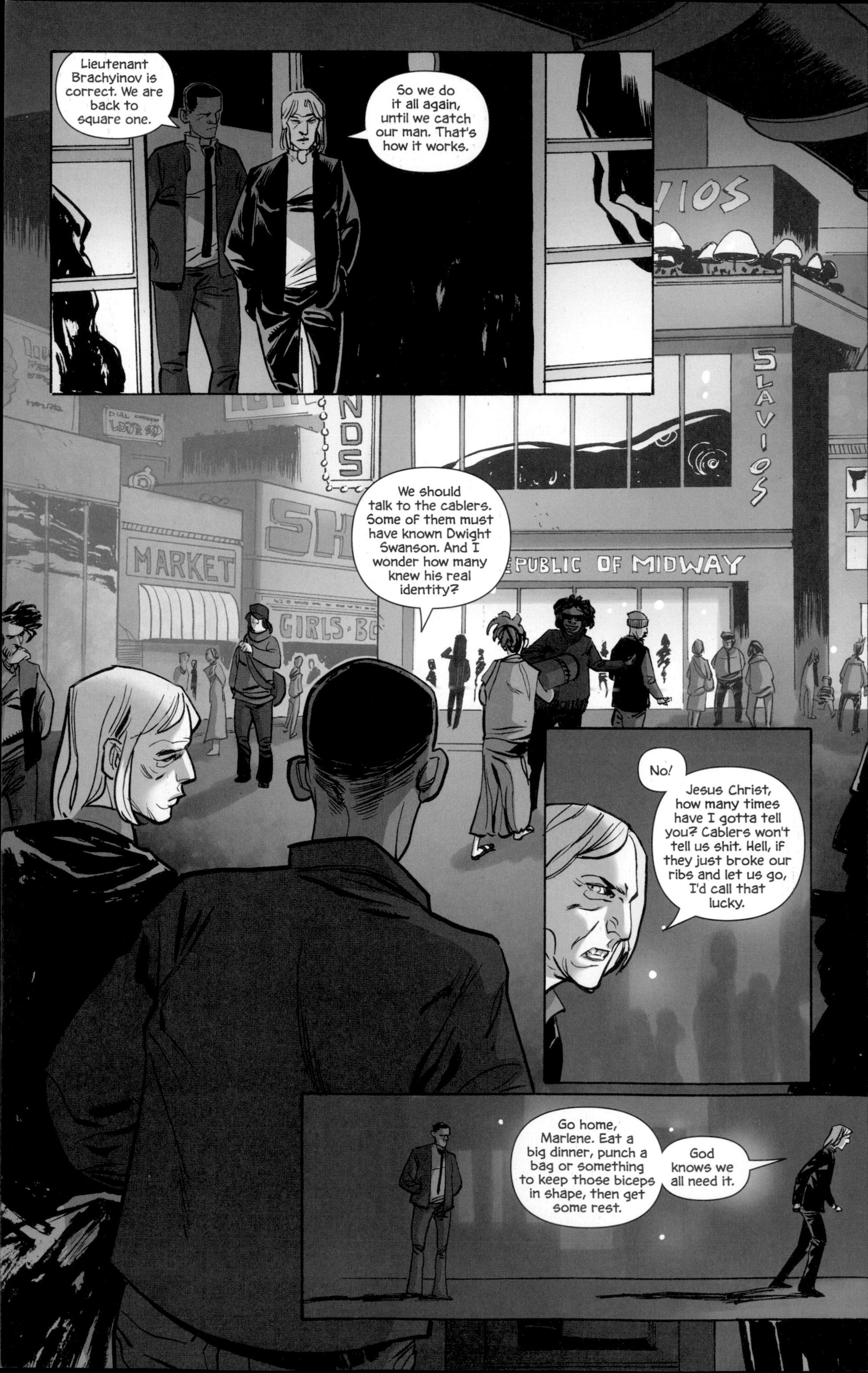
Lieutenant Brachyinov is correct. We are back to square one.
So we do it all again, until we catch our man. That's how it works.
IIOS
SLAVIOS
NDS
MARKET
GIRLS·BO
EPUBLIC OF MIDWAY
We should talk to the cablers. Some of them must have known Dwight Swanson. And I wonder how many knew his real identity?
No!
Jesus Christ, how many times have I gotta tell you? Cablers won't tell us shit. Hell, if they just broke our ribs and let us go, I'd call that lucky.
Go home, Marlene. Eat a big dinner, punch a bag or something to keep those biceps in shape, then get some rest.
God knows we all need it.

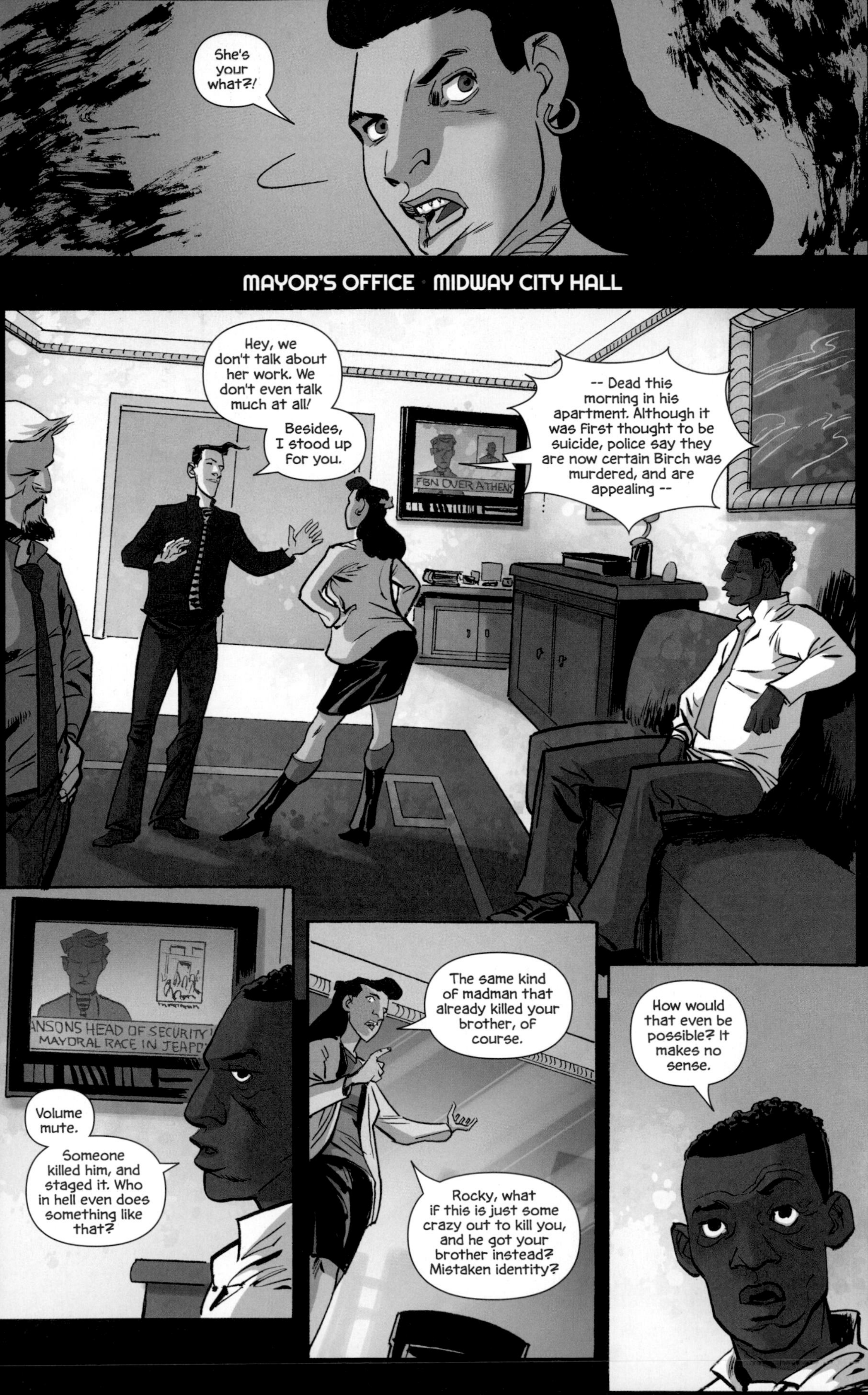
She's your what?!
MAYOR'S OFFICE · MIDWAY CITY HALL
Hey, we don't talk about her work. We don't even talk much at all!
Besides, I stood up for you.
FBN OVER ATHENS
-- Dead this morning in his apartment. Although it was first thought to be suicide, police say they are now certain Birch was murdered, and are appealing --
ANSONS HEAD OF SECURITY!
MAYORAL RACE IN JEAPO
Volume mute.
Someone killed him, and staged it. Who in hell even does something like that?
The same kind of madman that already killed your brother, of course.
Rocky, what if this is just some crazy out to kill you, and he got your brother instead? Mistaken identity?
How would that even be possible? It makes no sense.

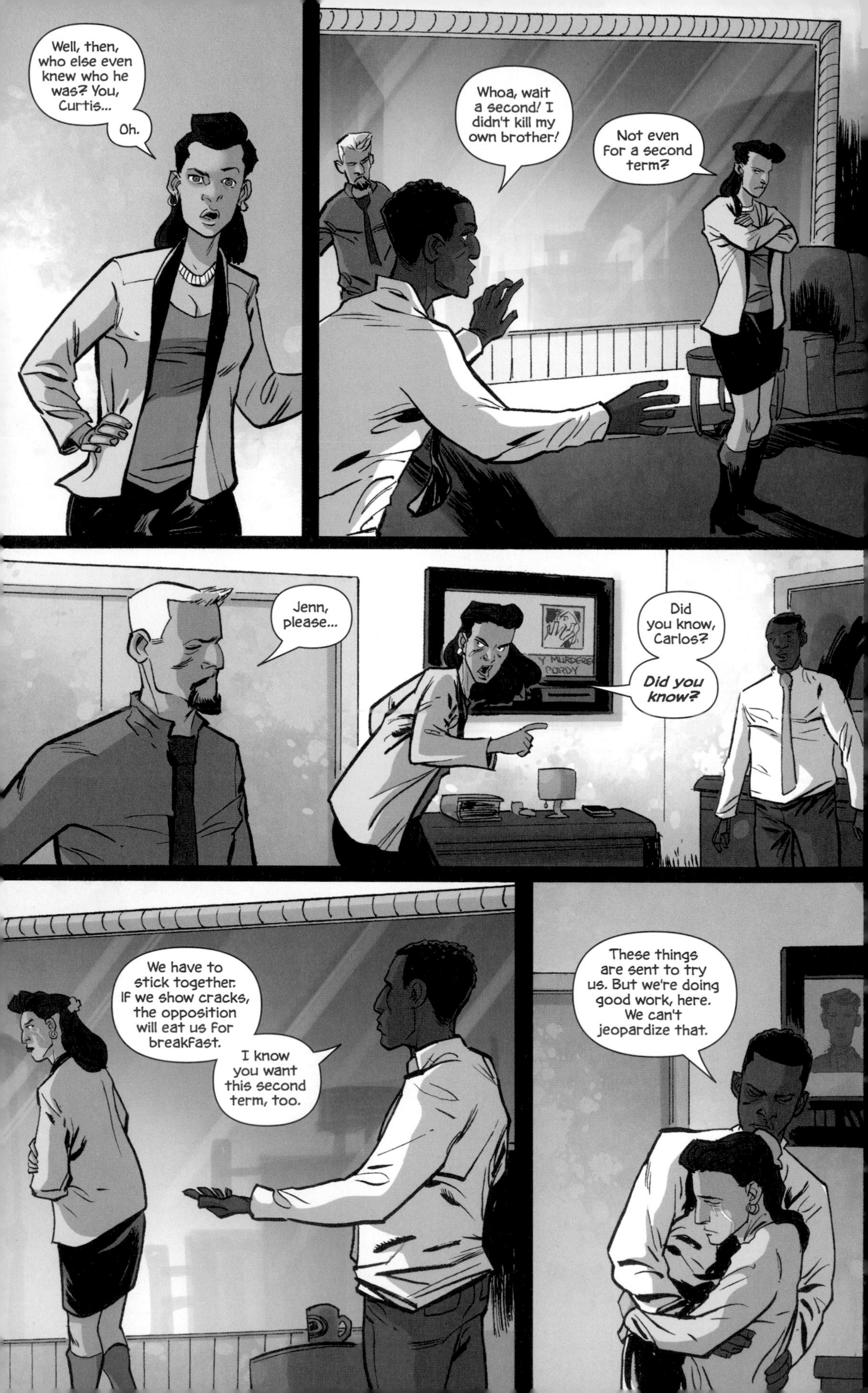
Well, then, who else even knew who he was? You, Curtis...
Oh.
Whoa, wait a second! I didn't kill my own brother!
Not even for a second term?
Jenn, please...
Did you know, Carlos?
Did you know?
We have to stick together. If we show cracks, the opposition will eat us for breakfast.
I know you want this second term, too.
These things are sent to try us. But we're doing good work, here. We can't jeopardize that.

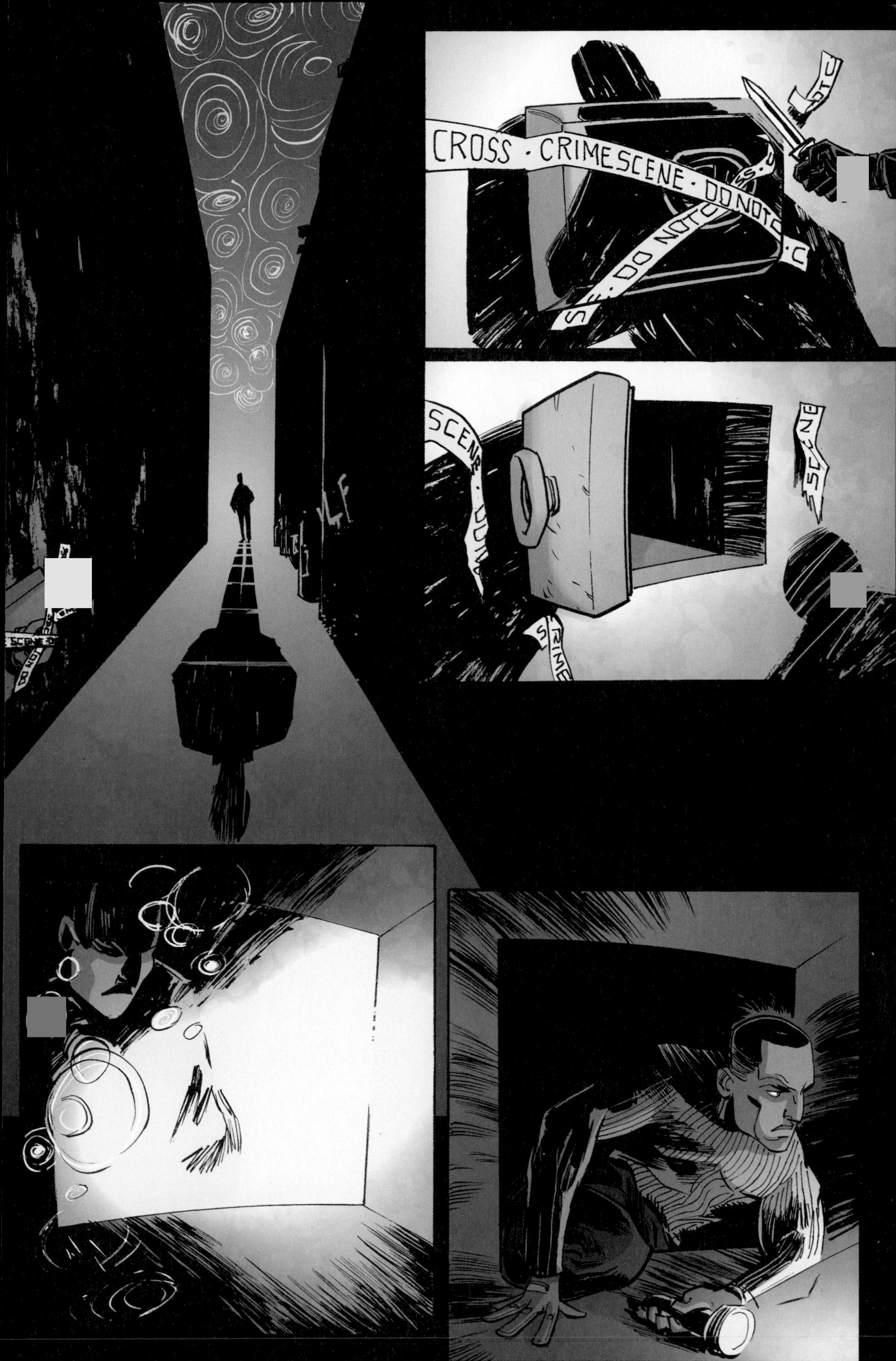
CROSS · CRIMESCENE · DO NOT C
DO NOT C
SCENE
SCENE
CRIME

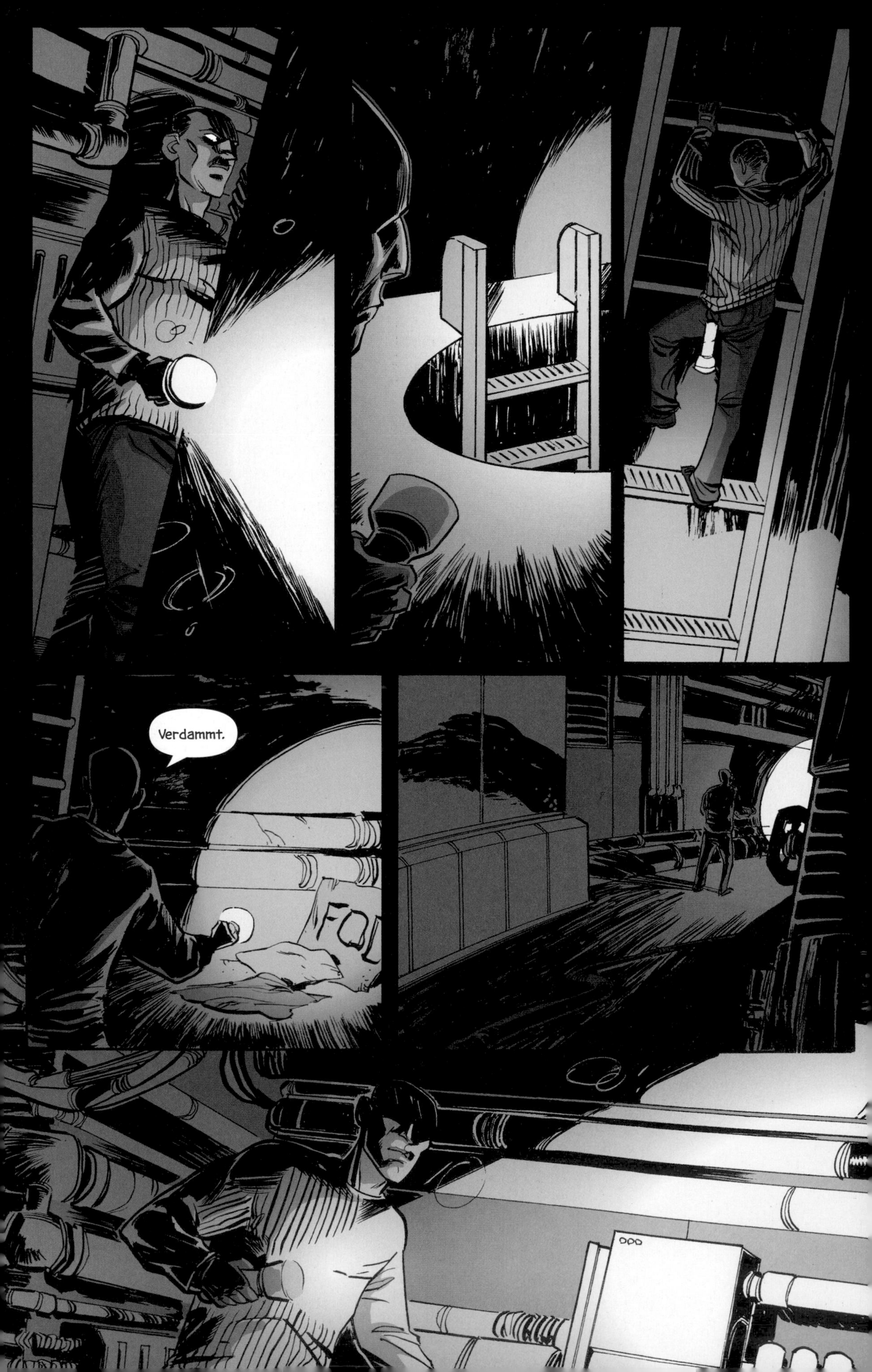
Verdammt.
FOL

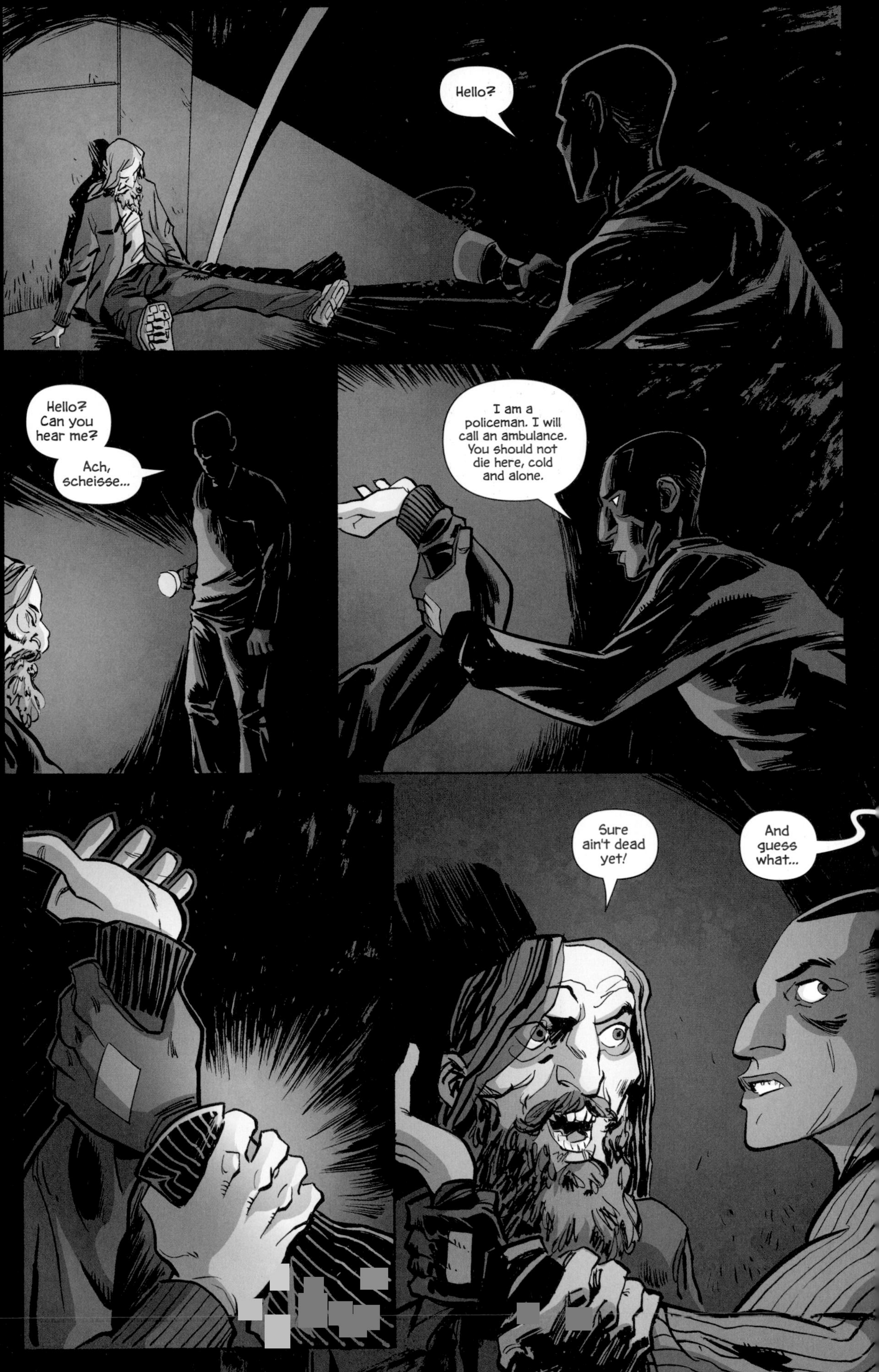
Hello?
Hello? Can you hear me?
Ach, scheisse...
I am a policeman. I will call an ambulance. You should not die here, cold and alone.
Sure ain't dead yet!
And guess what...

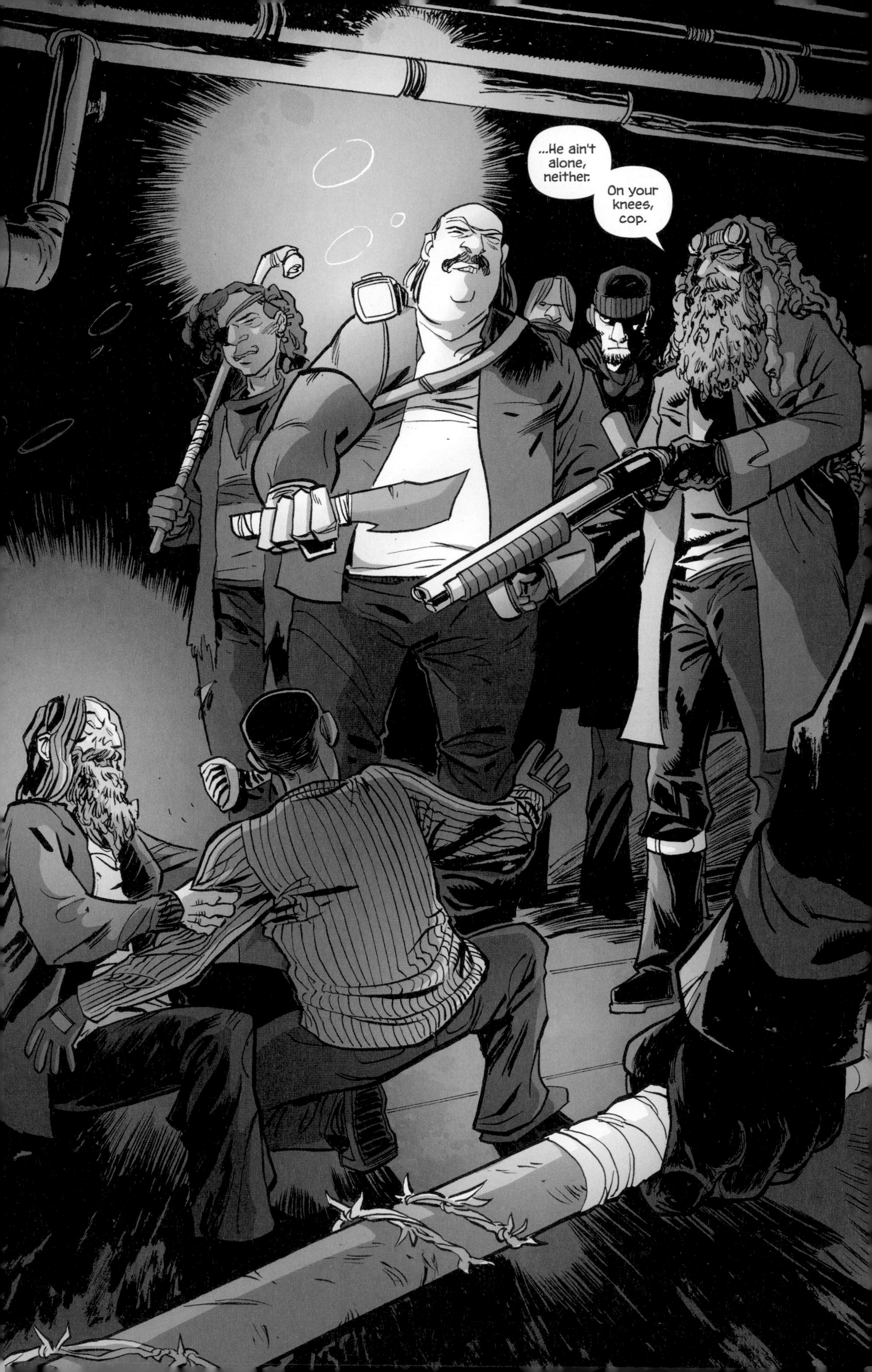
...He ain't alone, neither.
On your knees, cop.

PART 5

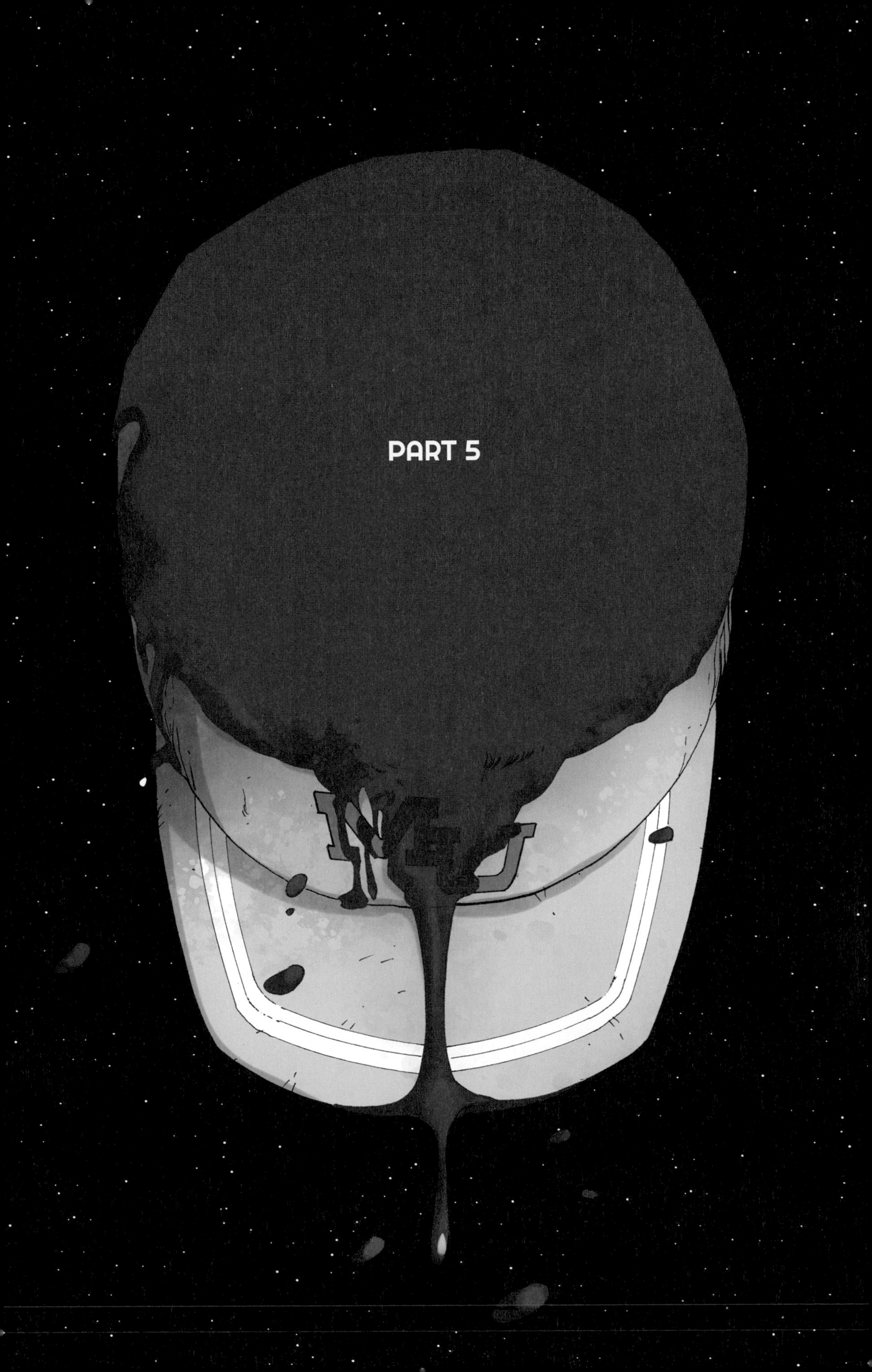

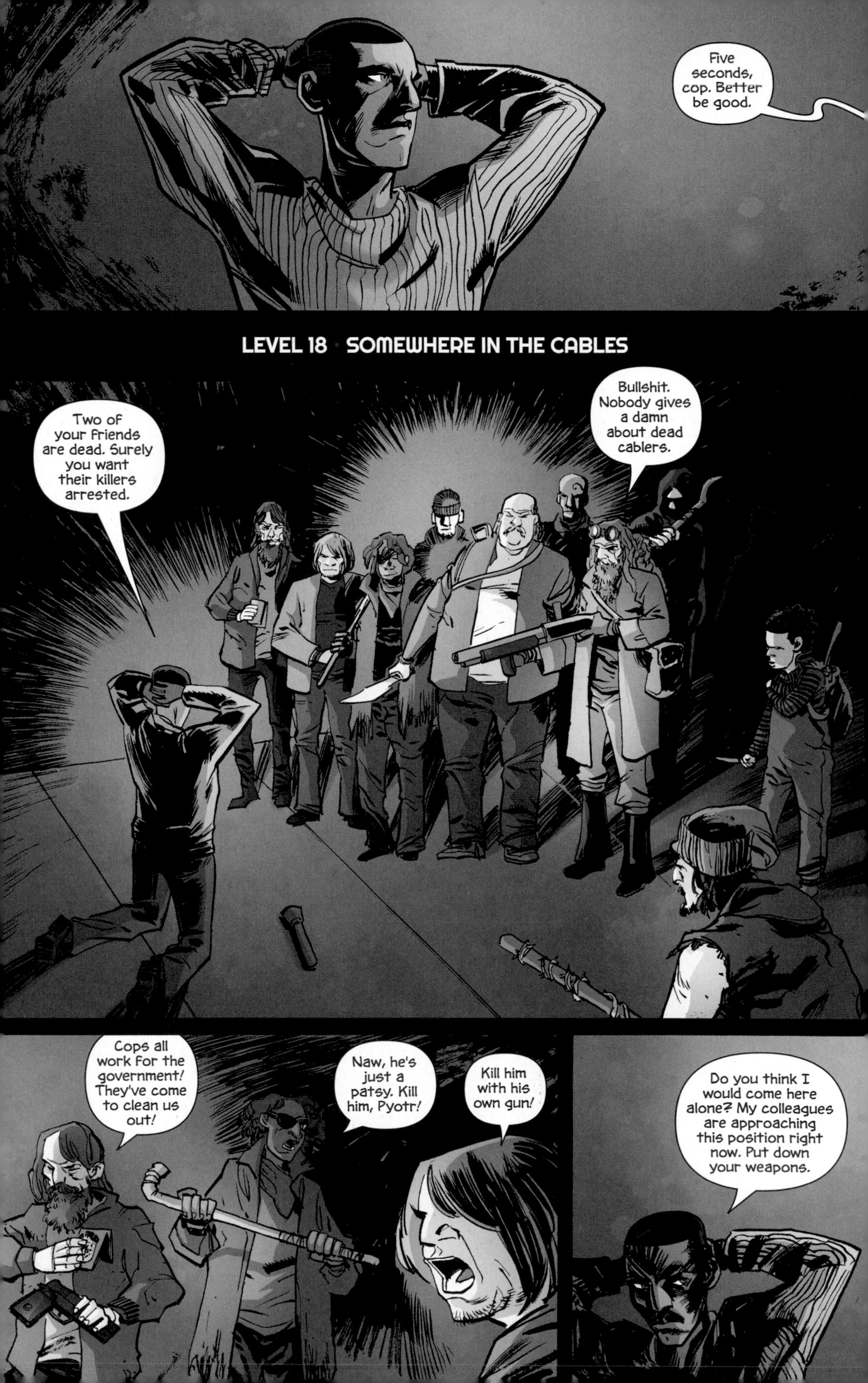
Five seconds, cop. Better be good.
LEVEL 18 · SOMEWHERE IN THE CABLES
Two of your friends are dead. Surely you want their killers arrested.
Bullshit. Nobody gives a damn about dead cablers.
Cops all work for the government! They've come to clean us out!
Naw, he's just a patsy. Kill him, Pyotr!
Kill him with his own gun!
Do you think I would come here alone? My colleagues are approaching this position right now. Put down your weapons.

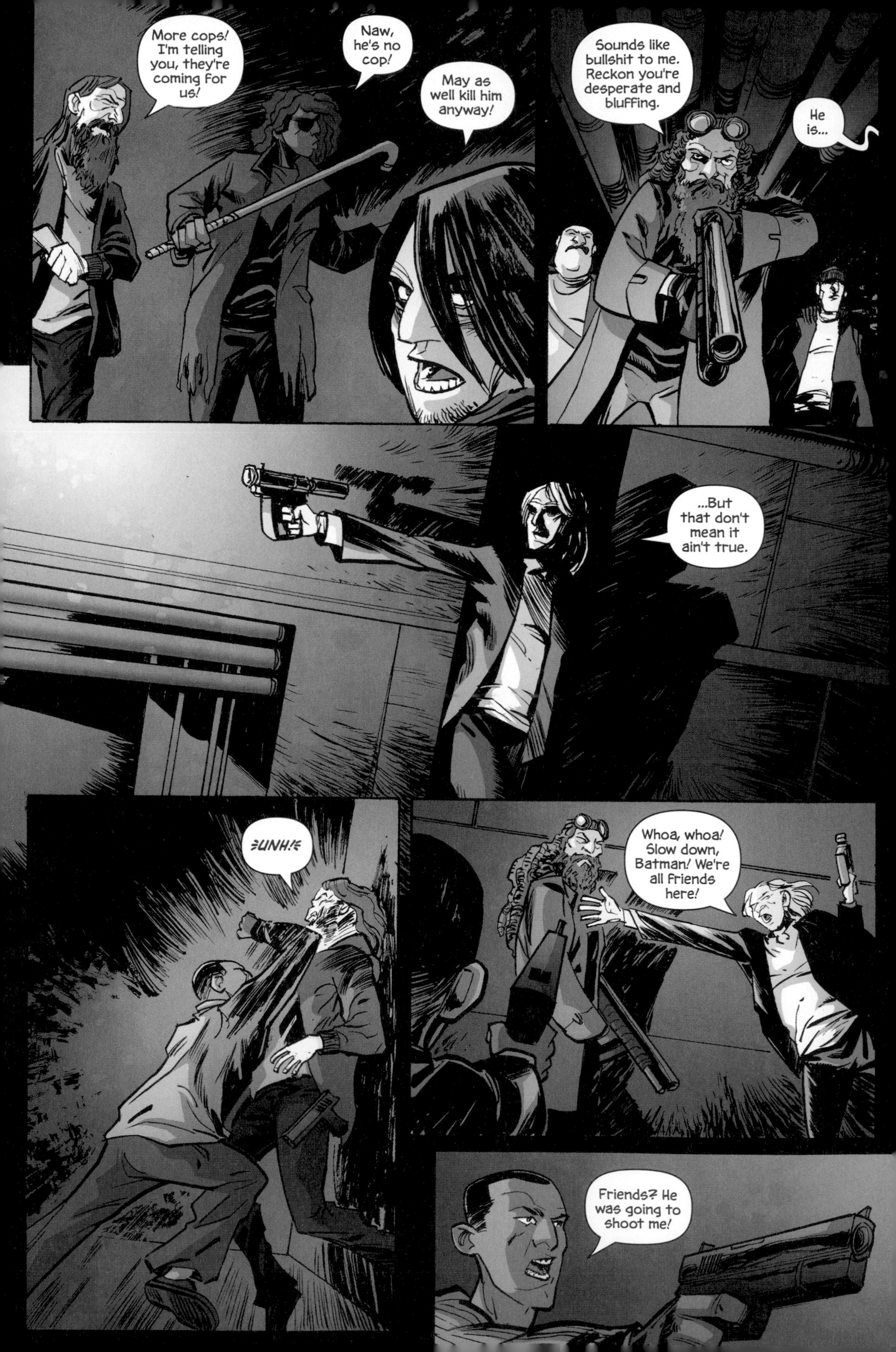
More cops! I'm telling you, they're coming for us!
Naw, he's no cop!
May as well kill him anyway!
Sounds like bullshit to me. Reckon you're desperate and bluffing.
He is...
...But that don't mean it ain't true.
UNH!
Whoa, whoa! Slow down, Batman! We're all friends here!
Friends? He was going to shoot me!

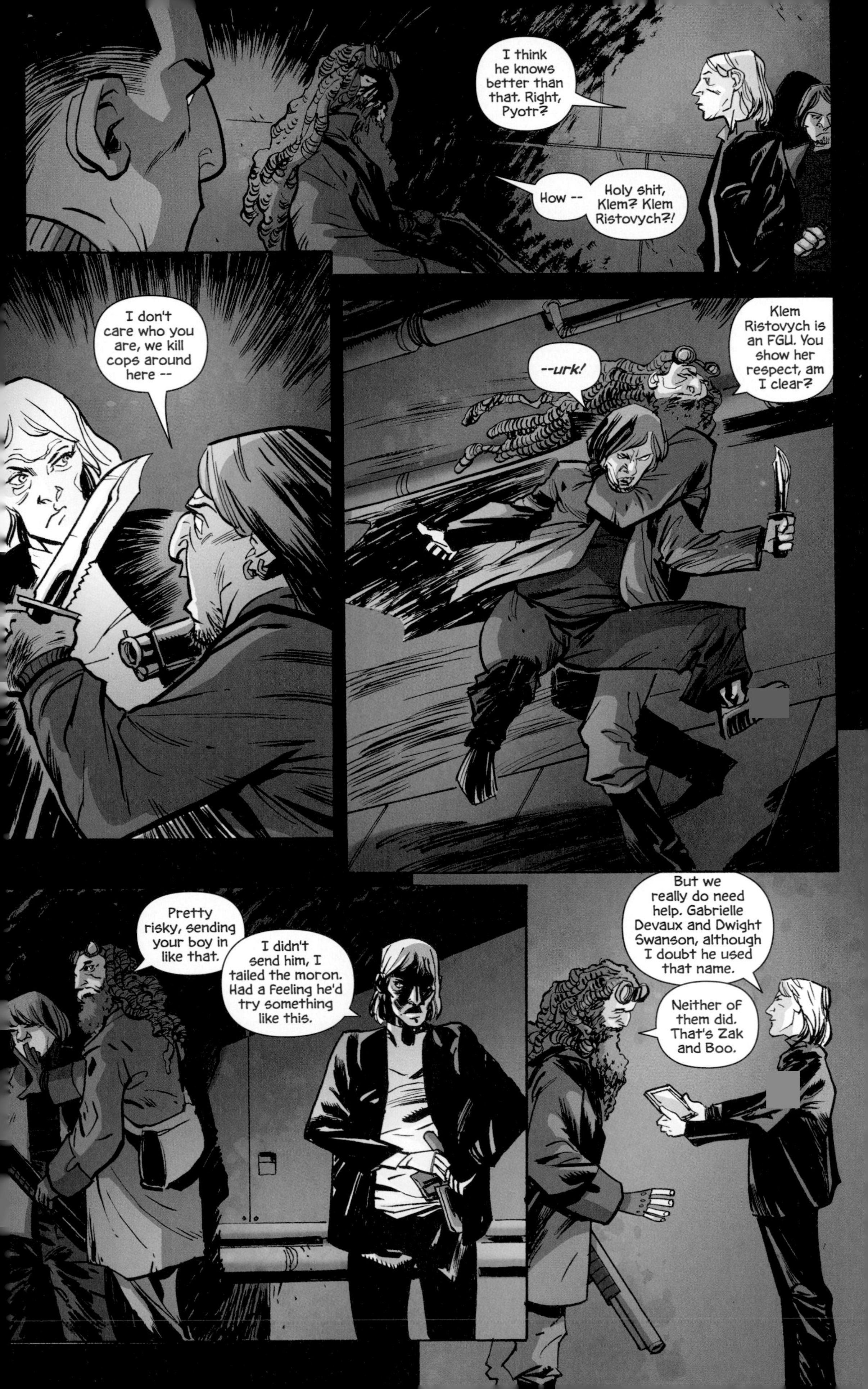
I think he knows better than that. Right, Pyotr?
How --
Holy shit, Klem? Klem Ristovych?!
I don't care who you are, we kill cops around here --
--urk!
Klem Ristovych is an FGU. You show her respect, am I clear?
Pretty risky, sending your boy in like that.
I didn't send him, I tailed the moron. Had a feeling he'd try something like this.
But we really do need help. Gabrielle Devaux and Dwight Swanson, although I doubt he used that name.
Neither of them did. That's Zak and Boo.

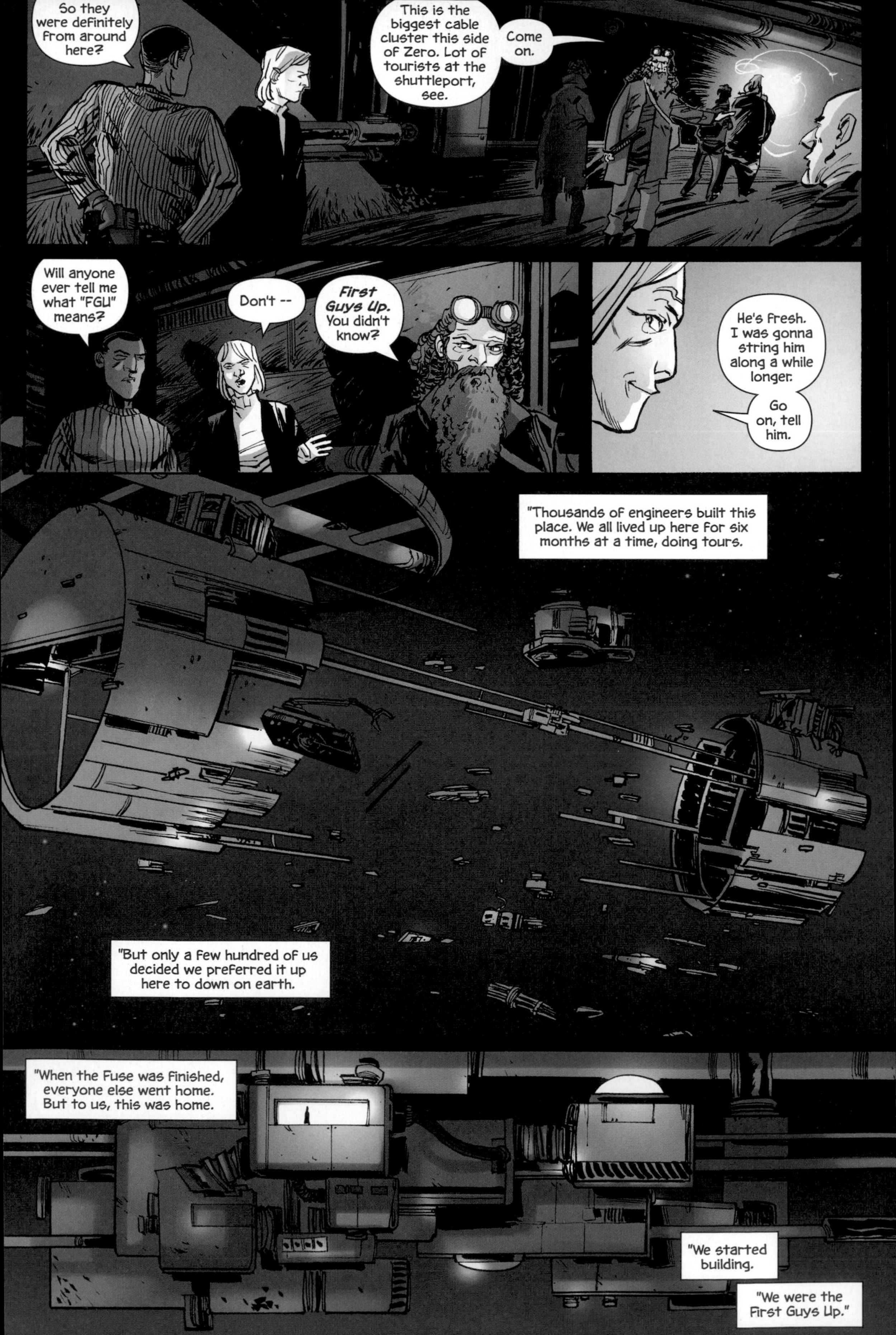
So they were definitely from around here?
This is the biggest cable cluster this side of Zero. Lot of tourists at the shuttleport, see.
Come on.
Will anyone ever tell me what "FGU" means?
Don't --
First Guys Up. You didn't know?
He's fresh. I was gonna string him along a while longer.
Go on, tell him.
"Thousands of engineers built this place. We all lived up here for six months at a time, doing tours.
"But only a few hundred of us decided we preferred it up here to down on earth.
"When the Fuse was finished, everyone else went home. But to us, this was home.
"We started building.
"We were the First Guys Up."

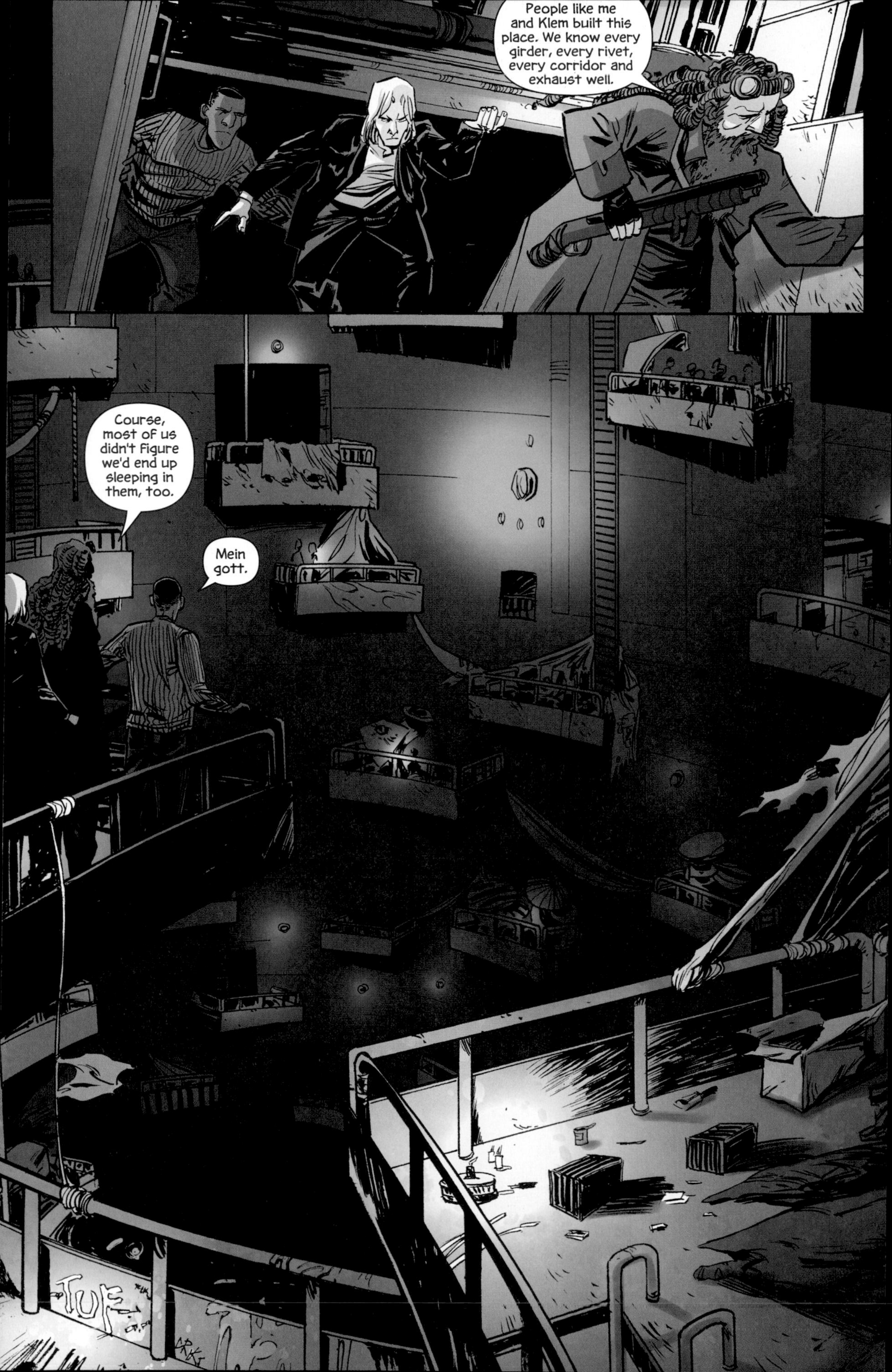
People like me and Klem built this place. We know every girder, every rivet, every corridor and exhaust well.
Course, most of us didn't figure we'd end up sleeping in them, too.
Mein gott.

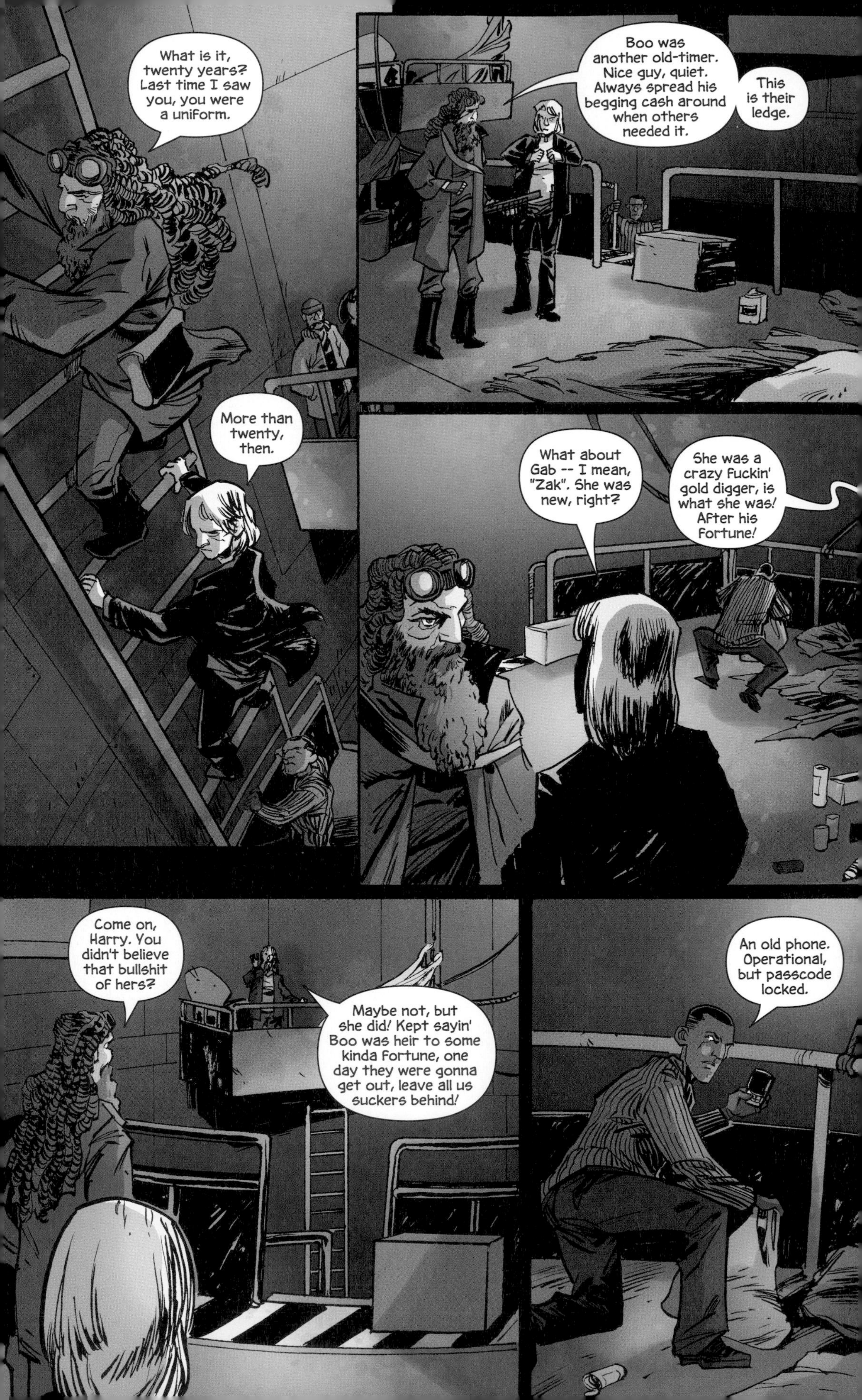
What is it, twenty years? Last time I saw you, you were a uniform.
More than twenty, then.
Boo was another old-timer. Nice guy, quiet. Always spread his begging cash around when others needed it.
This is their ledge.
What about Gab -- I mean, "Zak". She was new, right?
She was a crazy fuckin' gold digger, is what she was! After his fortune!
Come on, Harry. You didn't believe that bullshit of hers?
Maybe not, but she did! Kept sayin' Boo was heir to some kinda fortune, one day they were gonna get out, leave all us suckers behind!
An old phone. Operational, but passcode locked.

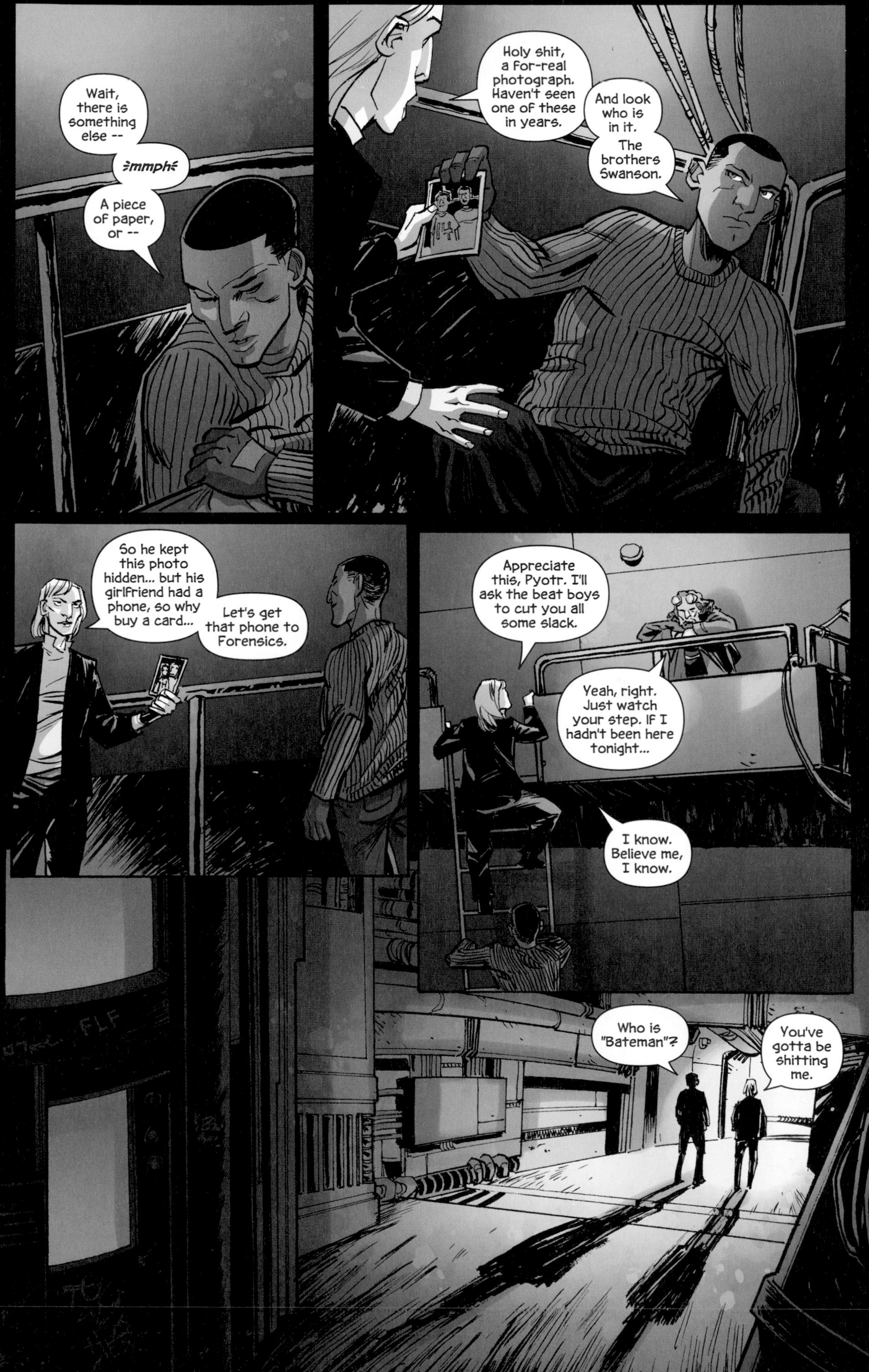
Wait, there is something else --
mmph
A piece of paper, or --
Holy shit, a for-real photograph. Haven't seen one of these in years.
And look who is in it.
The brothers Swanson.
So he kept this photo hidden... but his girlfriend had a phone, so why buy a card...
Let's get that phone to Forensics.
Appreciate this, Pyotr. I'll ask the beat boys to cut you all some slack.
Yeah, right. Just watch your step. If I hadn't been here tonight...
I know. Believe me, I know.
Who is "Bateman"?
You've gotta be shitting me.

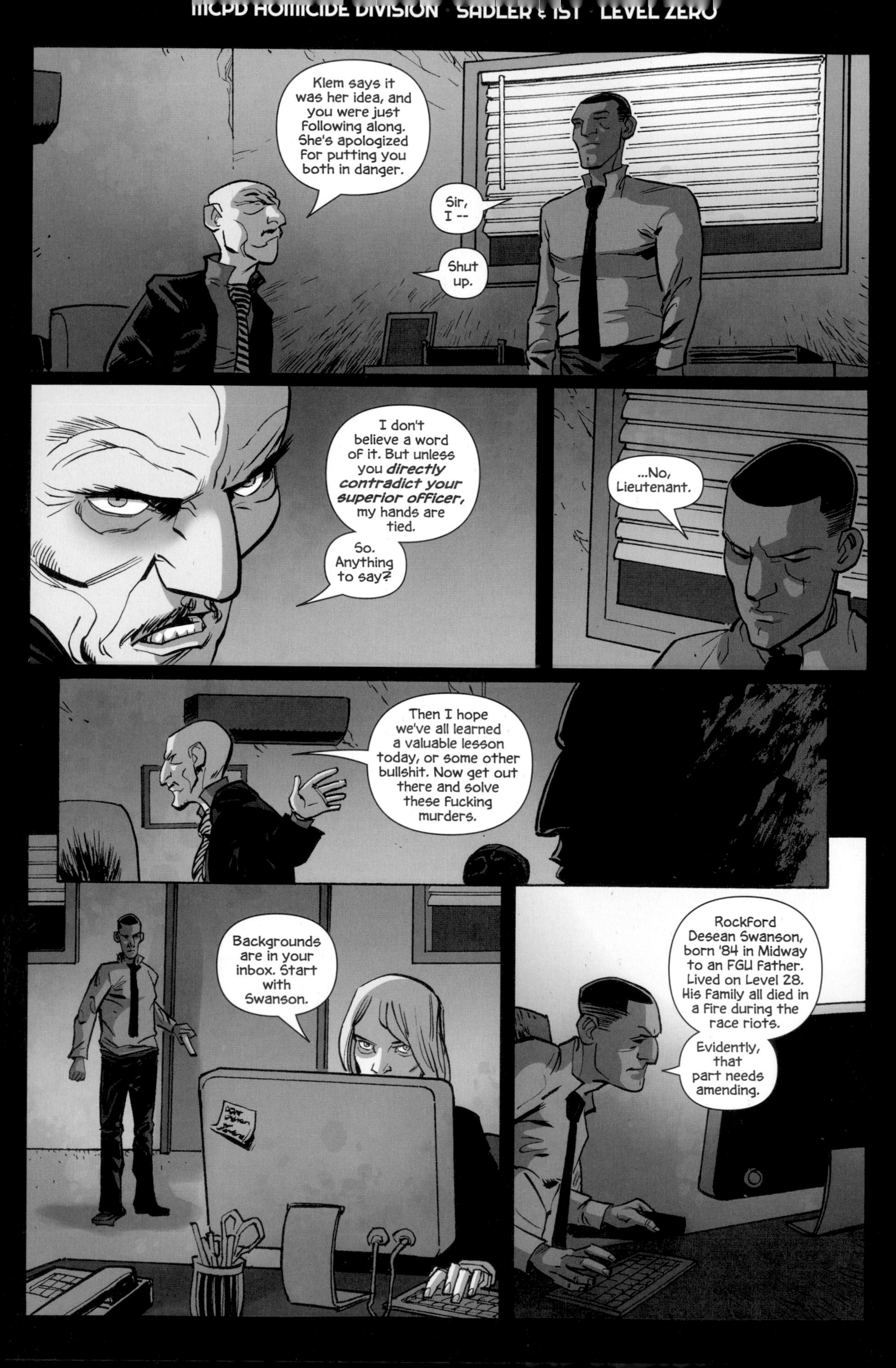
MCPD HOMICIDE DIVISION SADLER & 1ST LEVEL ZERO
Klem says it was her idea, and you were just following along. She's apologized for putting you both in danger.
Sir, I --
Shut up.
I don't believe a word of it. But unless you *directly contradict your superior officer,* my hands are tied.
So. Anything to say?
...No, Lieutenant.
Then I hope we've all learned a valuable lesson today, or some other bullshit. Now get out there and solve these fucking murders.
Backgrounds are in your inbox. Start with Swanson.
Rockford Desean Swanson, born '84 in Midway to an FGU father. Lived on Level 28. His family all died in a fire during the race riots.
Evidently, that part needs amending.

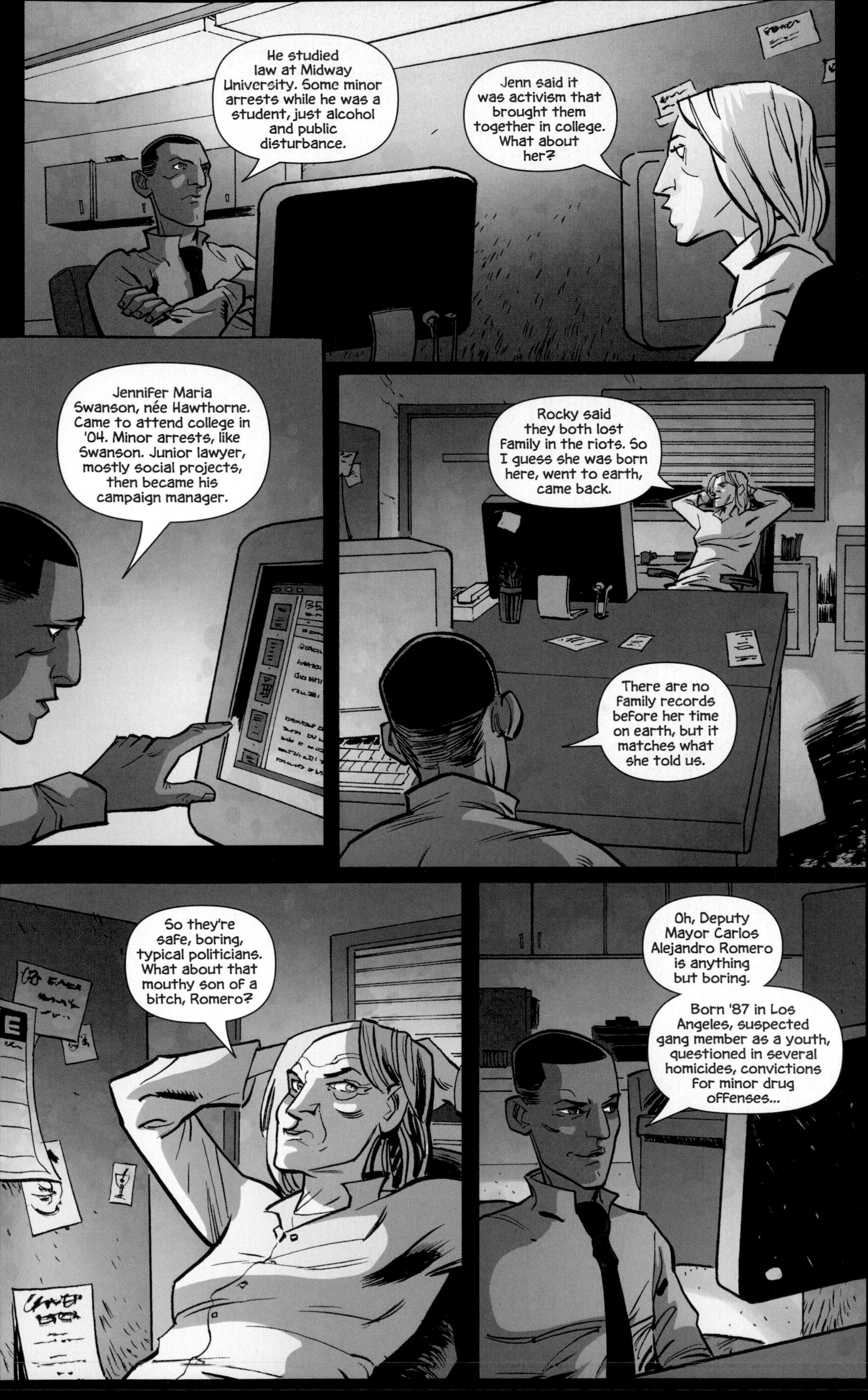

He studied law at Midway University. Some minor arrests while he was a student, just alcohol and public disturbance.
Jenn said it was activism that brought them together in college. What about her?
Jennifer Maria Swanson, née Hawthorne. Came to attend college in '04. Minor arrests, like Swanson. Junior lawyer, mostly social projects, then became his campaign manager.
Rocky said they both lost family in the riots. So I guess she was born here, went to earth, came back.
There are no family records before her time on earth, but it matches what she told us.
So they're safe, boring, typical politicians. What about that mouthy son of a bitch, Romero?
Oh, Deputy Mayor Carlos Alejandro Romero is anything but boring.
Born '87 in Los Angeles, suspected gang member as a youth, questioned in several homicides, convictions for minor drug offenses...

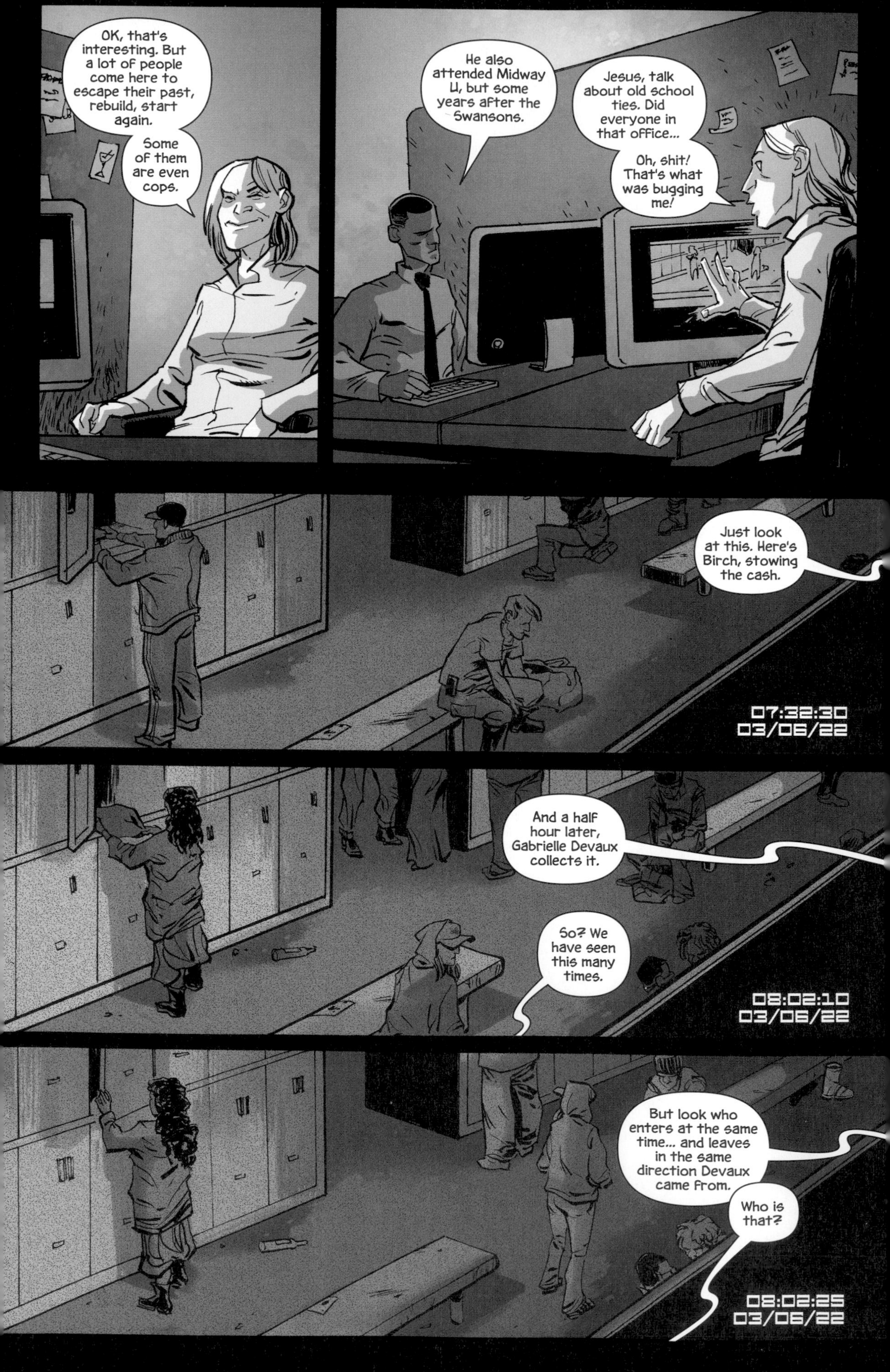
OK, that's interesting. But a lot of people come here to escape their past, rebuild, start again.
Some of them are even cops.
He also attended Midway U, but some years after the Swansons.
Jesus, talk about old school ties. Did everyone in that office...
Oh, shit! That's what was bugging me!
Just look at this. Here's Birch, stowing the cash.
07:32:30
03/06/22
And a half hour later, Gabrielle Devaux collects it.
So? We have seen this many times.
08:02:10
03/06/22
But look who enters at the same time... and leaves in the same direction Devaux came from.
Who is that?
08:02:25
03/06/22

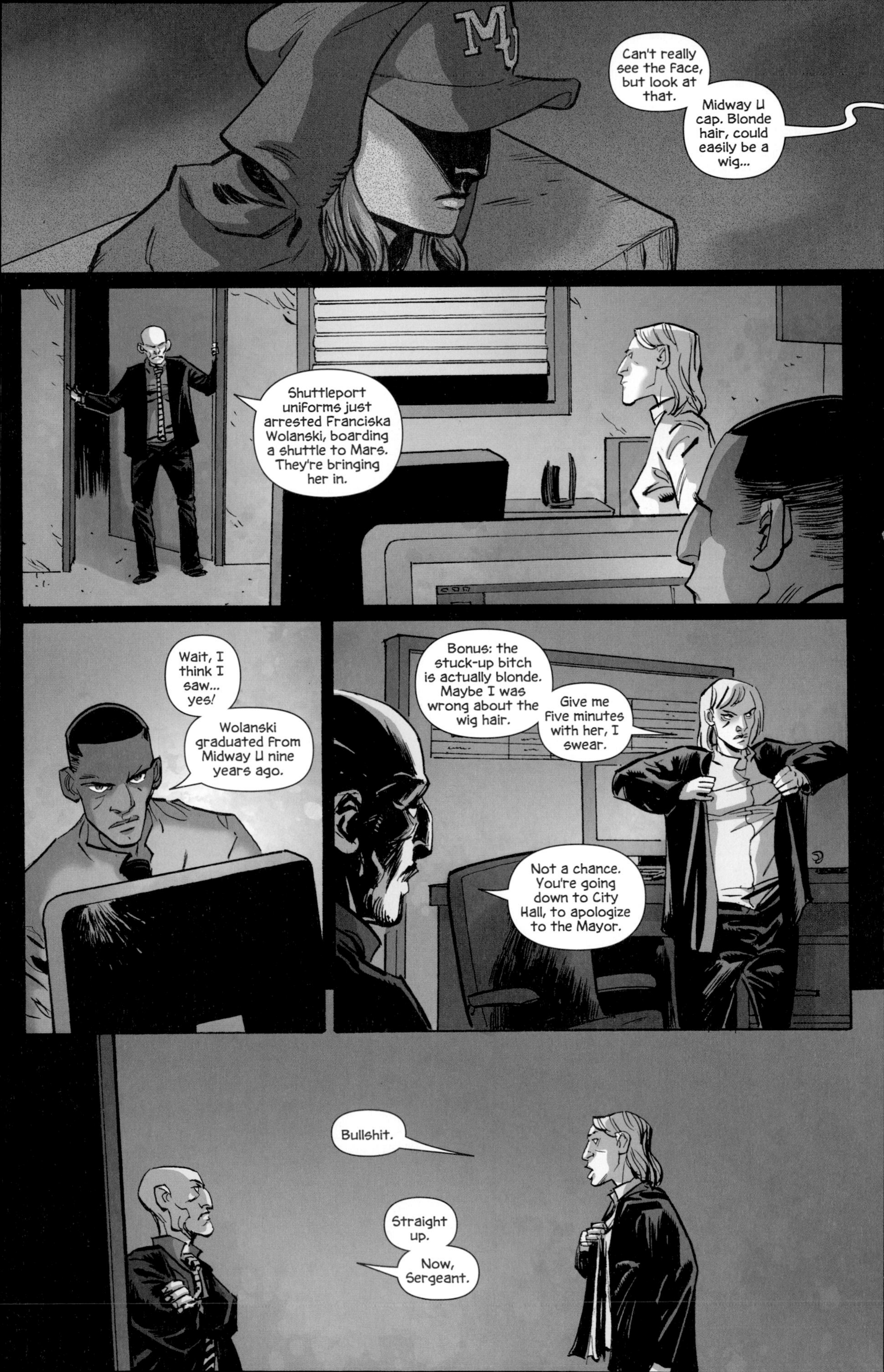
Can't really see the Face, but look at that.
Midway U cap. Blonde hair, could easily be a wig...
Shuttleport uniforms just arrested Franciska Wolanski, boarding a shuttle to Mars. They're bringing her in.
Wait, I think I saw... yes!
Wolanski graduated from Midway U nine years ago.
Bonus: the stuck-up bitch is actually blonde. Maybe I was wrong about the wig hair.
Give me five minutes with her, I swear.
Not a chance. You're going down to City Hall, to apologize to the Mayor.
Bullshit.
Straight up.
Now, Sergeant.

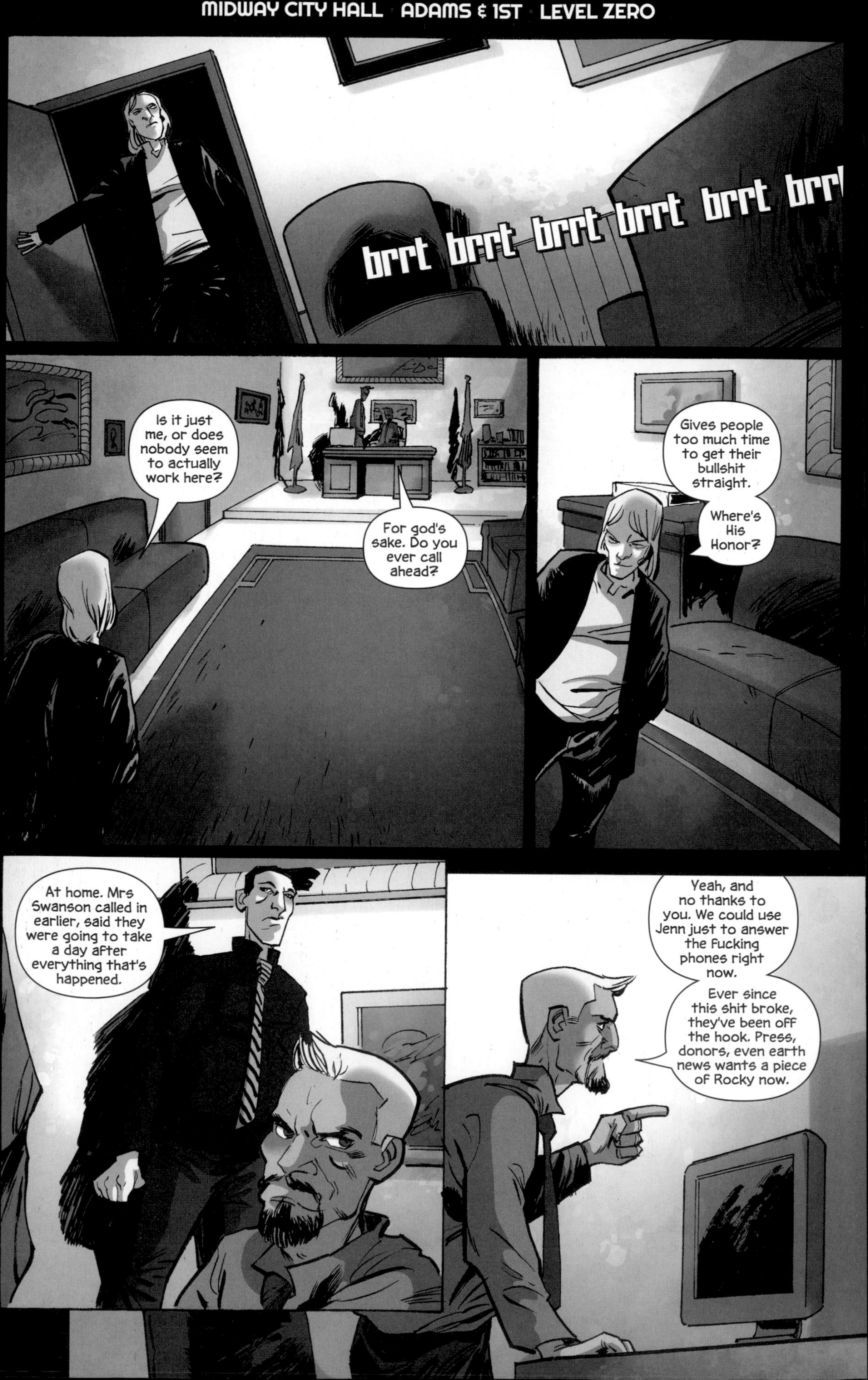
MIDWAY CITY HALL · ADAMS & 1ST · LEVEL ZERO
brrt brrt brrt brrt brrt brrt
Is it just me, or does nobody seem to actually work here?
For god's sake. Do you ever call ahead?
Gives people too much time to get their bullshit straight.
Where's His Honor?
At home. Mrs Swanson called in earlier, said they were going to take a day after everything that's happened.
Yeah, and no thanks to you. We could use Jenn just to answer the fucking phones right now.
Ever since this shit broke, they've been off the hook. Press, donors, even earth news wants a piece of Rocky now.

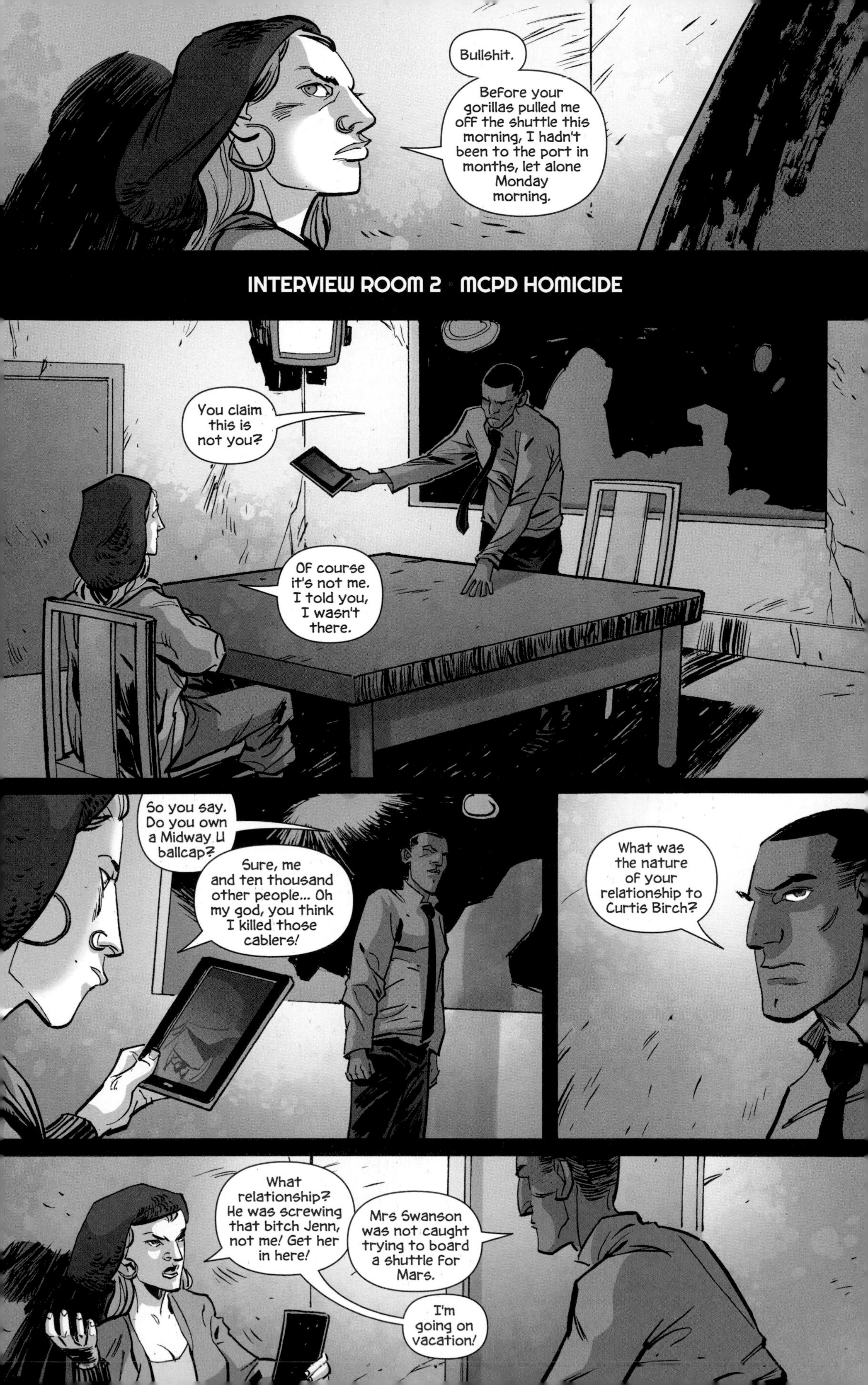
Bullshit.
Before your gorillas pulled me off the shuttle this morning, I hadn't been to the port in months, let alone Monday morning.
INTERVIEW ROOM 2 MCPD HOMICIDE
You claim this is not you?
Of course it's not me. I told you, I wasn't there.
So you say. Do you own a Midway U ballcap?
Sure, me and ten thousand other people... Oh my god, you think I killed those cablers!
What was the nature of your relationship to Curtis Birch?
What relationship? He was screwing that bitch Jenn, not me! Get her in here!
Mrs Swanson was not caught trying to board a shuttle for Mars.
I'm going on vacation!

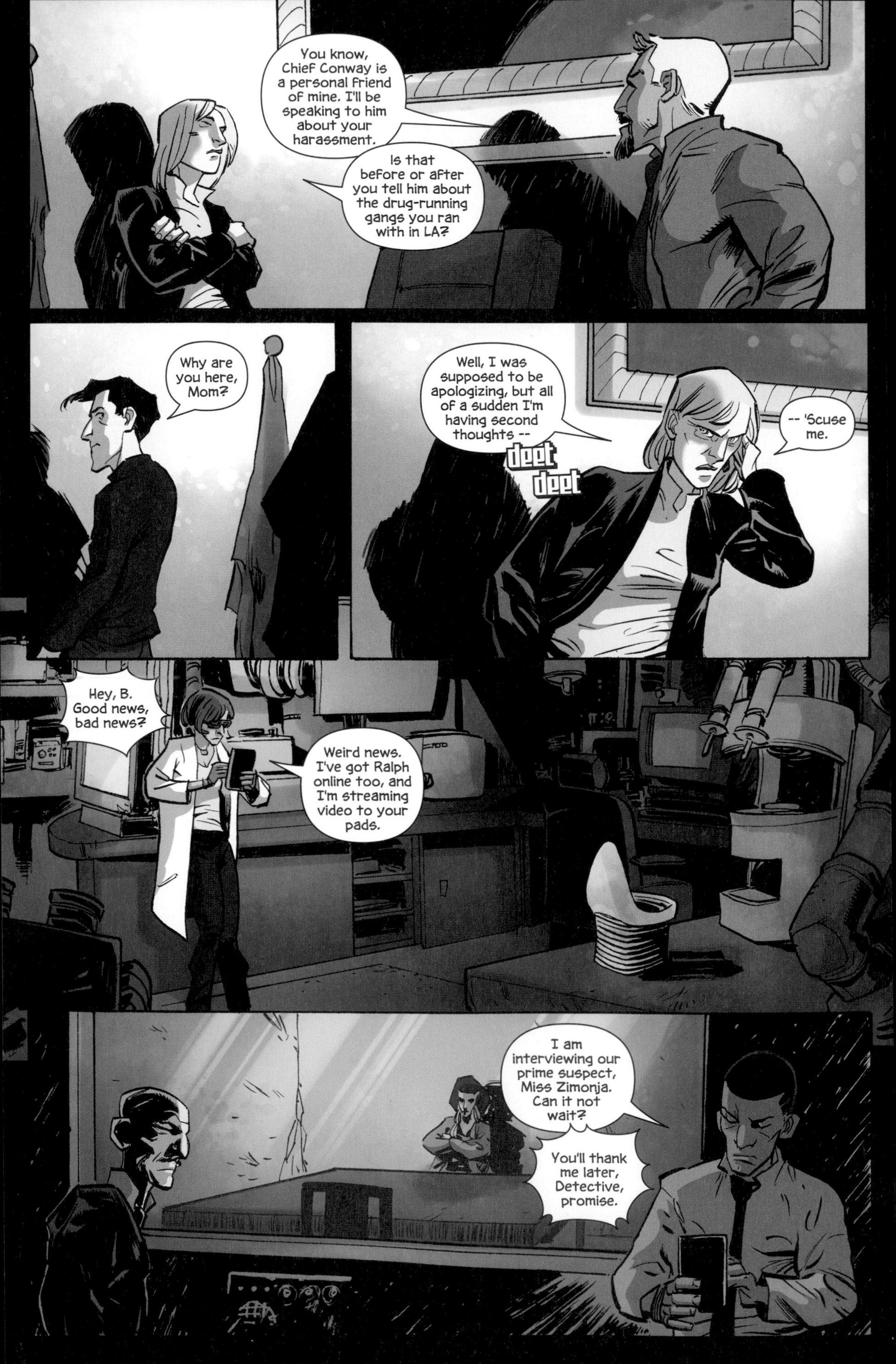
You know, Chief Conway is a personal friend of mine. I'll be speaking to him about your harassment.
Is that before or after you tell him about the drug-running gangs you ran with in LA?
Why are you here, Mom?
Well, I was supposed to be apologizing, but all of a sudden I'm having second thoughts --
deet deet
-- 'Scuse me.
Hey, B. Good news, bad news?
Weird news. I've got Ralph online too, and I'm streaming video to your pads.
I am interviewing our prime suspect, Miss Zimonja. Can it not wait?
You'll thank me later, Detective, promise.

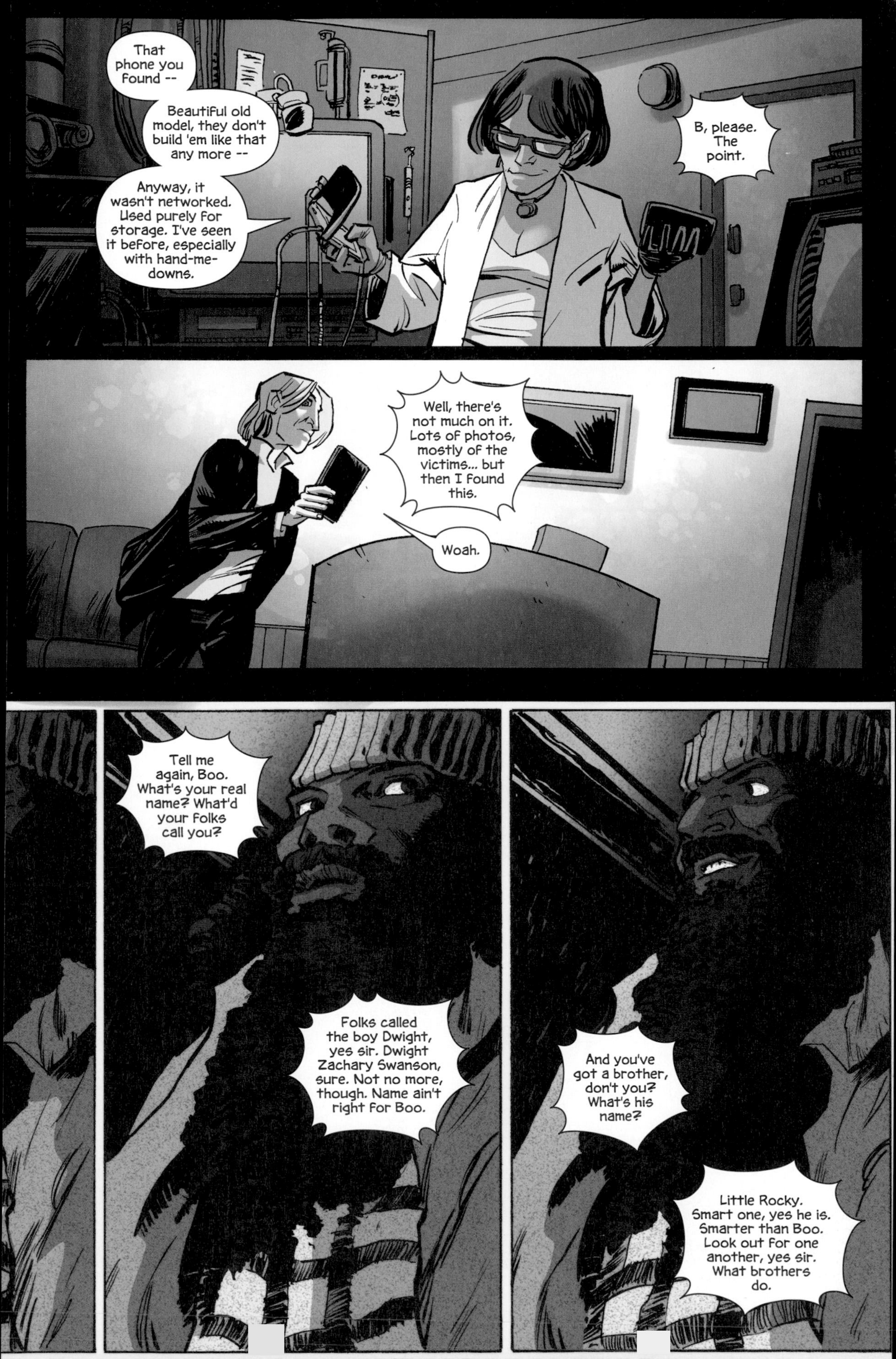
That phone you found --
Beautiful old model, they don't build 'em like that any more --
Anyway, it wasn't networked. Used purely for storage. I've seen it before, especially with hand-me-downs.
B, please. The point.
Well, there's not much on it. Lots of photos, mostly of the victims... but then I found this.
Woah.
Tell me again, Boo. What's your real name? What'd your folks call you?
Folks called the boy Dwight, yes sir. Dwight Zachary Swanson, sure. Not no more, though. Name ain't right for Boo.
And you've got a brother, don't you? What's his name?
Little Rocky. Smart one, yes he is. Smarter than Boo. Look out for one another, yes sir. What brothers do.

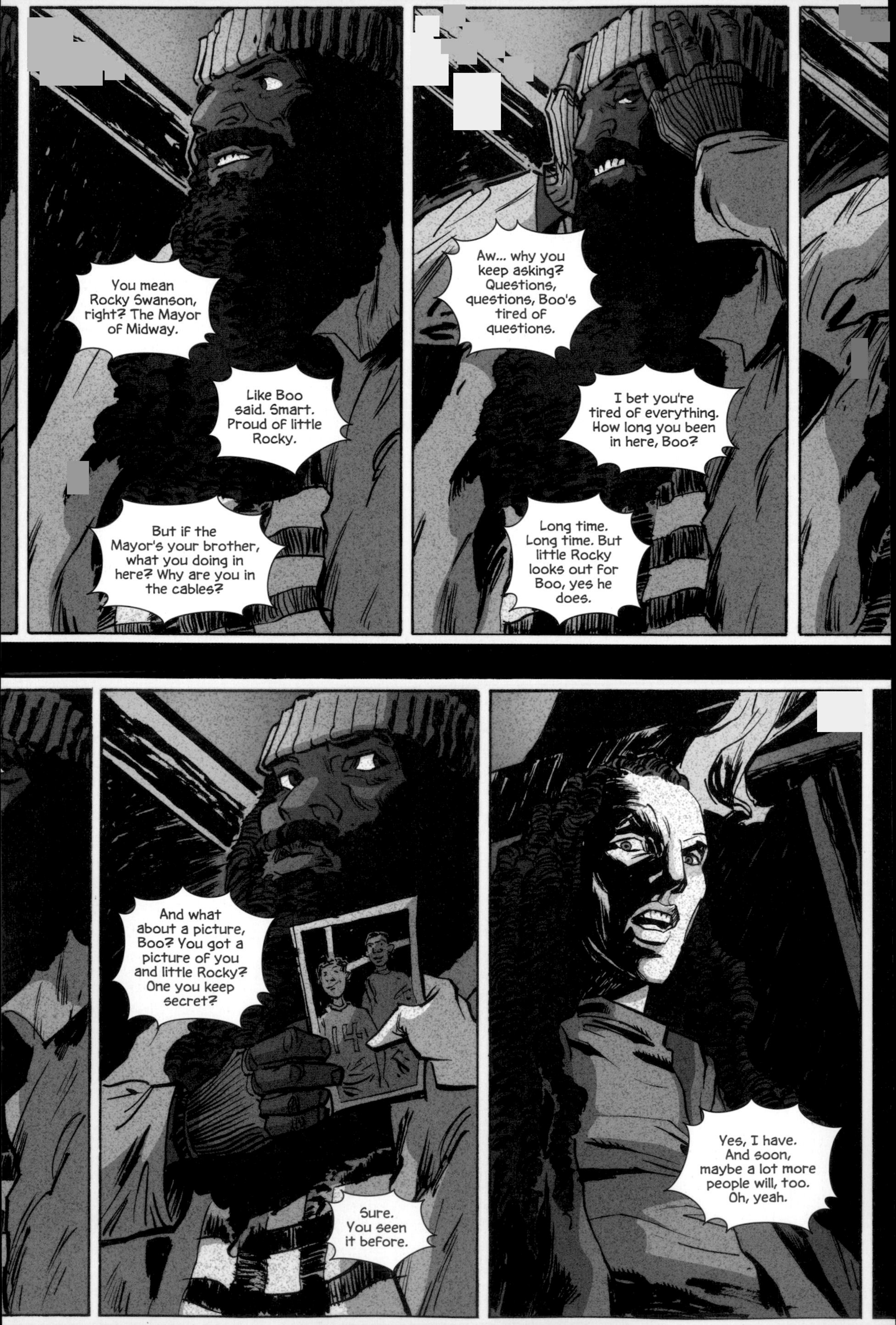
You mean Rocky Swanson, right? The Mayor of Midway.
Like Boo said. Smart. Proud of little Rocky.
But if the Mayor's your brother, what you doing in here? Why are you in the cables?
Aw... why you keep asking? Questions, questions, Boo's tired of questions.
I bet you're tired of everything. How long you been in here, Boo?
Long time. Long time. But little Rocky looks out for Boo, yes he does.
And what about a picture, Boo? You got a picture of you and little Rocky? One you keep secret?
Sure. You seen it before.
Yes, I have. And soon, maybe a lot more people will, too. Oh, yeah.

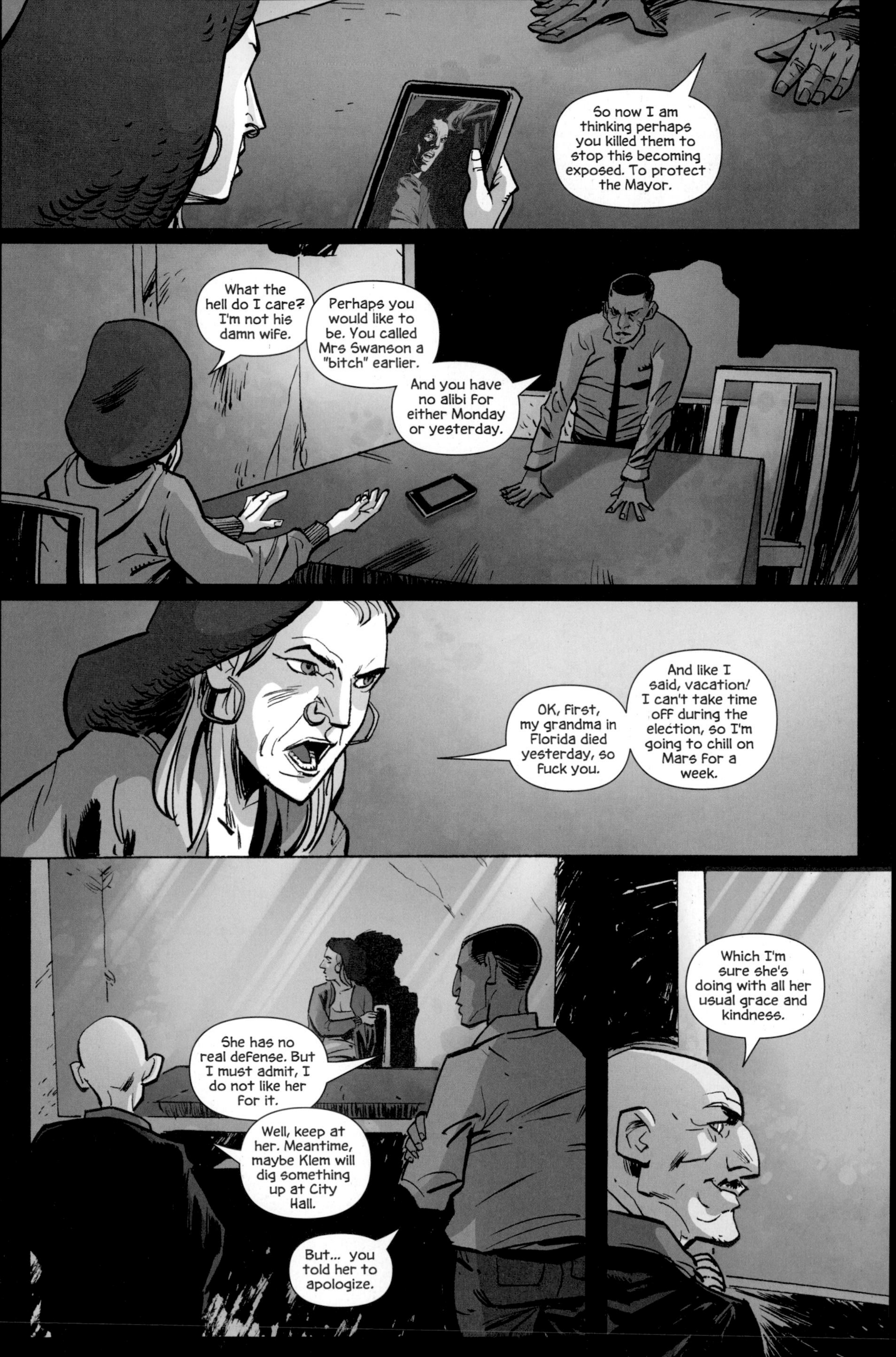
So now I am thinking perhaps you killed them to stop this becoming exposed. To protect the Mayor.
What the hell do I care? I'm not his damn wife.
Perhaps you would like to be. You called Mrs Swanson a "bitch" earlier.
And you have no alibi for either Monday or yesterday.
OK, first, my grandma in Florida died yesterday, so fuck you.
And like I said, vacation! I can't take time off during the election, so I'm going to chill on Mars for a week.
She has no real defense. But I must admit, I do not like her for it.
Well, keep at her. Meantime, maybe Klem will dig something up at City Hall.
But... you told her to apologize.
Which I'm sure she's doing with all her usual grace and kindness.

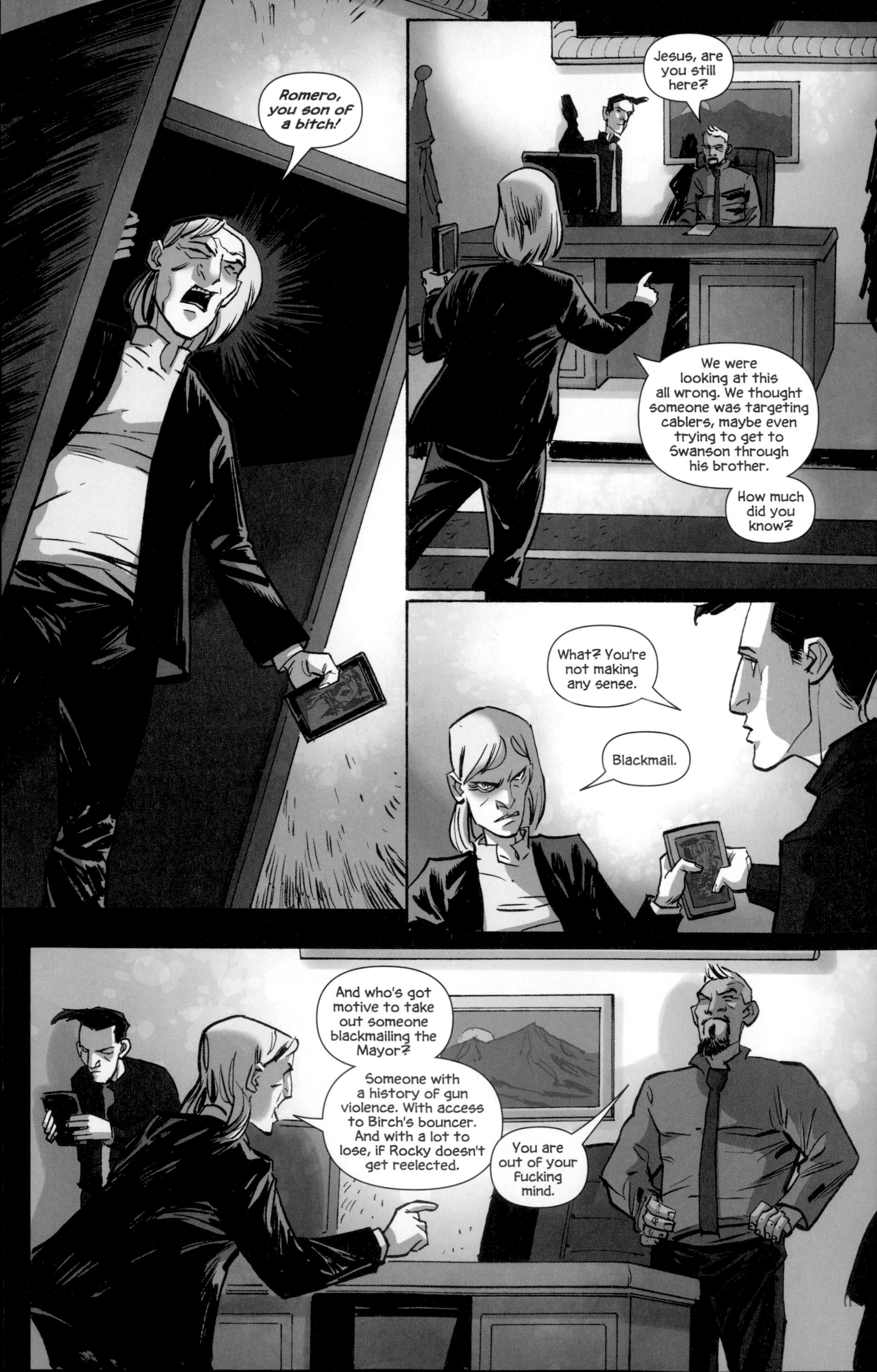
Romero, you son of a bitch!
Jesus, are you still here?
We were looking at this all wrong. We thought someone was targeting cablers, maybe even trying to get to Swanson through his brother.
How much did you know?
What? You're not making any sense.
Blackmail.
And who's got motive to take out someone blackmailing the Mayor?
Someone with a history of gun violence. With access to Birch's bouncer. And with a lot to lose, if Rocky doesn't get reelected.
You are out of your fucking mind.

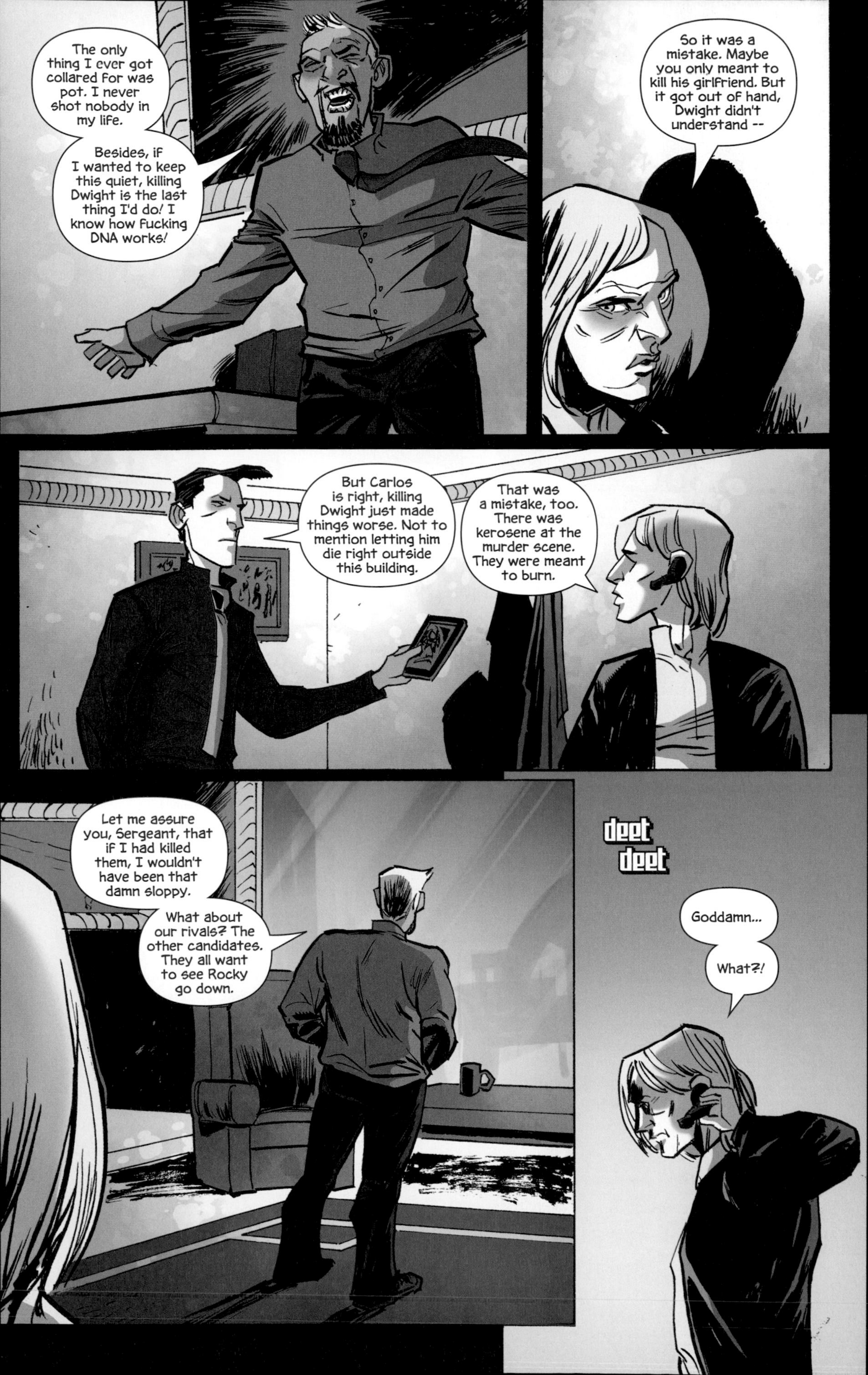

The only thing I ever got collared for was pot. I never shot nobody in my life.
Besides, if I wanted to keep this quiet, killing Dwight is the last thing I'd do! I know how fucking DNA works!
So it was a mistake. Maybe you only meant to kill his girlfriend. But it got out of hand, Dwight didn't understand --
But Carlos is right, killing Dwight just made things worse. Not to mention letting him die right outside this building.
That was a mistake, too. There was kerosene at the murder scene. They were meant to burn.
Let me assure you, Sergeant, that if I had killed them, I wouldn't have been that damn sloppy.
What about our rivals? The other candidates. They all want to see Rocky go down.
deet
deet
Goddamn...
What?!

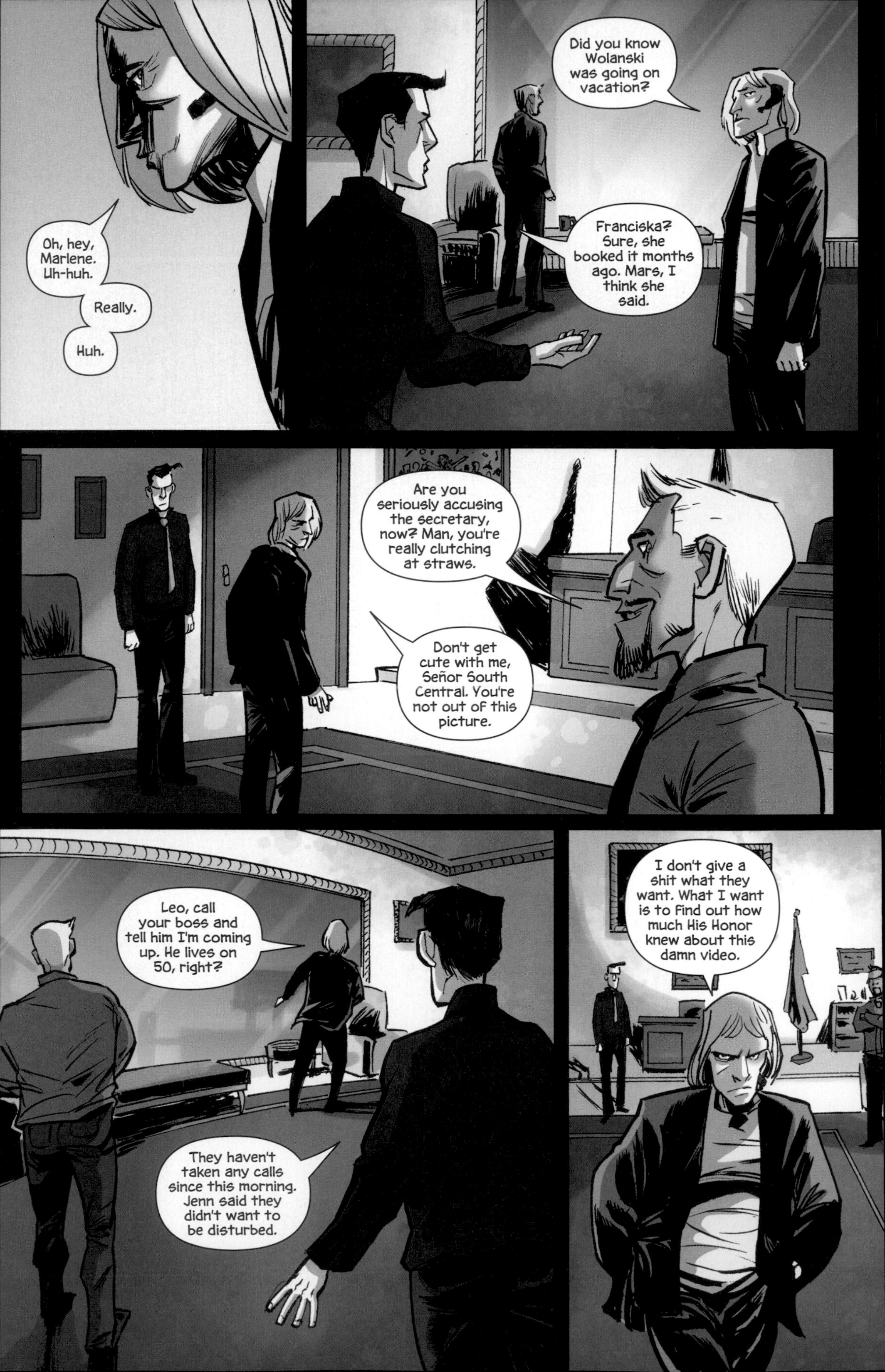
Oh, hey, Marlene. Uh-huh.
Really.
Huh.
Did you know Wolanski was going on vacation?
Franciska? Sure, she booked it months ago. Mars, I think she said.
Are you seriously accusing the secretary, now? Man, you're really clutching at straws.
Don't get cute with me, Señor South Central. You're not out of this picture.
Leo, call your boss and tell him I'm coming up. He lives on 50, right?
They haven't taken any calls since this morning. Jenn said they didn't want to be disturbed.
I don't give a shit what they want. What I want is to find out how much His Honor knew about this damn video.

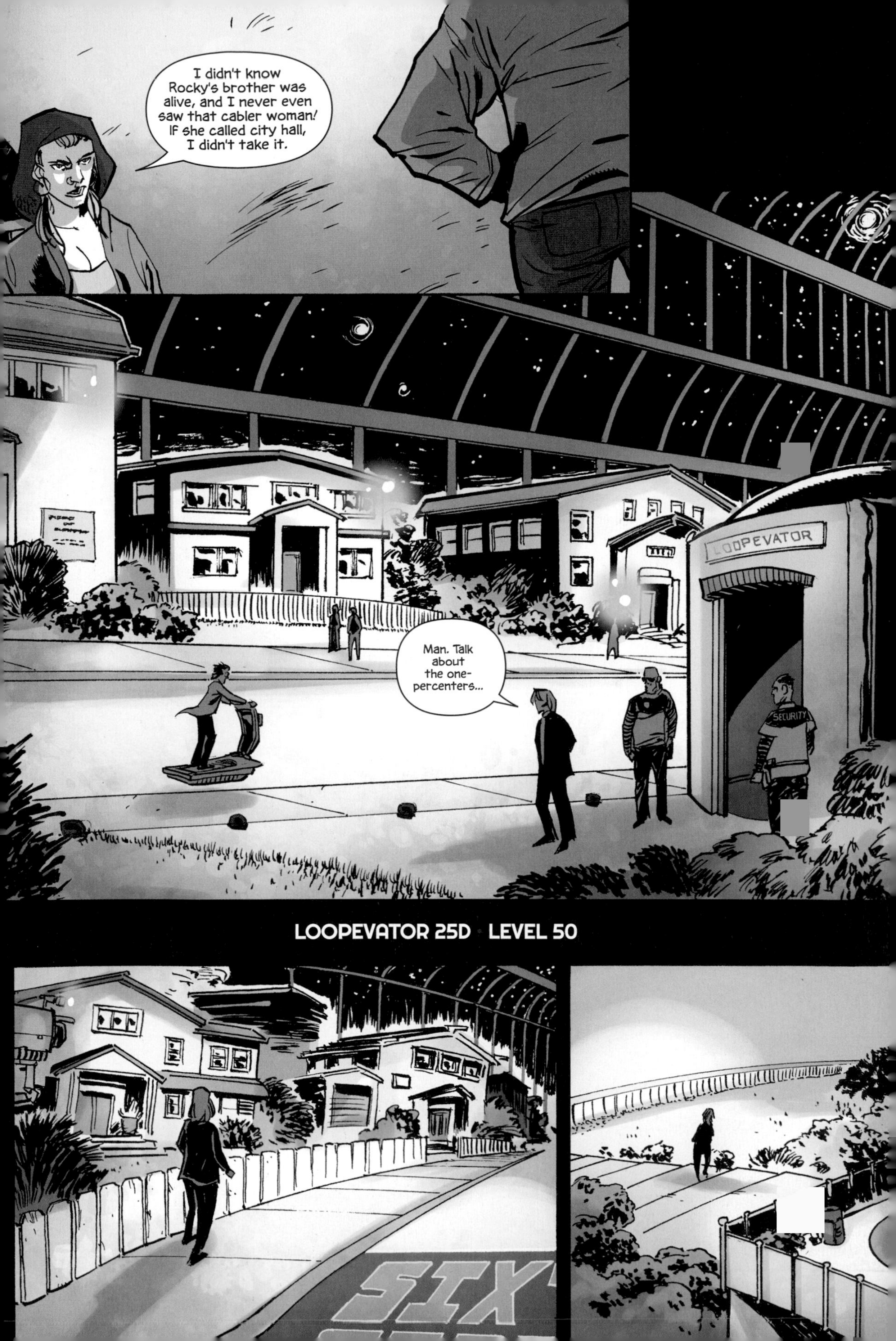
I didn't know Rocky's brother was alive, and I never even saw that cabler woman! If she called city hall, I didn't take it.
LOOPEVATOR
Man. Talk about the one-percenters...
SECURITY
LOOPEVATOR 25D · LEVEL 50
SIX

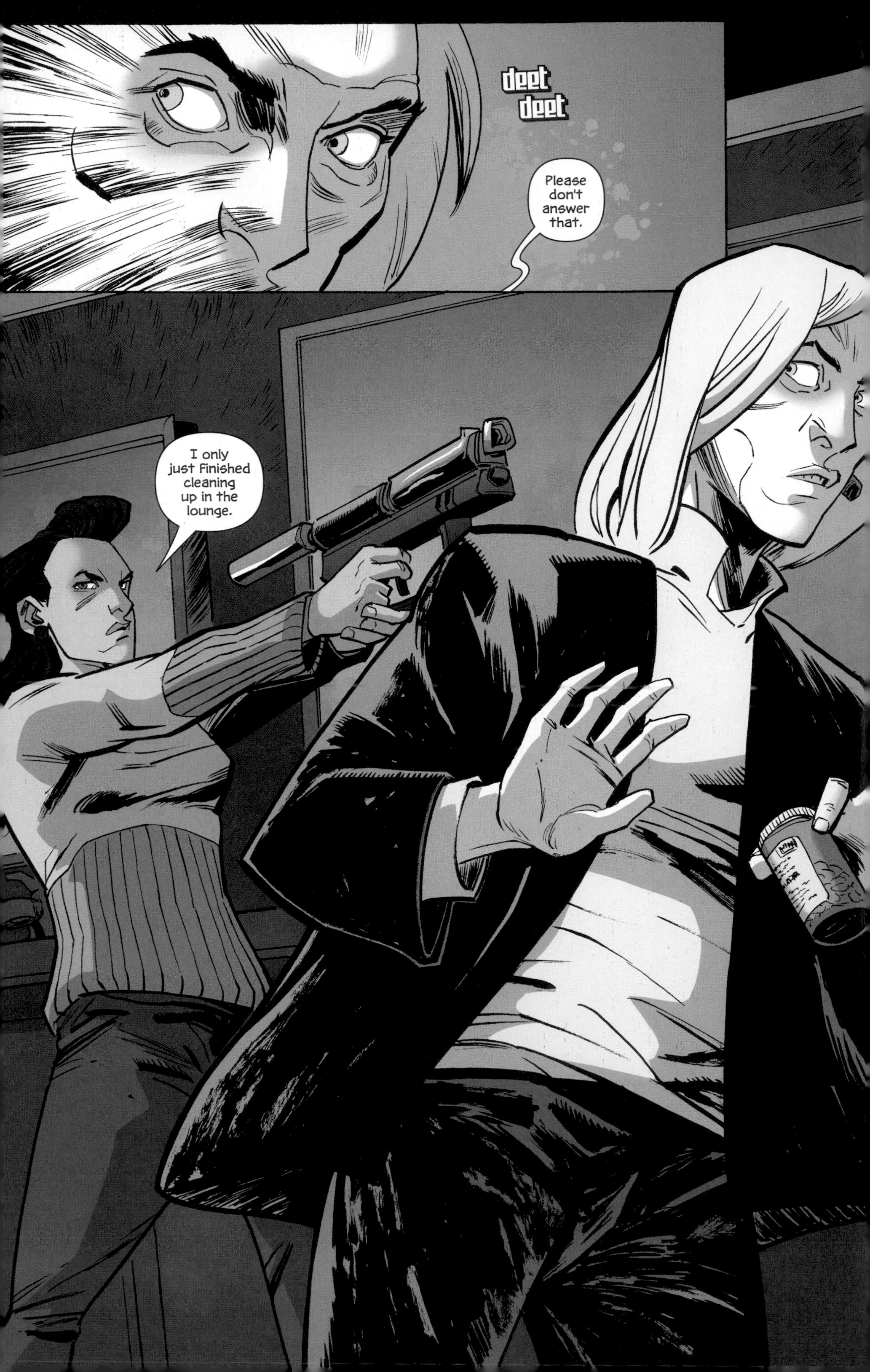
deet deet
Please don't answer that.
I only just finished cleaning up in the lounge.

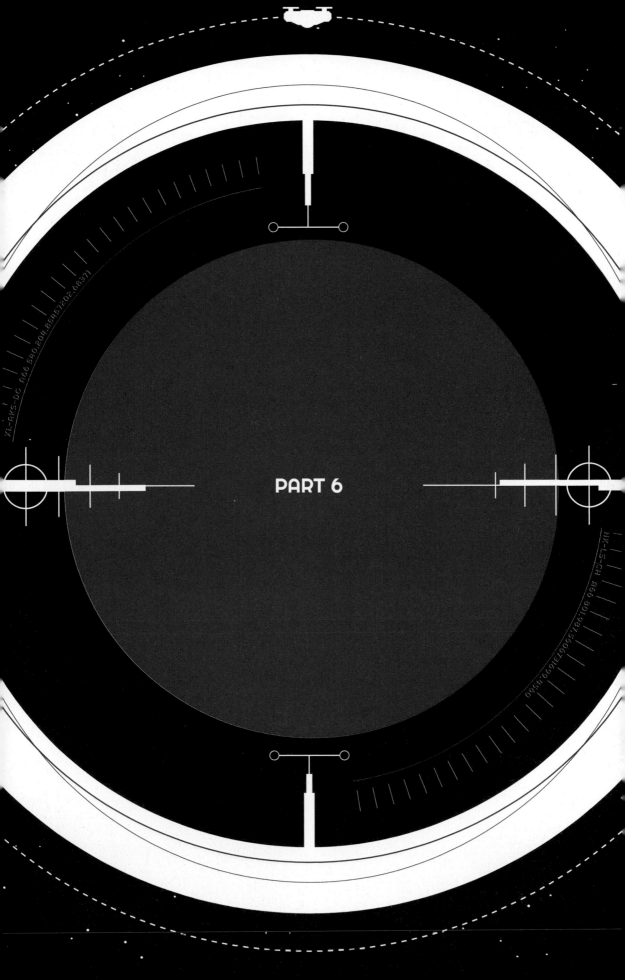

PART 6

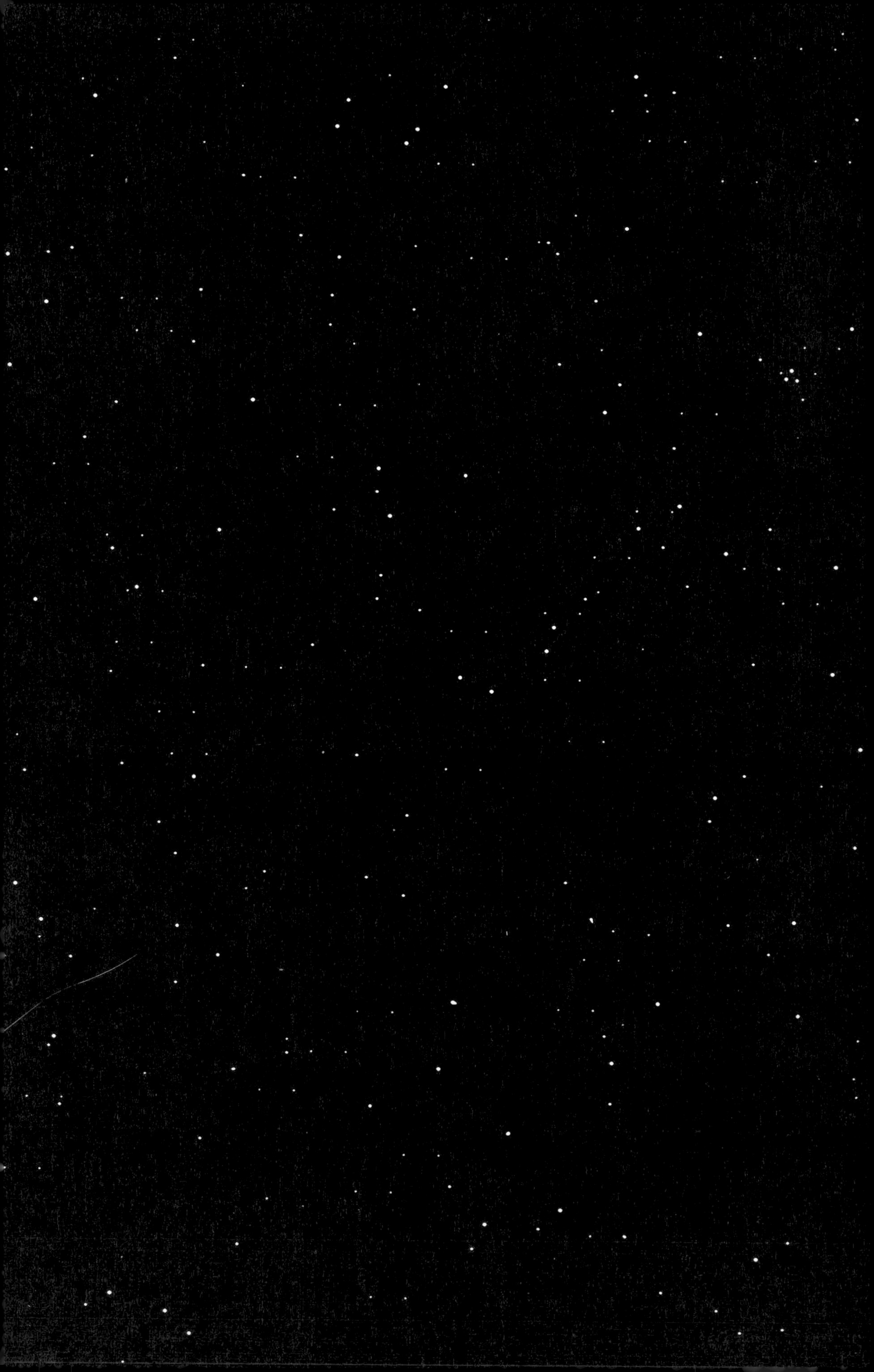

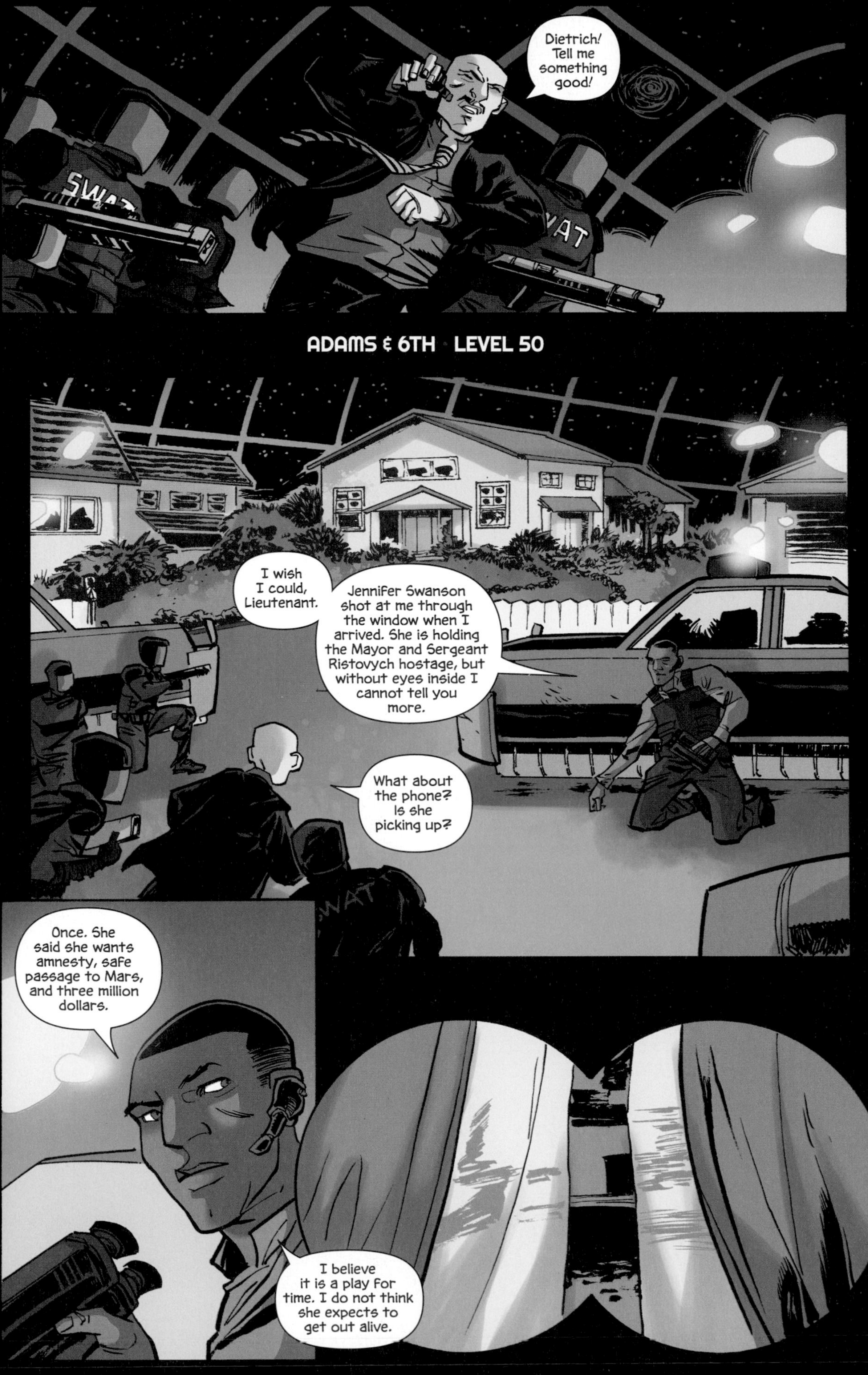
Dietrich! Tell me something good!
SWAT
SWAT
ADAMS & 6TH LEVEL 50
I wish I could, Lieutenant.
Jennifer Swanson shot at me through the window when I arrived. She is holding the Mayor and Sergeant Ristovych hostage, but without eyes inside I cannot tell you more.
What about the phone? Is she picking up?
SWAT
Once. She said she wants amnesty, safe passage to Mars, and three million dollars.
I believe it is a play for time. I do not think she expects to get out alive.

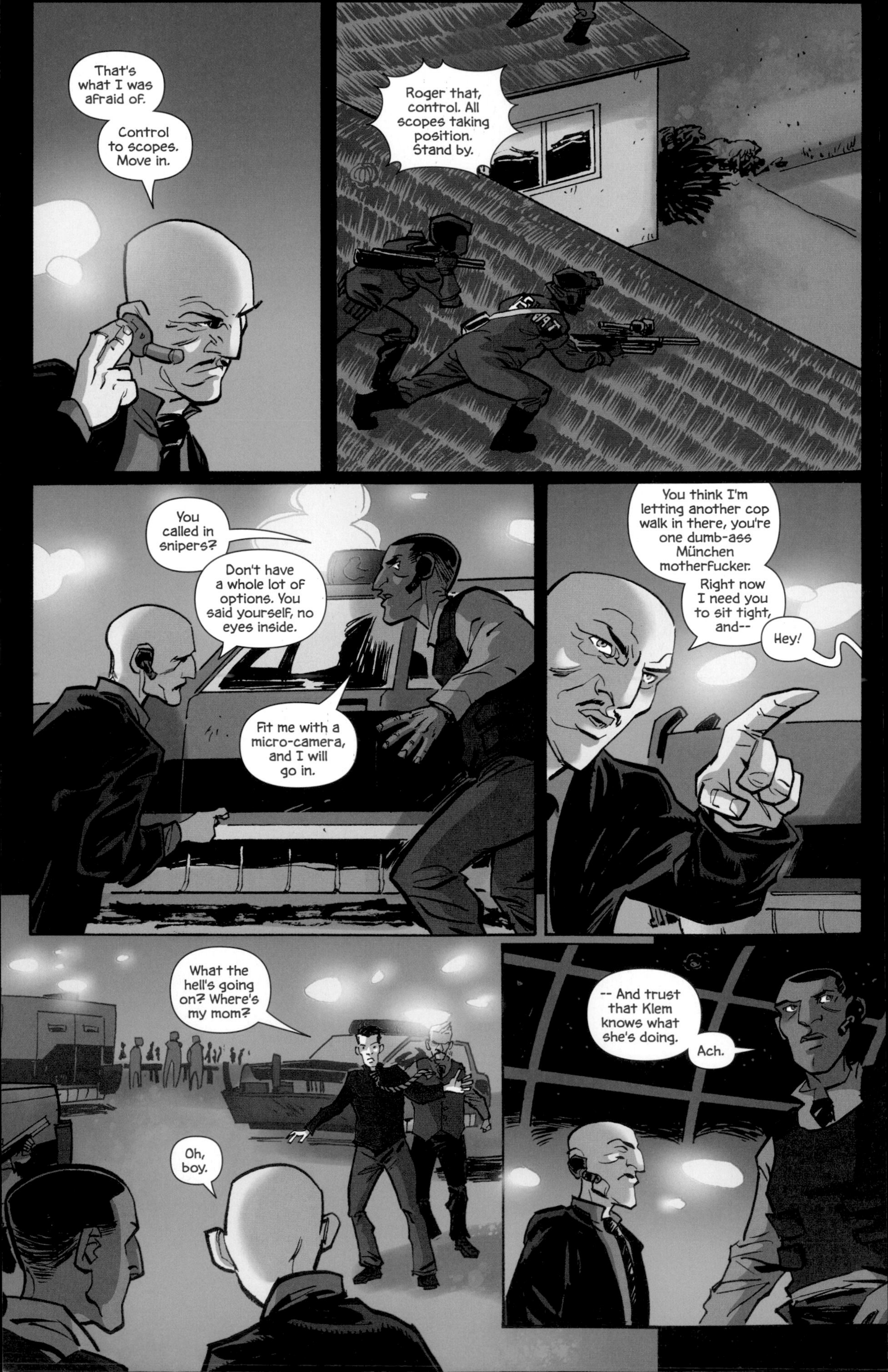
That's what I was afraid of.
Control to scopes. Move in.
Roger that, control. All scopes taking position. Stand by.
You called in snipers?
Don't have a whole lot of options. You said yourself, no eyes inside.
Fit me with a micro-camera, and I will go in.
You think I'm letting another cop walk in there, you're one dumb-ass München motherfucker.
Right now I need you to sit tight, and--
Hey!
What the hell's going on? Where's my mom?
Oh, boy.
-- And trust that Klem knows what she's doing.
Ach.

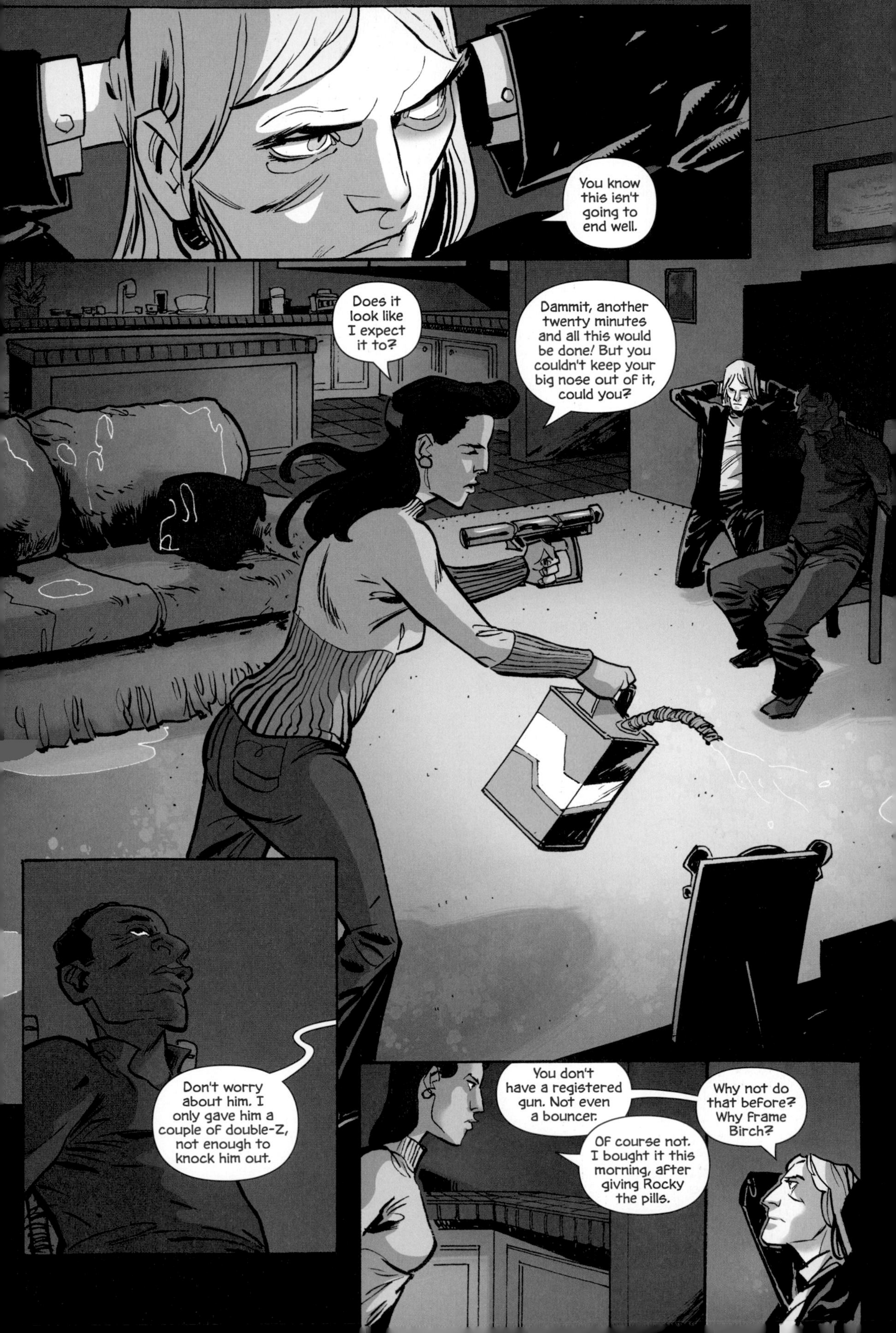
You know this isn't going to end well.
Does it look like I expect it to?
Dammit, another twenty minutes and all this would be done! But you couldn't keep your big nose out of it, could you?
Don't worry about him. I only gave him a couple of double-Z, not enough to knock him out.
You don't have a registered gun. Not even a bouncer.
Of course not. I bought it this morning, after giving Rocky the pills.
Why not do that before? Why frame Birch?

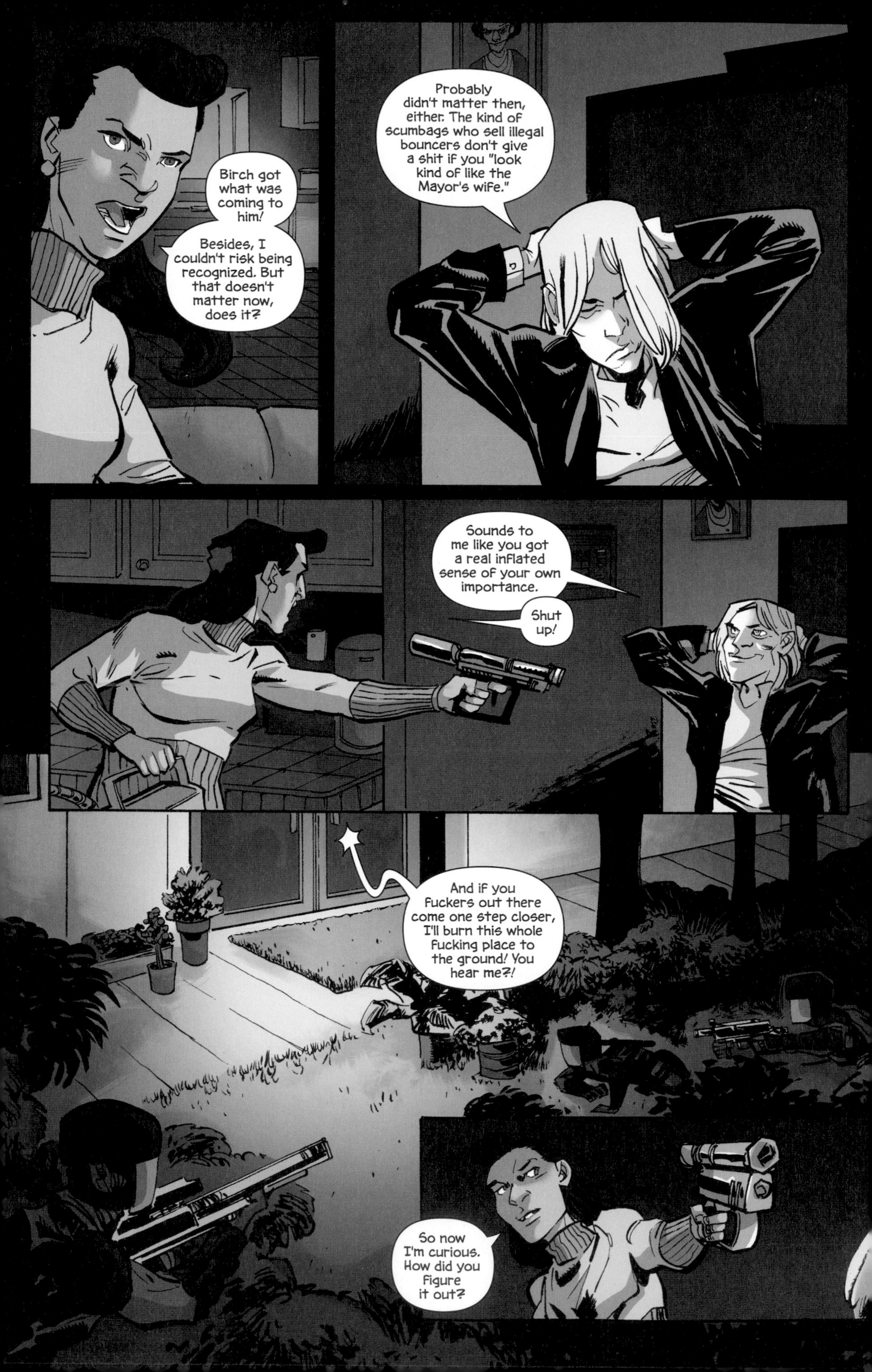
Birch got what was coming to him!
Besides, I couldn't risk being recognized. But that doesn't matter now, does it?
Probably didn't matter then, either. The kind of scumbags who sell illegal bouncers don't give a shit if you "look kind of like the Mayor's wife."
Sounds to me like you got a real inflated sense of your own importance.
Shut up!
And if you fuckers out there come one step closer, I'll burn this whole fucking place to the ground! You hear me?!
So now I'm curious. How did you figure it out?

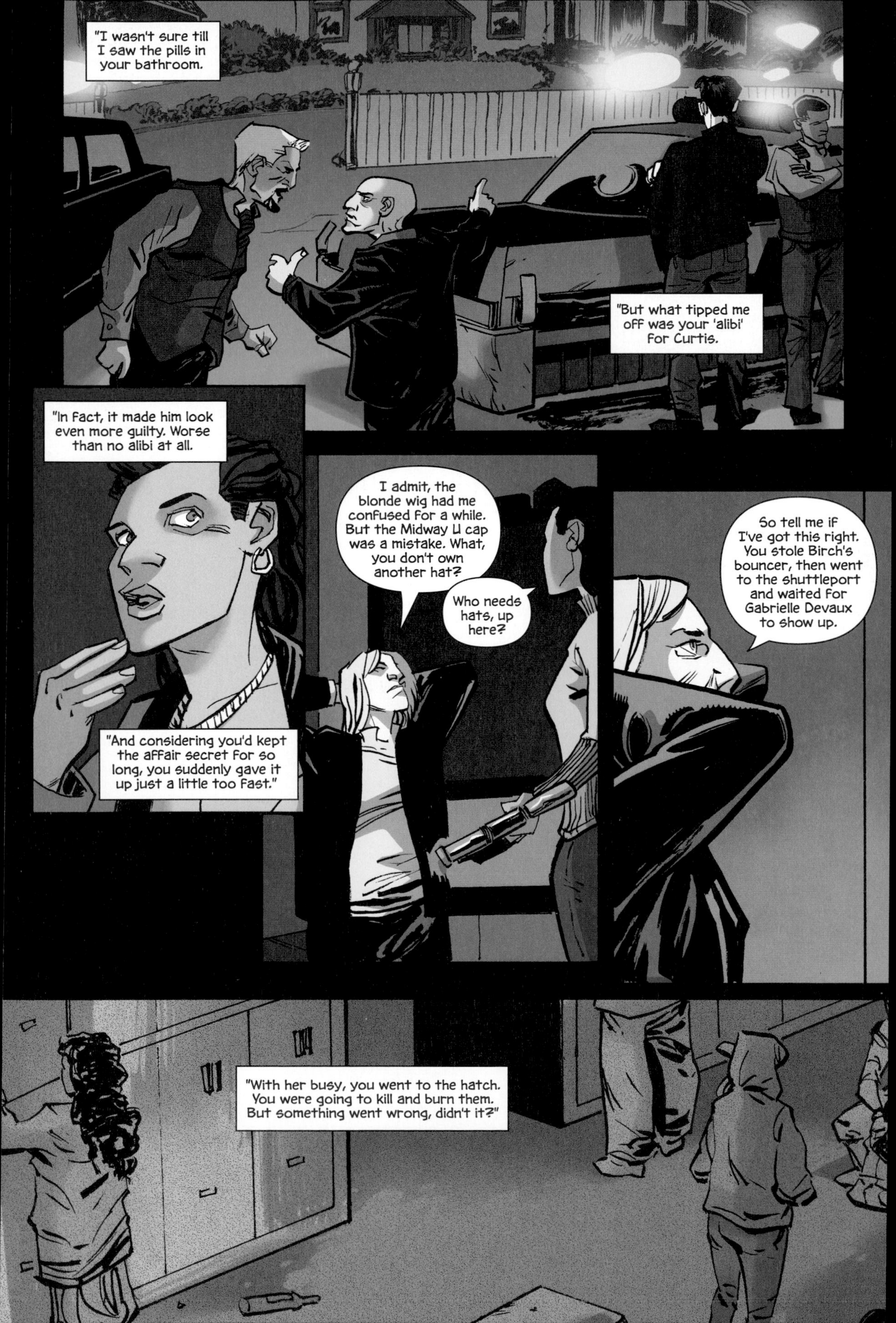
"I wasn't sure till I saw the pills in your bathroom.
"But what tipped me off was your 'alibi' for Curtis.
"In fact, it made him look even more guilty. Worse than no alibi at all.
"And considering you'd kept the affair secret for so long, you suddenly gave it up just a little too fast."
I admit, the blonde wig had me confused for a while. But the Midway U cap was a mistake. What, you don't own another hat?
Who needs hats, up here?
So tell me if I've got this right. You stole Birch's bouncer, then went to the shuttleport and waited for Gabrielle Devaux to show up.
"With her busy, you went to the hatch. You were going to kill and burn them. But something went wrong, didn't it?"

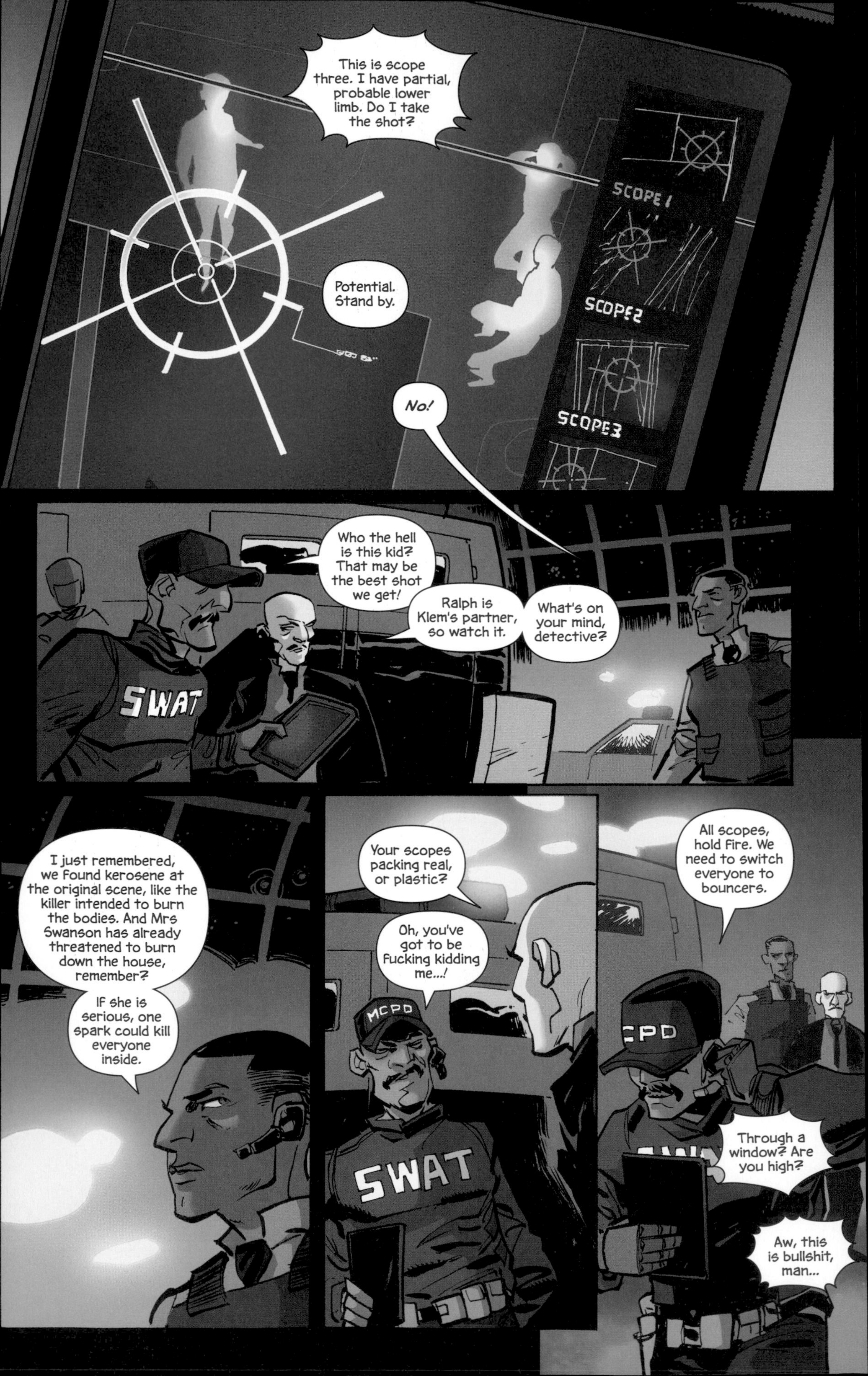
This is scope three. I have partial, probable lower limb. Do I take the shot?
SCOPE 1
SCOPE 2
SCOPE 3
Potential. Stand by.
No!
Who the hell is this kid? That may be the best shot we get!
Ralph is Klem's partner, so watch it.
What's on your mind, detective?
SWAT
I just remembered, we found kerosene at the original scene, like the killer intended to burn the bodies. And Mrs Swanson has already threatened to burn down the house, remember?
If she is serious, one spark could kill everyone inside.
Your scopes packing real, or plastic?
Oh, you've got to be fucking kidding me...!
MCPD
SWAT
All scopes, hold fire. We need to switch everyone to bouncers.
CPD
Through a window? Are you high?
Aw, this is bullshit, man...

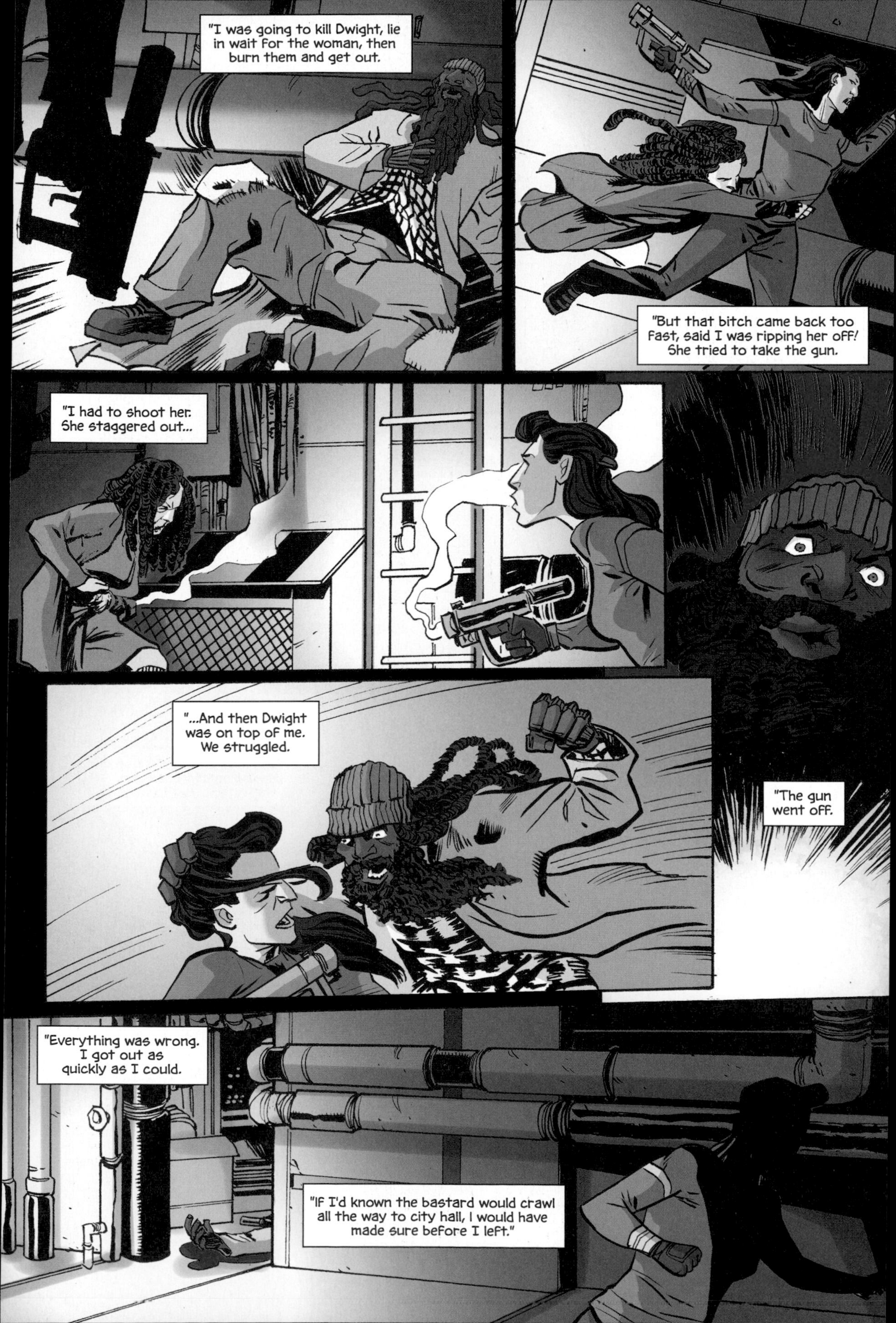
"I was going to kill Dwight, lie in wait for the woman, then burn them and get out.
"But that bitch came back too fast, said I was ripping her off! She tried to take the gun.
"I had to shoot her. She staggered out...
"...And then Dwight was on top of me. We struggled.
"The gun went off.
"Everything was wrong. I got out as quickly as I could.
"If I'd known the bastard would crawl all the way to city hall, I would have made sure before I left."

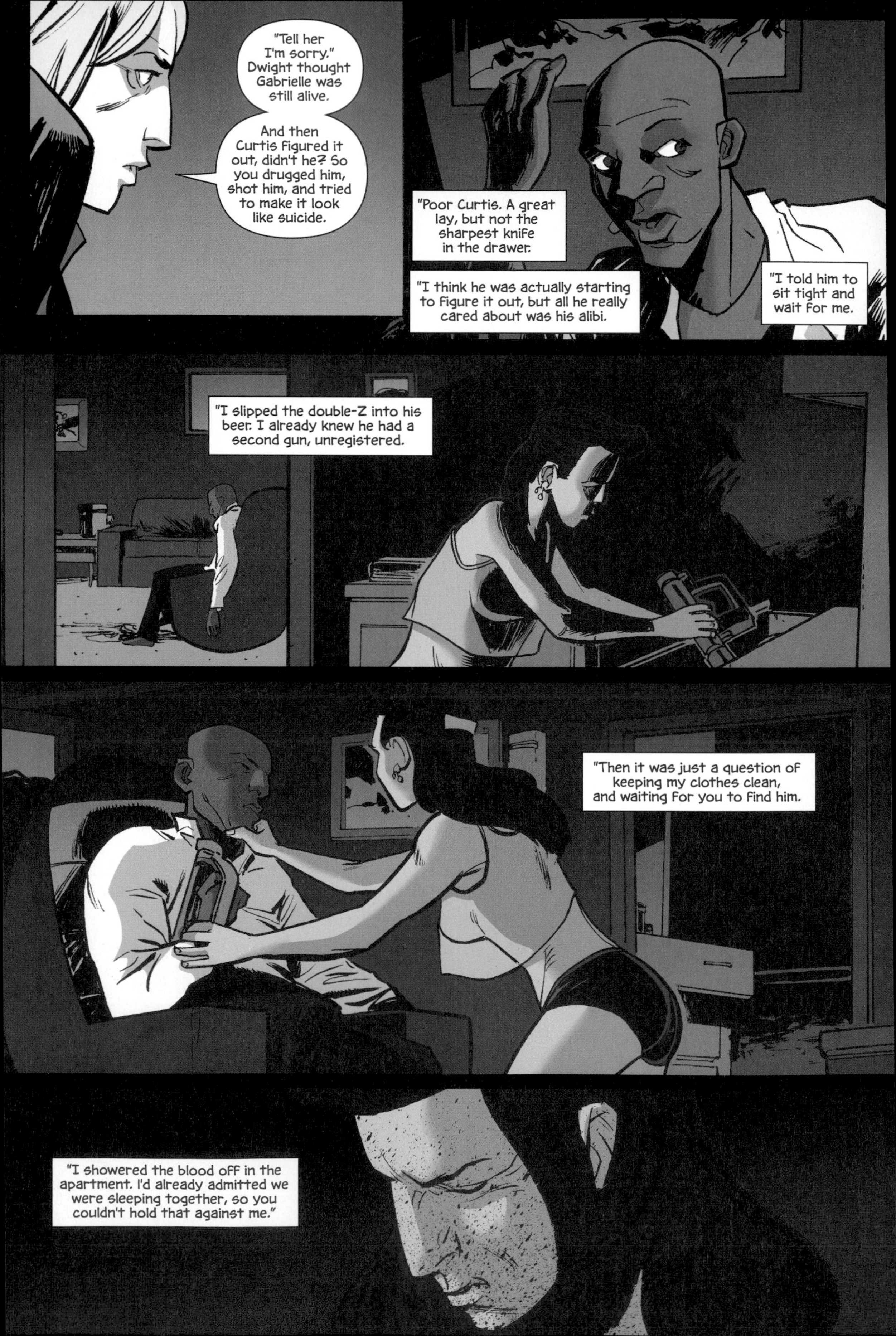
"Tell her I'm sorry." Dwight thought Gabrielle was still alive.
And then Curtis figured it out, didn't he? So you drugged him, shot him, and tried to make it look like suicide.
"Poor Curtis. A great lay, but not the sharpest knife in the drawer.
"I think he was actually starting to figure it out, but all he really cared about was his alibi.
"I told him to sit tight and wait for me.
"I slipped the double-Z into his beer. I already knew he had a second gun, unregistered.
"Then it was just a question of keeping my clothes clean, and waiting for you to find him.
"I showered the blood off in the apartment. I'd already admitted we were sleeping together, so you couldn't hold that against me."

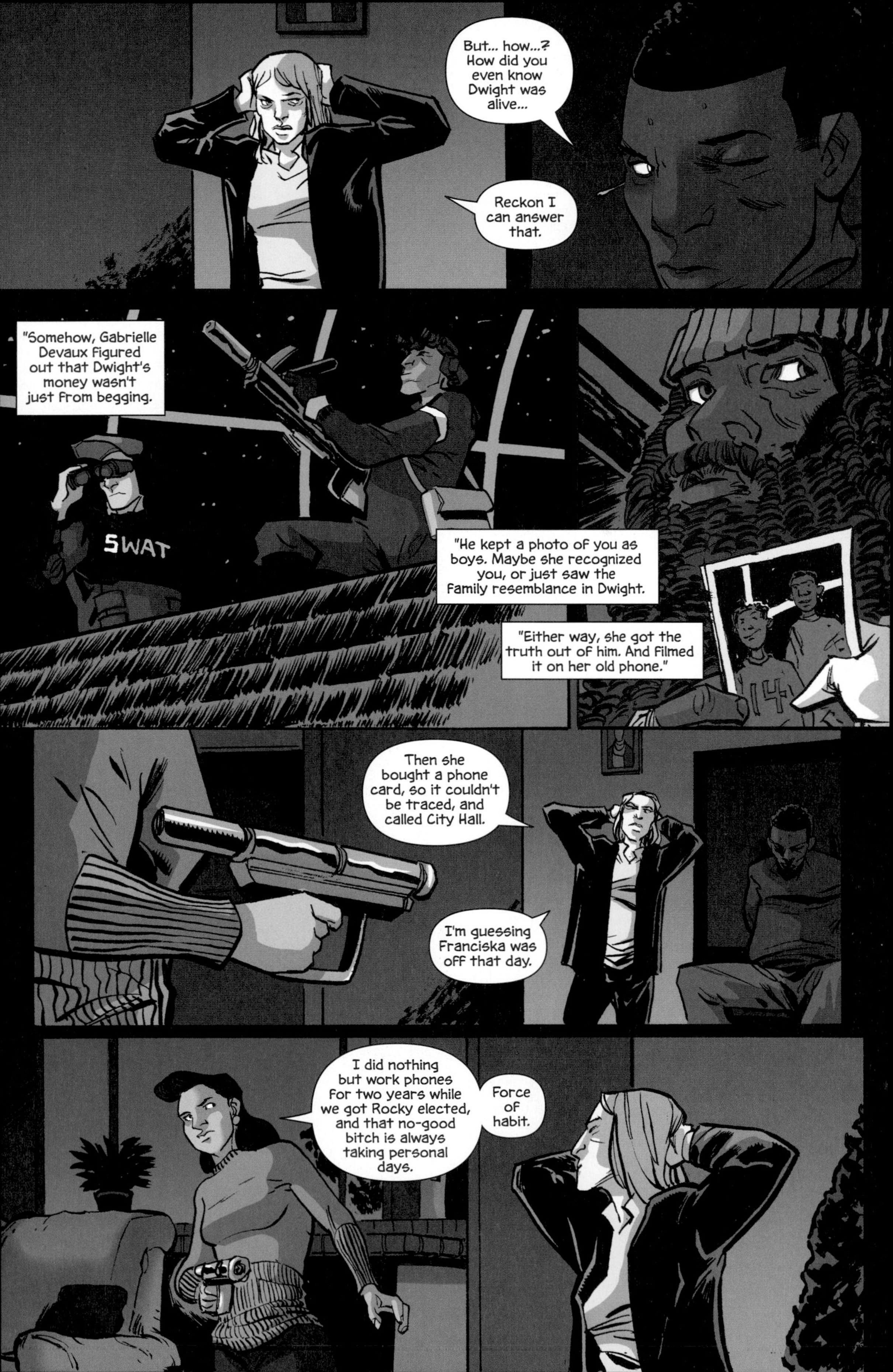
But... how...?
How did you even know Dwight was alive...
Reckon I can answer that.
"Somehow, Gabrielle Devaux figured out that Dwight's money wasn't just from begging.
"He kept a photo of you as boys. Maybe she recognized you, or just saw the family resemblance in Dwight.
"Either way, she got the truth out of him. And filmed it on her old phone."
SWAT
Then she bought a phone card, so it couldn't be traced, and called City Hall.
I'm guessing Franciska was off that day.
I did nothing but work phones for two years while we got Rocky elected, and that no-good bitch is always taking personal days.
Force of habit.

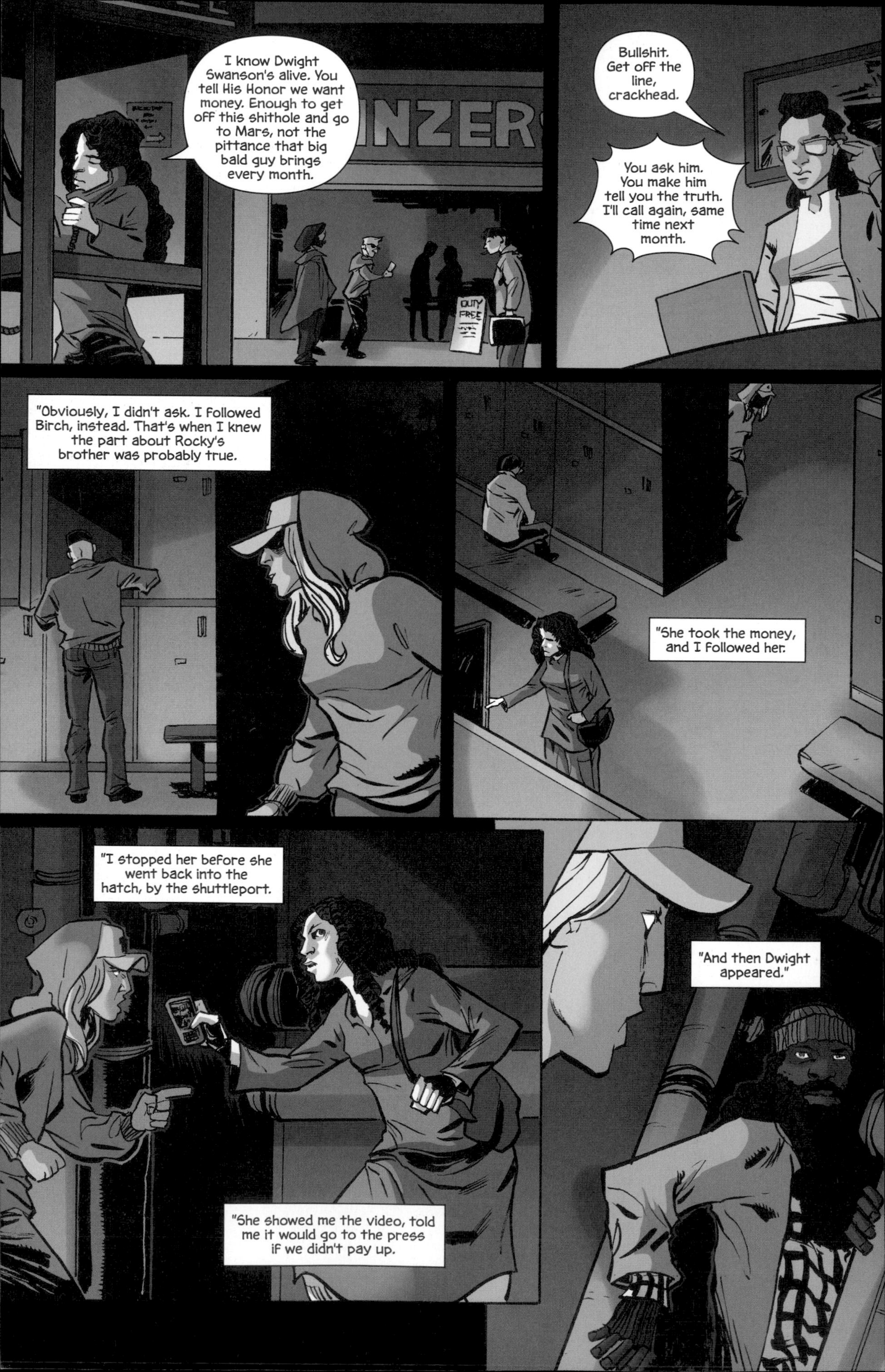

I know Dwight Swanson's alive. You tell His Honor we want money. Enough to get off this shithole and go to Mars, not the pittance that big bald guy brings every month.
INZER
DUTY FREE
Bullshit. Get off the line, crackhead.
You ask him. You make him tell you the truth. I'll call again, same time next month.
"Obviously, I didn't ask. I followed Birch, instead. That's when I knew the part about Rocky's brother was probably true.
"She took the money, and I followed her.
"I stopped her before she went back into the hatch, by the shuttleport.
"She showed me the video, told me it would go to the press if we didn't pay up.
"And then Dwight appeared."

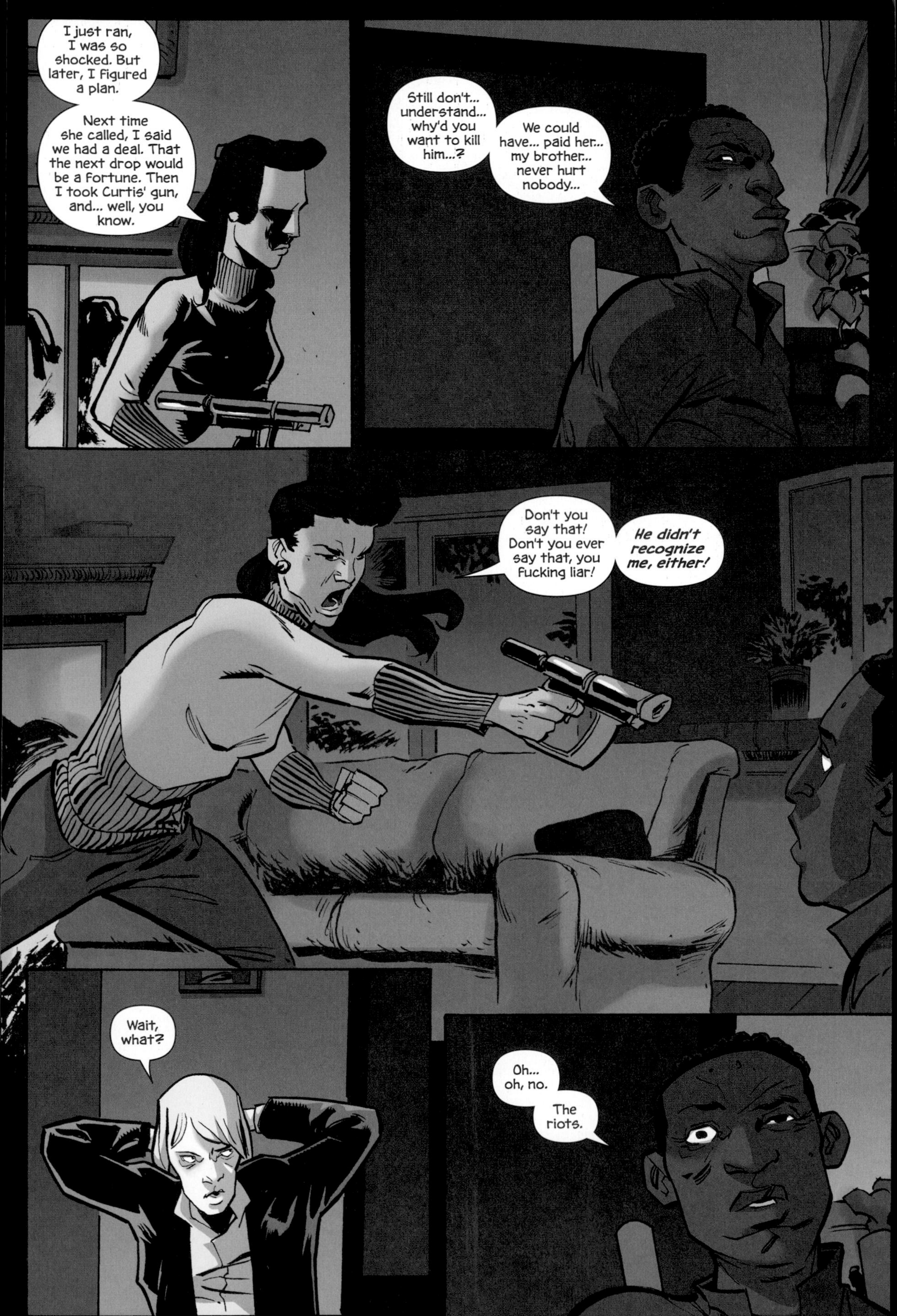

I just ran, I was so shocked. But later, I figured a plan.
Next time she called, I said we had a deal. That the next drop would be a fortune. Then I took Curtis' gun, and... well, you know.
Still don't... understand... why'd you want to kill him...?
We could have... paid her... my brother... never hurt nobody...
Don't you say that! Don't you ever say that, you fucking liar!
He didn't recognize me, either!
Wait, what?
Oh... oh, no.
The riots.

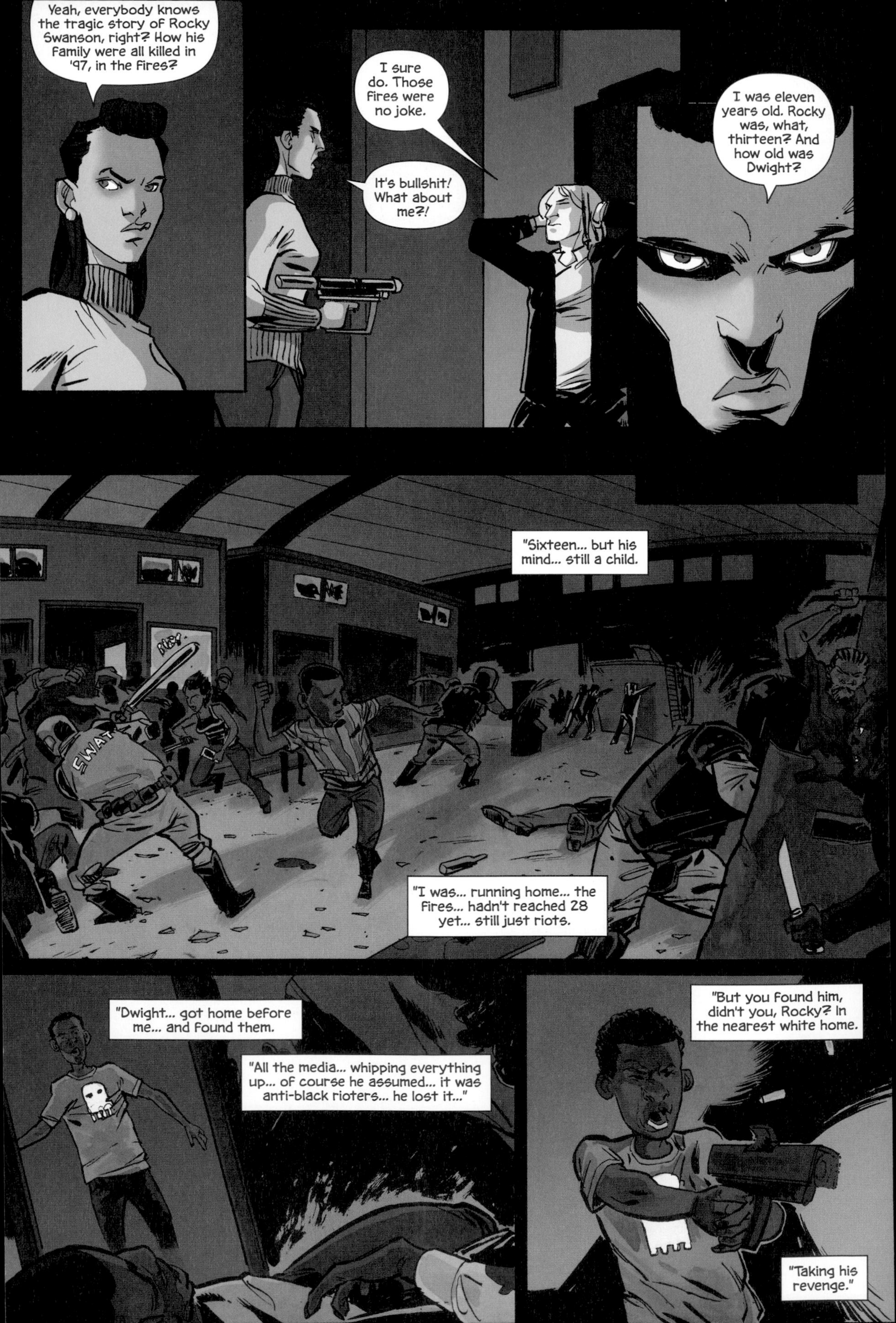
Yeah, everybody knows the tragic story of Rocky Swanson, right? How his family were all killed in '97, in the fires?
I sure do. Those fires were no joke.
It's bullshit! What about me?!
I was eleven years old. Rocky was, what, thirteen? And how old was Dwight?
"Sixteen... but his mind... still a child.
SWAT
"I was... running home... the fires... hadn't reached 28 yet... still just riots.
"Dwight... got home before me... and found them.
"All the media... whipping everything up... of course he assumed... it was anti-black rioters... he lost it..."
"But you found him, didn't you, Rocky? In the nearest white home.
"Taking his revenge."

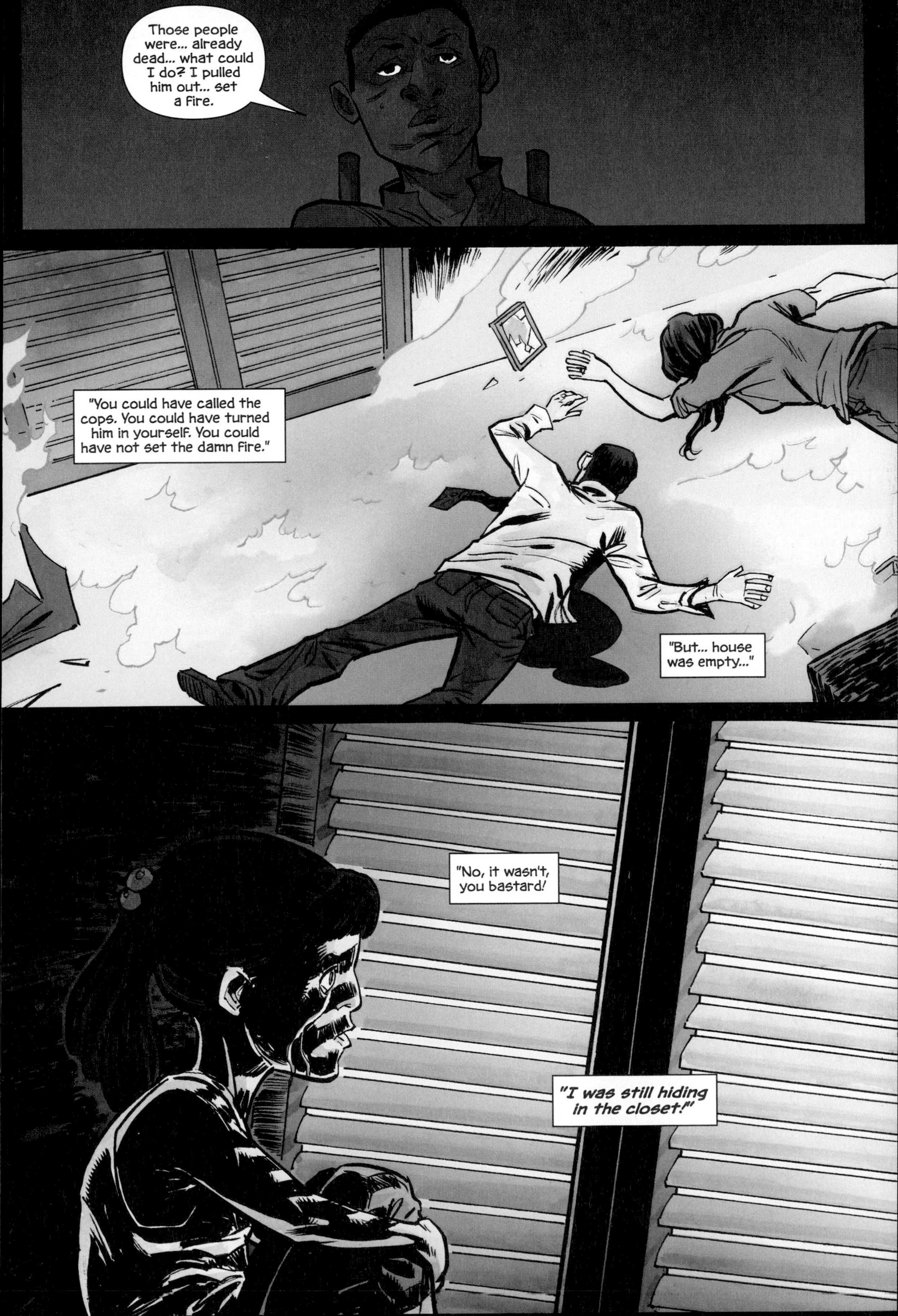
Those people were... already dead... what could I do? I pulled him out... set a fire.
"You could have called the cops. You could have turned him in yourself. You could have not set the damn fire."
"But... house was empty..."
"No, it wasn't, you bastard!
"I was still hiding in the closet!"

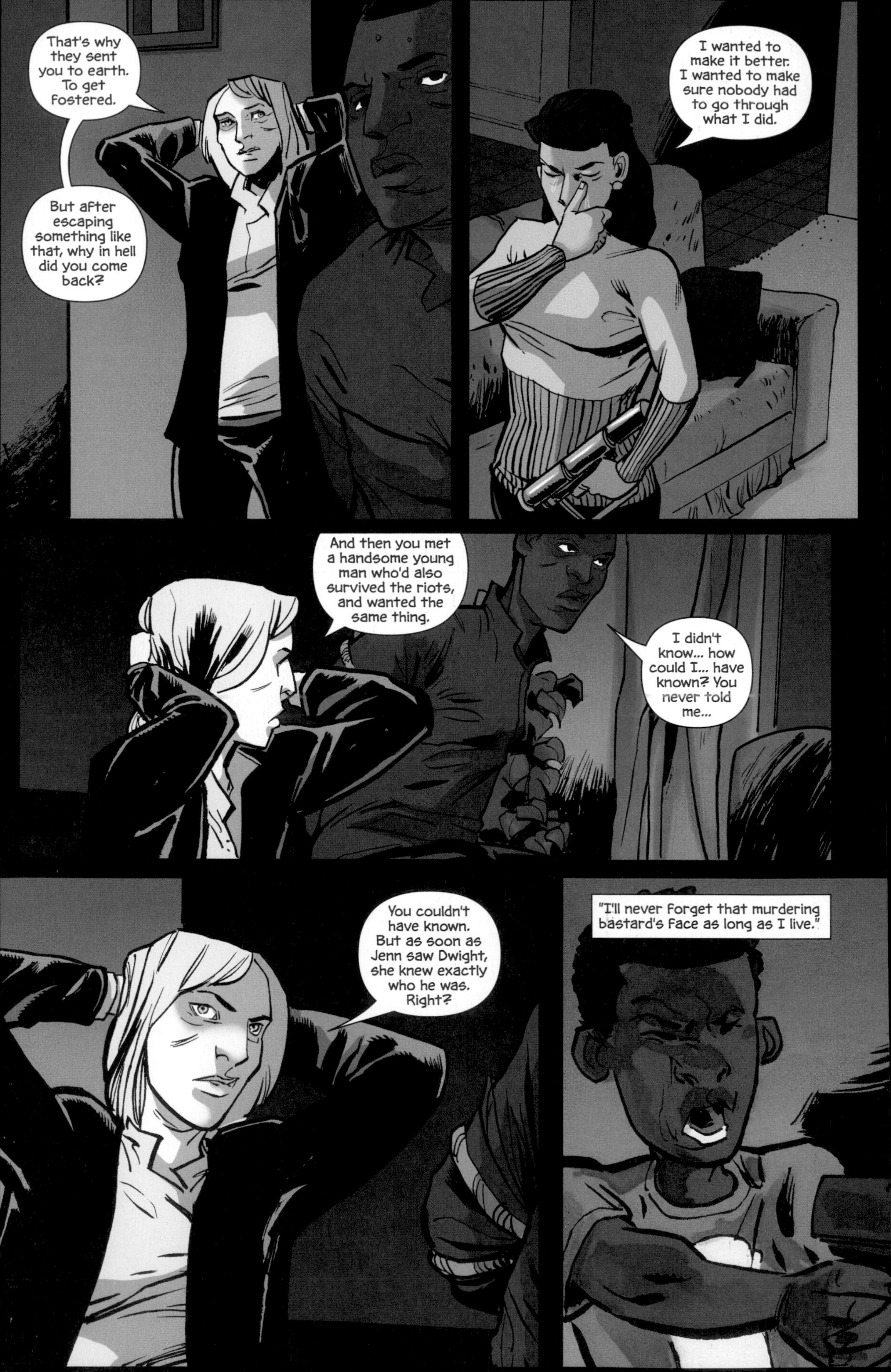

That's why they sent you to earth. To get fostered.
But after escaping something like that, why in hell did you come back?
I wanted to make it better. I wanted to make sure nobody had to go through what I did.
And then you met a handsome young man who'd also survived the riots, and wanted the same thing.
I didn't know... how could I... have known? You never told me...
You couldn't have known. But as soon as Jenn saw Dwight, she knew exactly who he was. Right?
"I'll never forget that murdering bastard's face as long as I live."

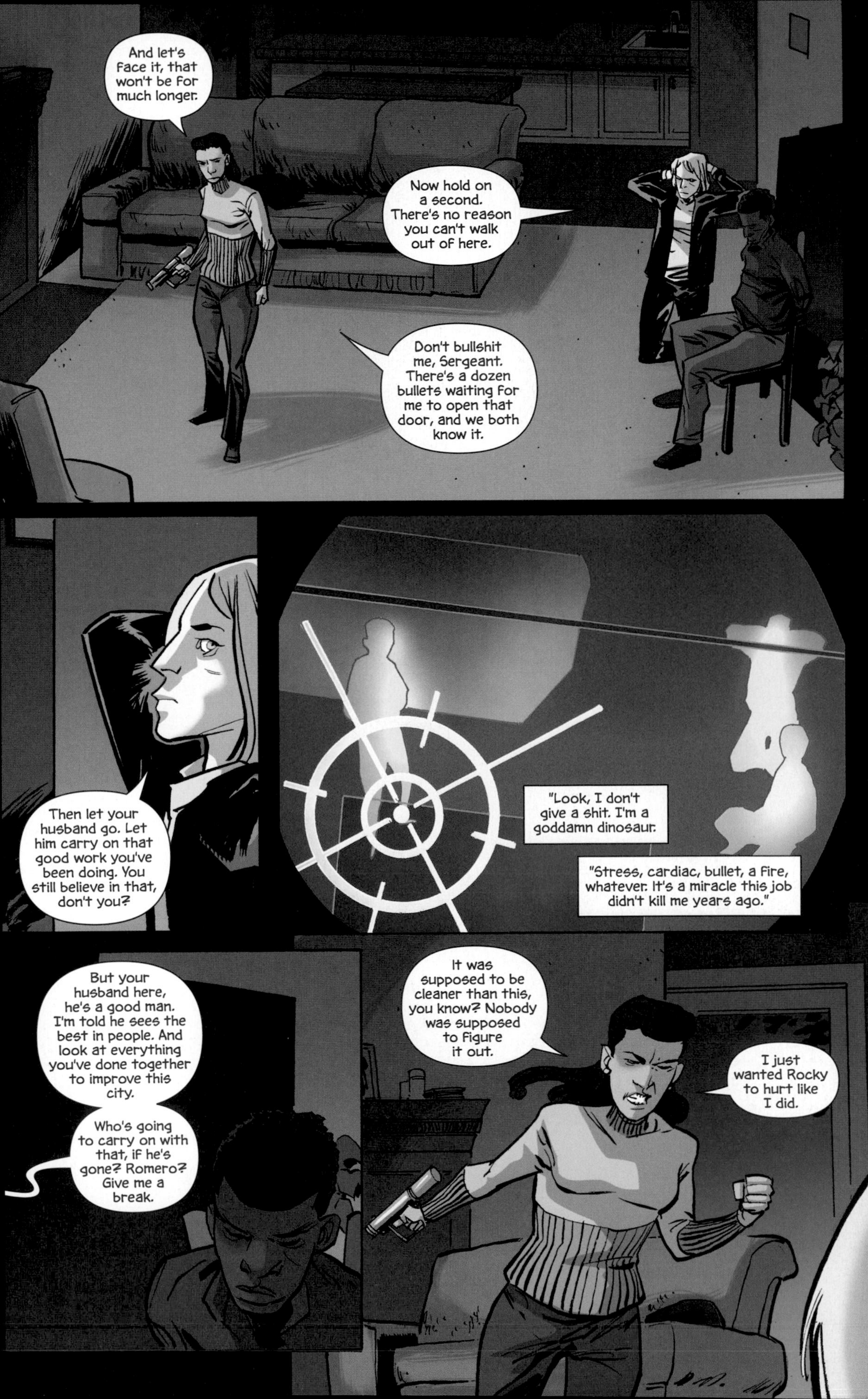
And let's face it, that won't be for much longer.
Now hold on a second. There's no reason you can't walk out of here.
Don't bullshit me, Sergeant. There's a dozen bullets waiting for me to open that door, and we both know it.
Then let your husband go. Let him carry on that good work you've been doing. You still believe in that, don't you?
"Look, I don't give a shit. I'm a goddamn dinosaur.
"Stress, cardiac, bullet, a fire, whatever. It's a miracle this job didn't kill me years ago."
But your husband here, he's a good man. I'm told he sees the best in people. And look at everything you've done together to improve this city.
Who's going to carry on with that, if he's gone? Romero? Give me a break.
It was supposed to be cleaner than this, you know? Nobody was supposed to figure it out.
I just wanted Rocky to hurt like I did.

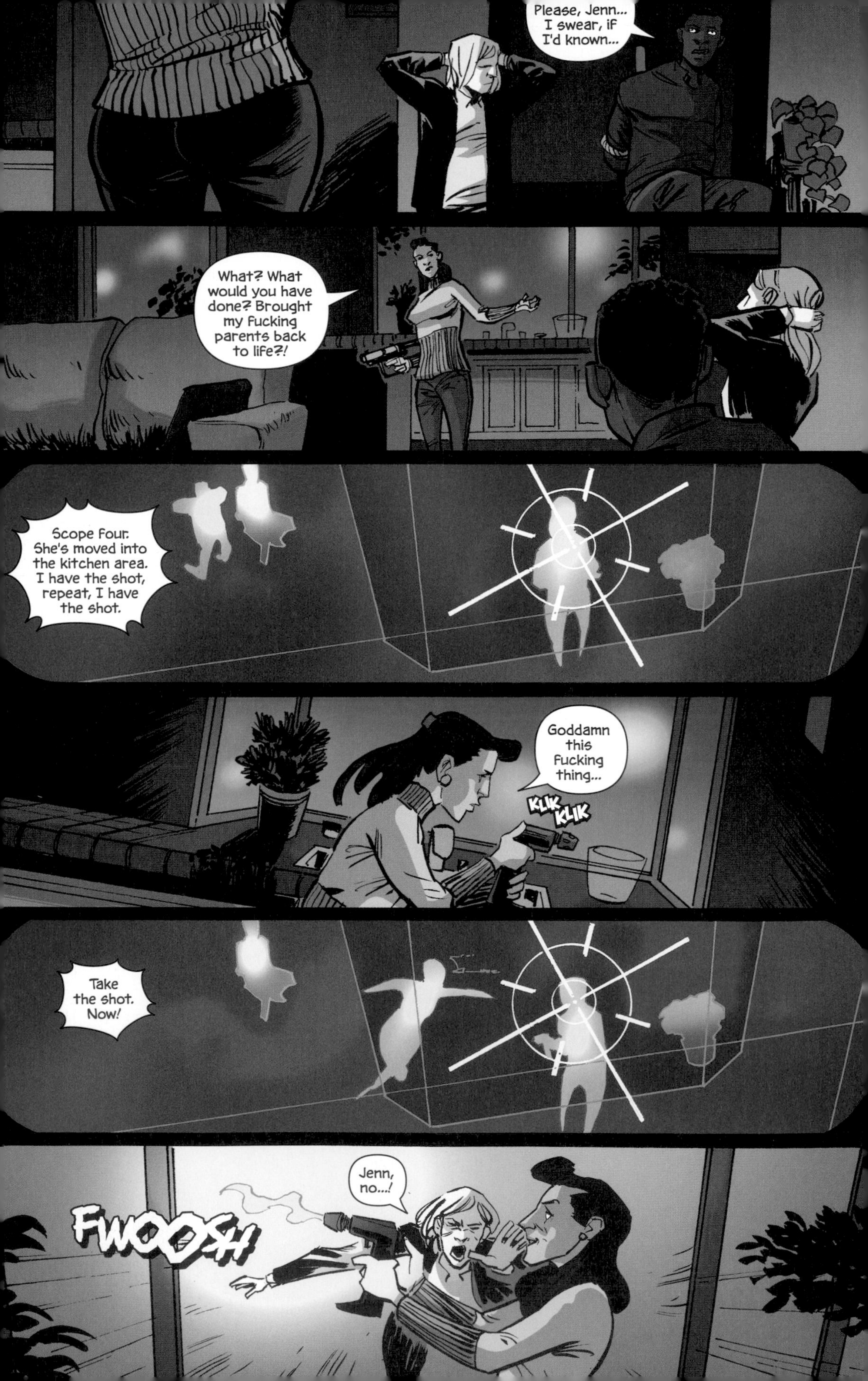
Please, Jenn... I swear, if I'd known...
What? What would you have done? Brought my fucking parents back to life?!
Scope four. She's moved into the kitchen area. I have the shot, repeat, I have the shot.
Goddamn this fucking thing...
KLIK KLIK
Take the shot. Now!
Jenn, no...!
FWOOSH

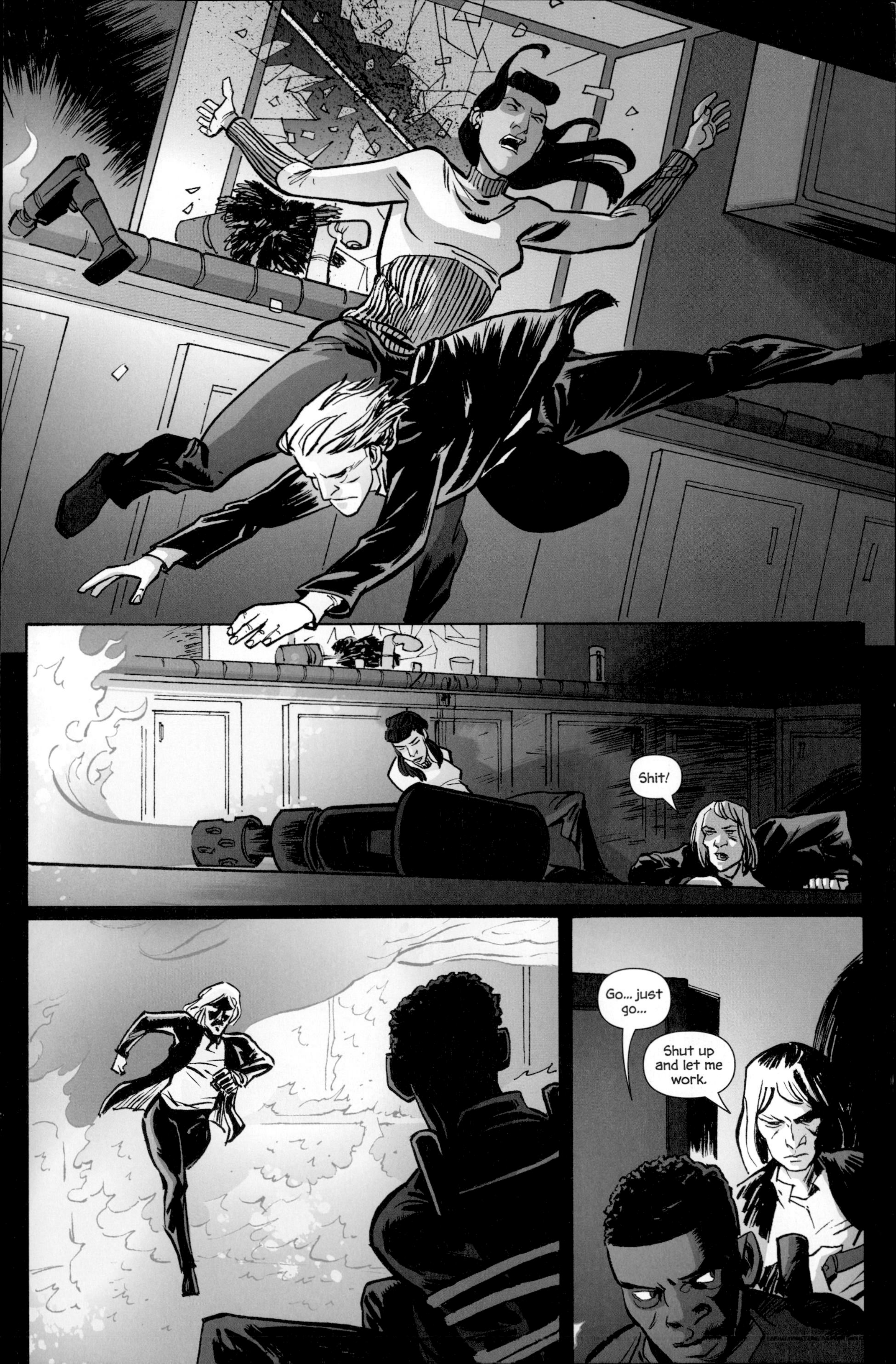
Shit!
Go... just go...
Shut up and let me work.

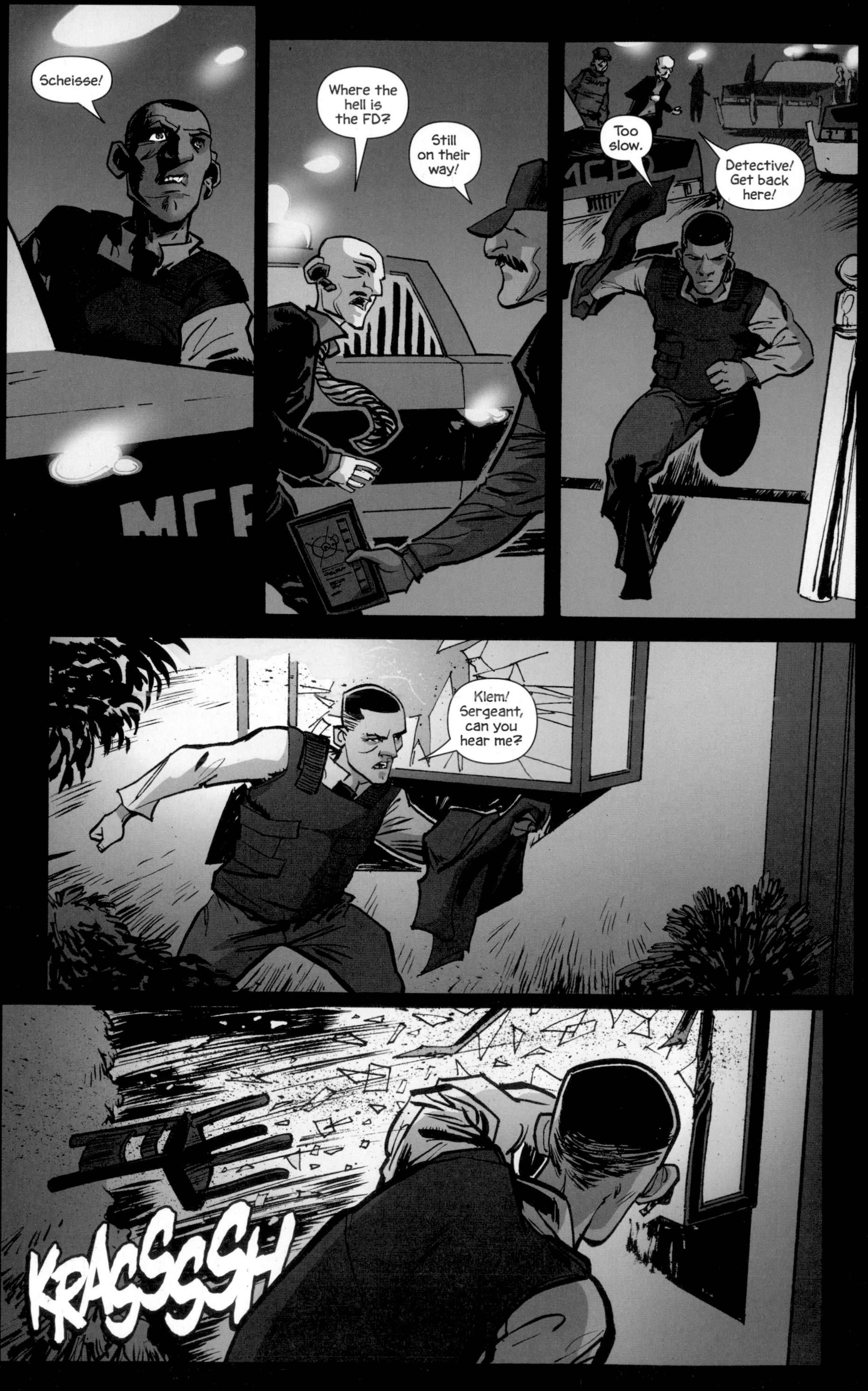
Scheisse!
Where the hell is the FD?
Still on their way!
Too slow.
Detective! Get back here!
Klem! Sergeant, can you hear me?
KRASSSSH

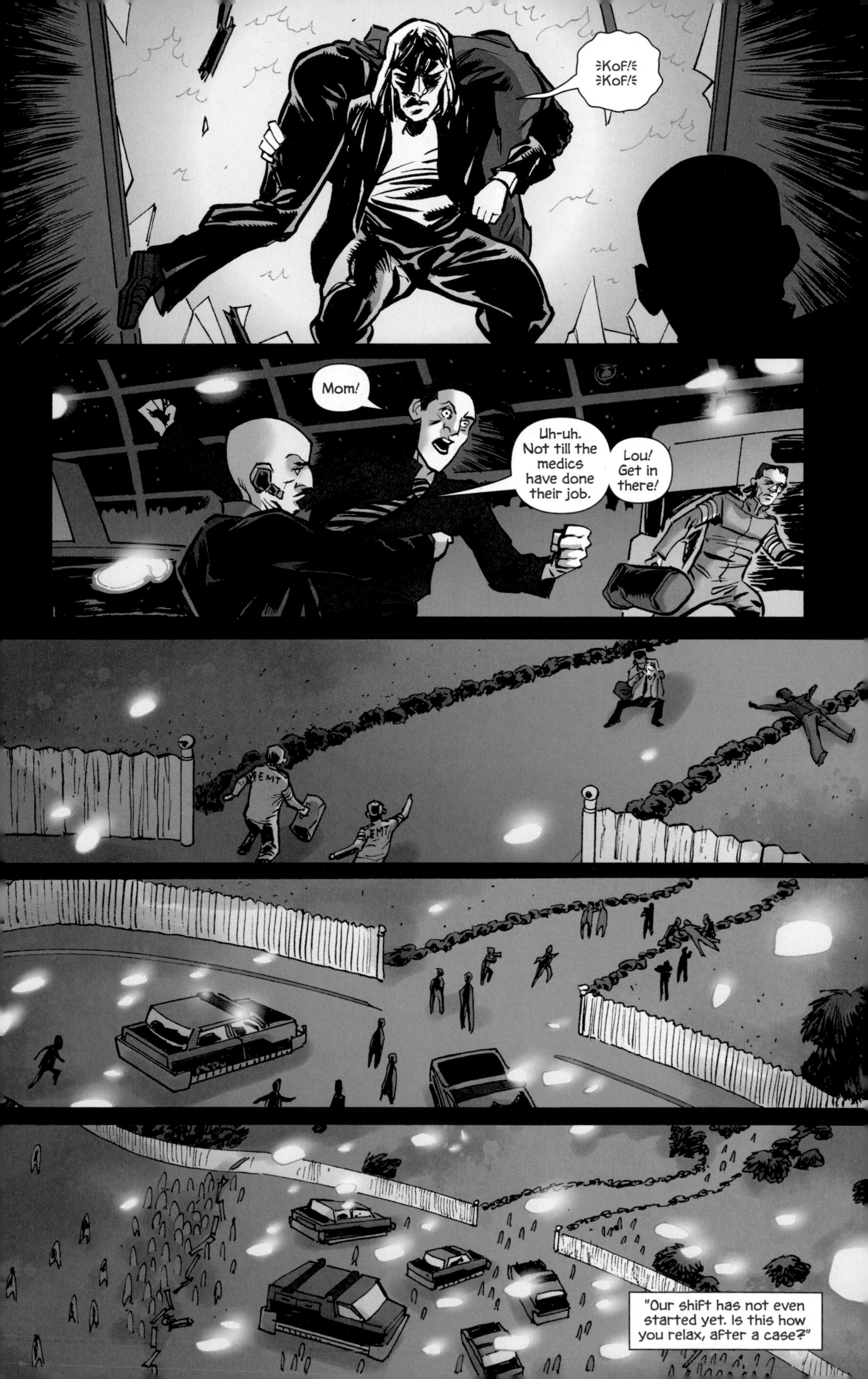

Kof! Kof!
Mom!
Uh-uh. Not till the medics have done their job.
Lou! Get in there!
EMT
EMT
"Our shift has not even started yet. Is this how you relax, after a case?"

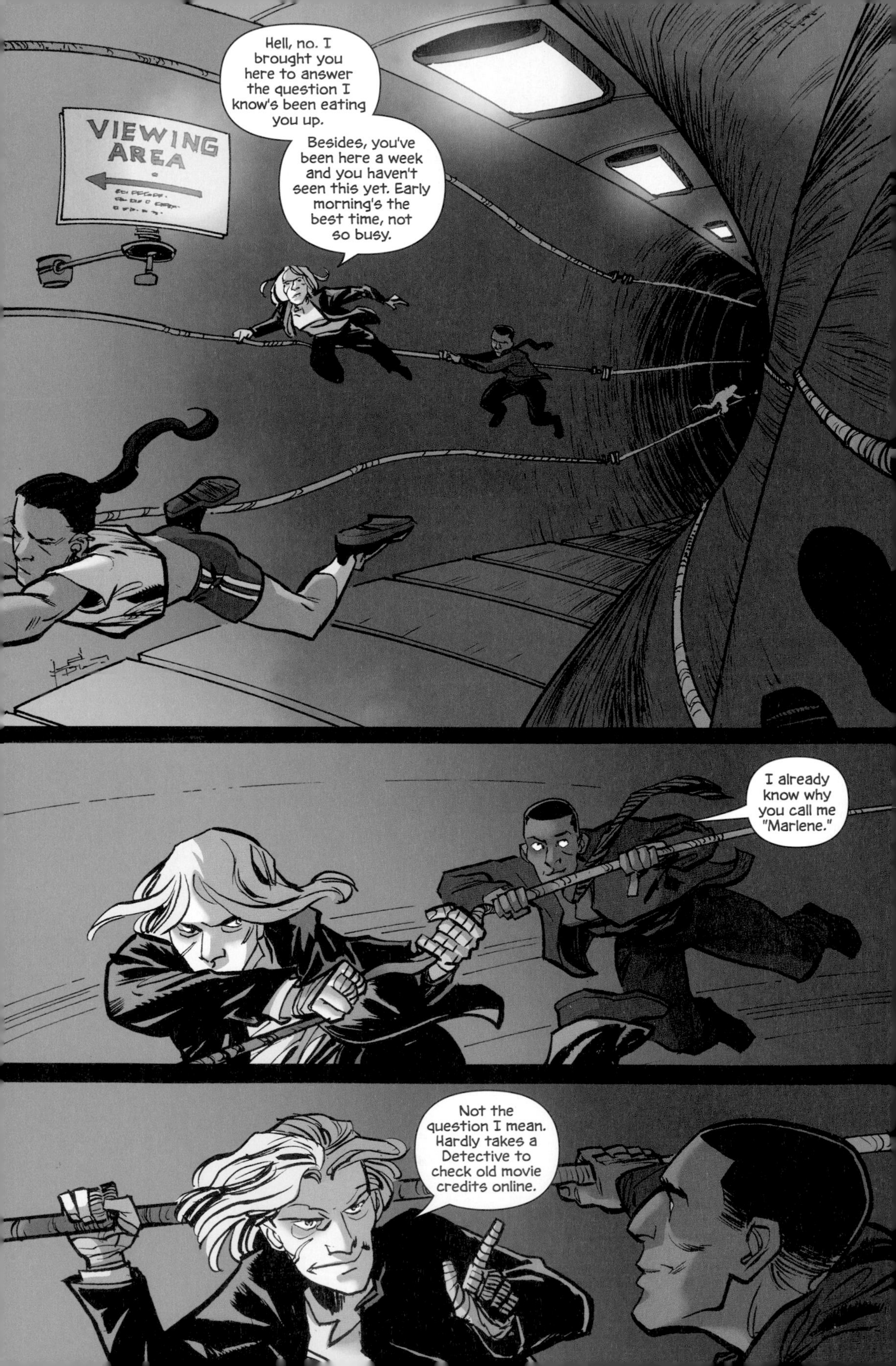
VIEWING AREA
Hell, no. I brought you here to answer the question I know's been eating you up.
Besides, you've been here a week and you haven't seen this yet. Early morning's the best time, not so busy.
I already know why you call me "Marlene."
Not the question I mean. Hardly takes a Detective to check old movie credits online.

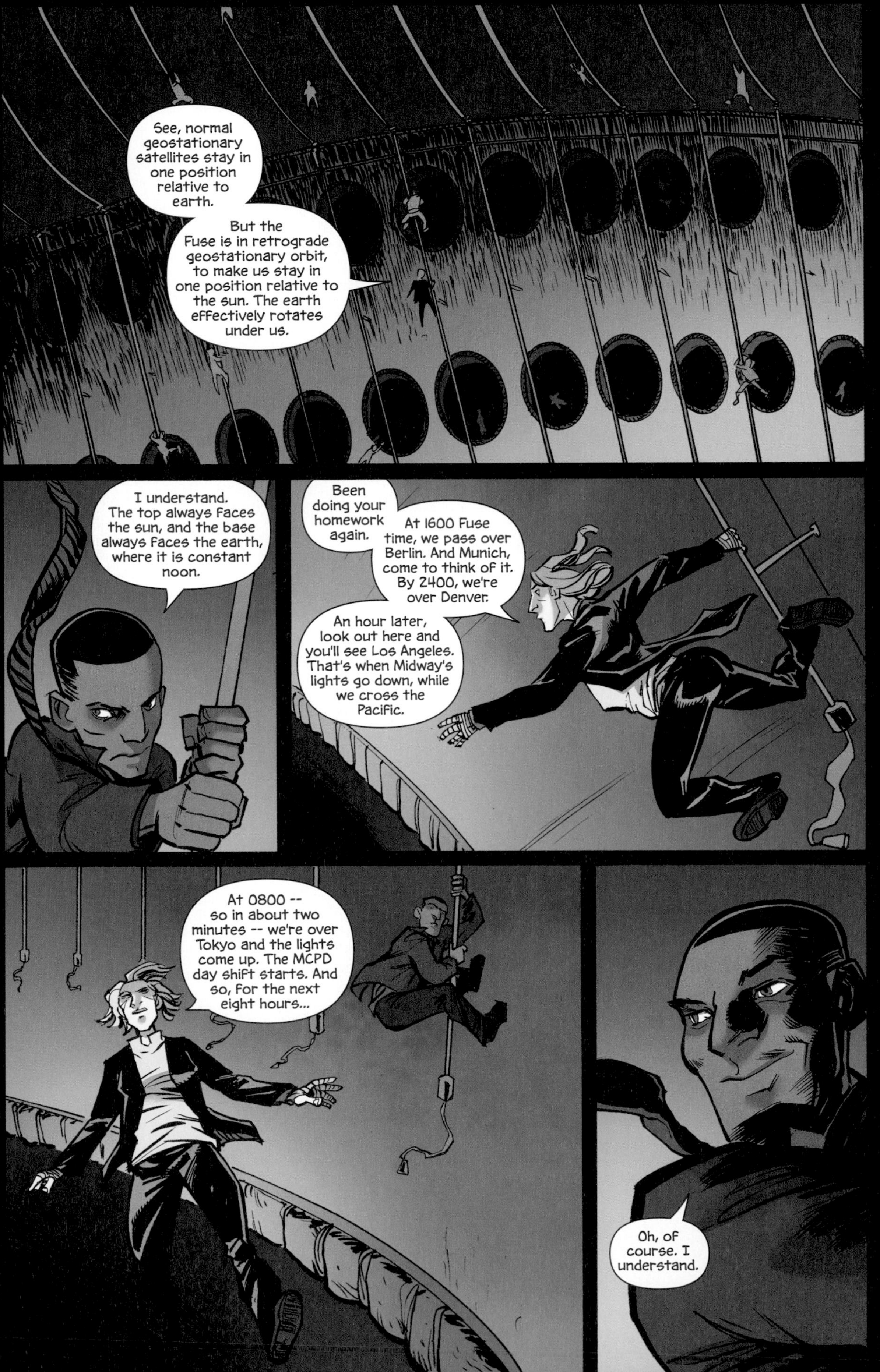
See, normal geostationary satellites stay in one position relative to earth.
But the Fuse is in retrograde geostationary orbit, to make us stay in one position relative to the sun. The earth effectively rotates under us.
I understand. The top always faces the sun, and the base always faces the earth, where it is constant noon.
Been doing your homework again.
At 1600 Fuse time, we pass over Berlin. And Munich, come to think of it. By 2400, we're over Denver.
An hour later, look out here and you'll see Los Angeles. That's when Midway's lights go down, while we cross the Pacific.
At 0800 -- so in about two minutes -- we're over Tokyo and the lights come up. The MCPD day shift starts. And so, for the next eight hours...
Oh, of course. I understand.

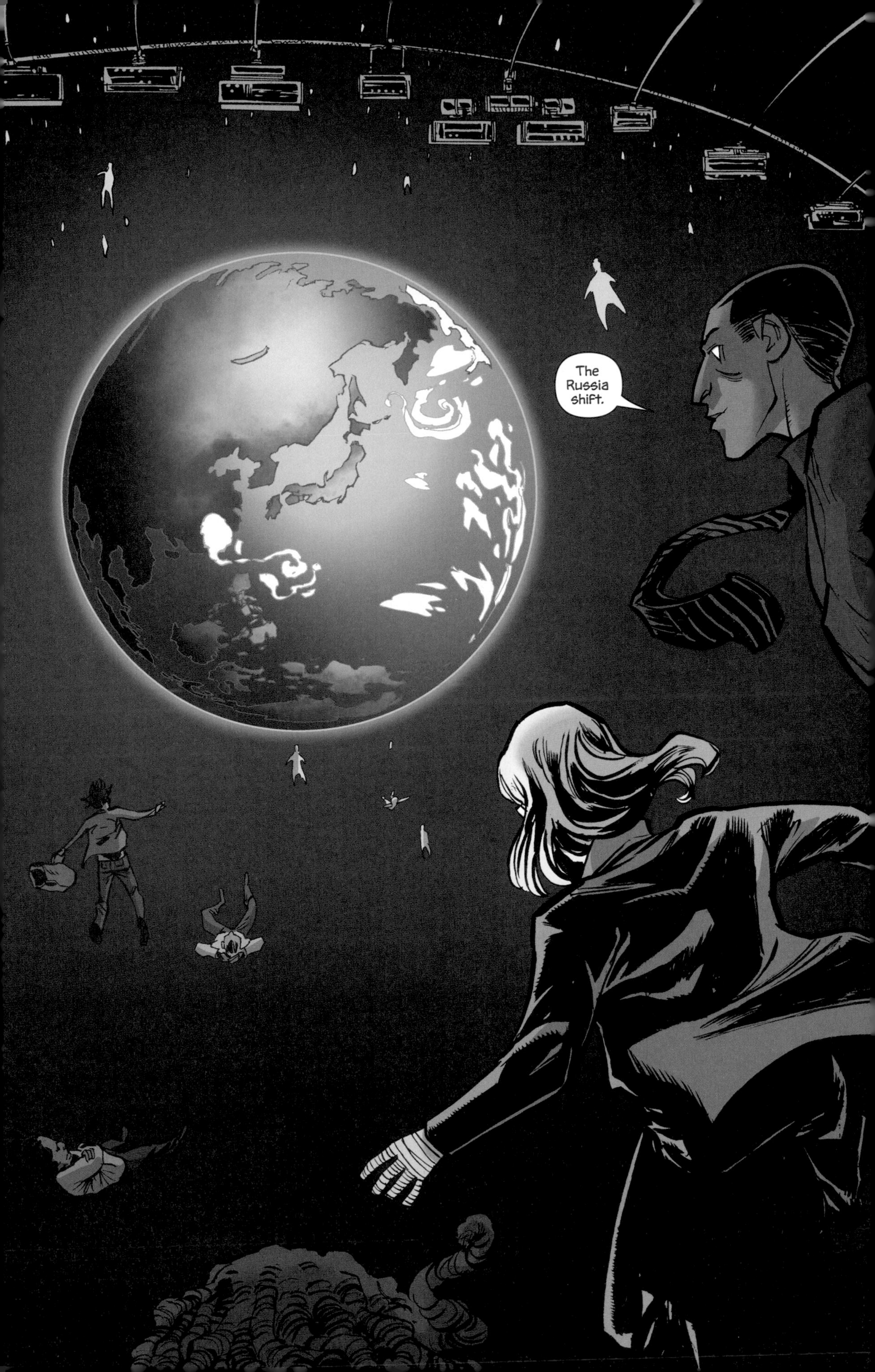
The Russia shift.

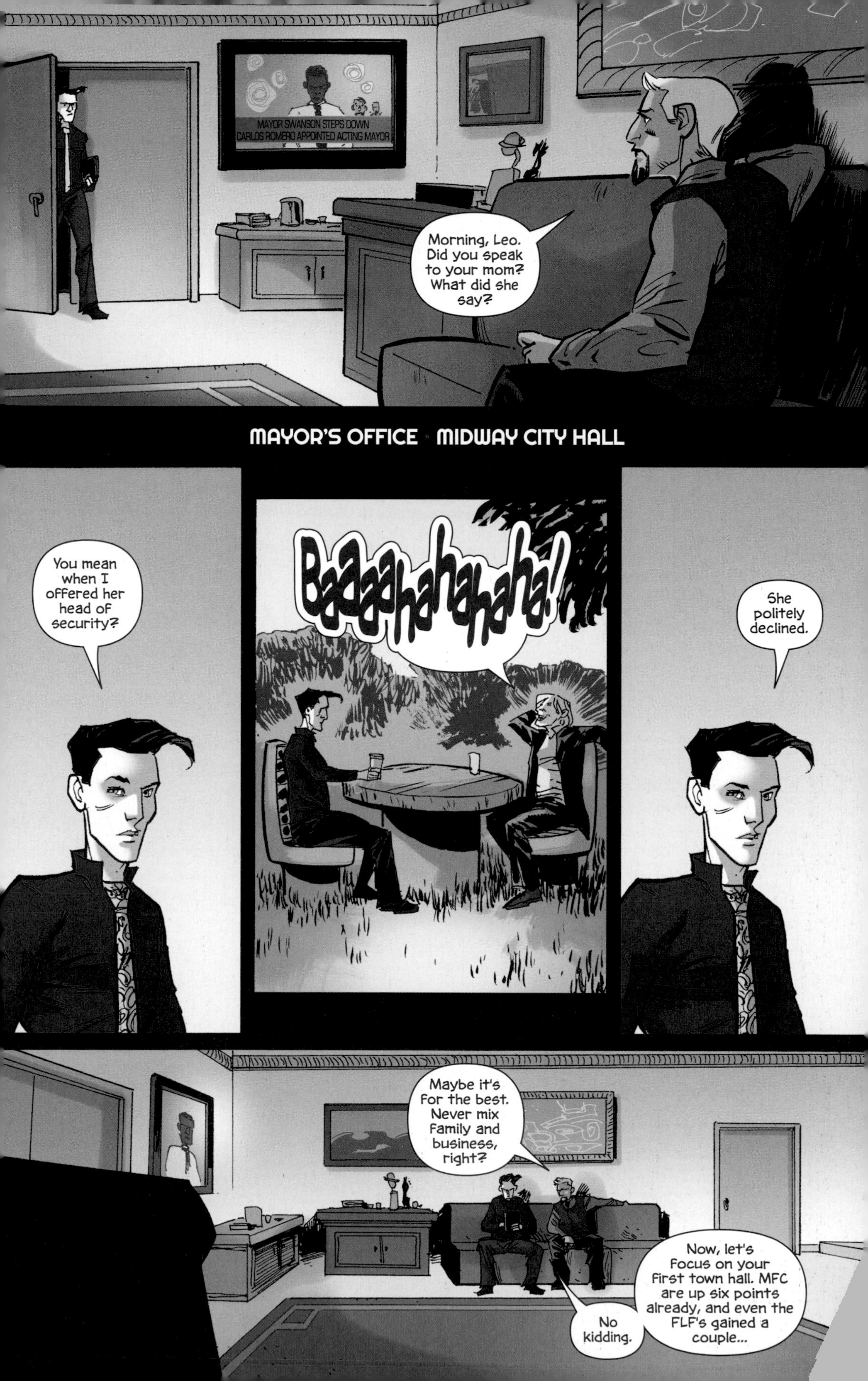
MAYOR SWANSON STEPS DOWN
CARLOS ROMERO APPOINTED ACTING MAYOR
Morning, Leo. Did you speak to your mom? What did she say?
MAYOR'S OFFICE • MIDWAY CITY HALL
You mean when I offered her head of security?
Baaaahahahahaha!
She politely declined.
Maybe it's for the best. Never mix family and business, right?
No kidding.
Now, let's focus on your first town hall. MFC are up six points already, and even the FLF's gained a couple...

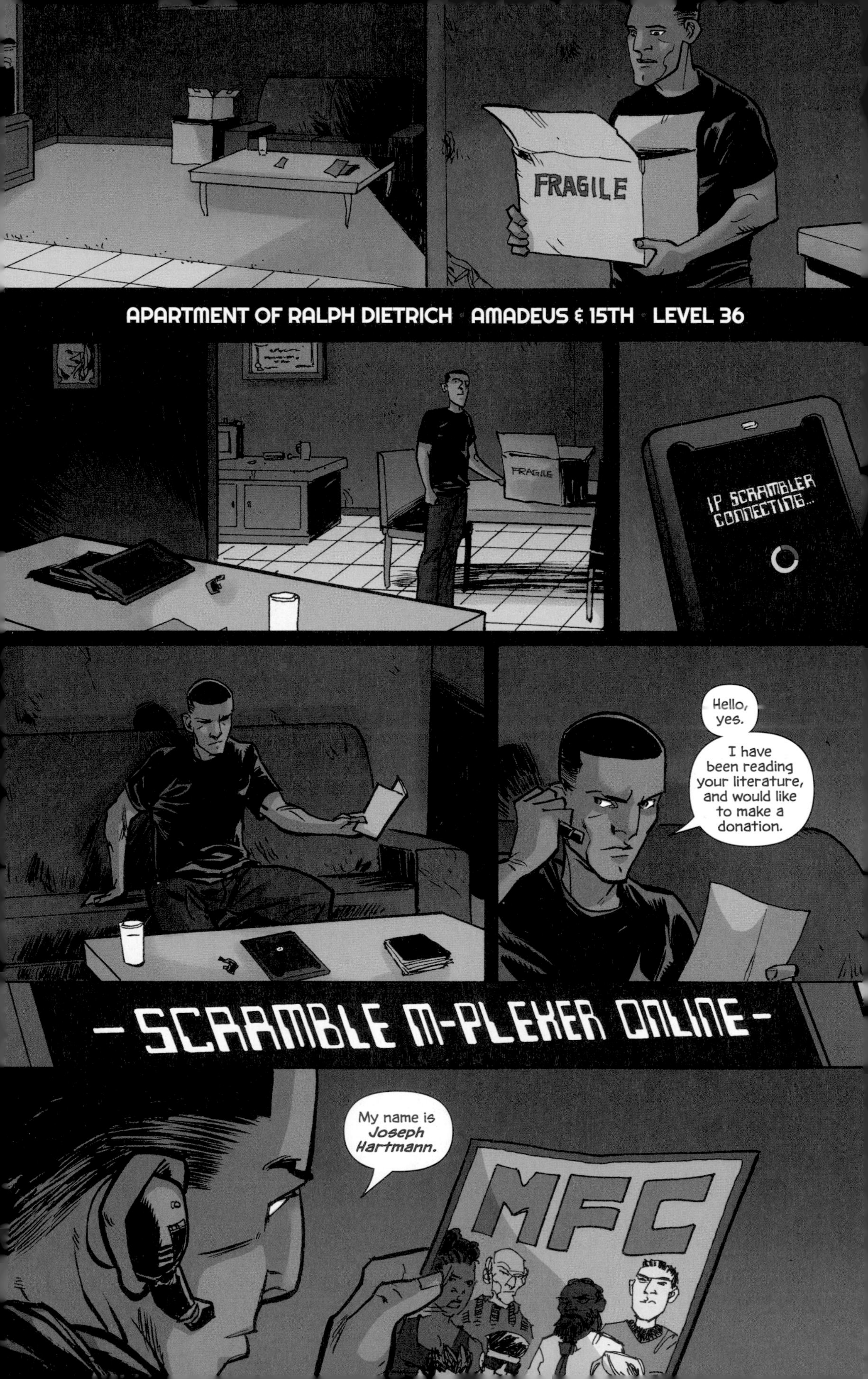
FRAGILE
APARTMENT OF RALPH DIETRICH · AMADEUS & 15TH · LEVEL 36
FRAGILE
IP SCRAMBLER CONNECTING...
Hello, yes.
I have been reading your literature, and would like to make a donation.
- SCRAMBLE M-PLEXER ONLINE -
My name is *Joseph Hartmann.*
MFC

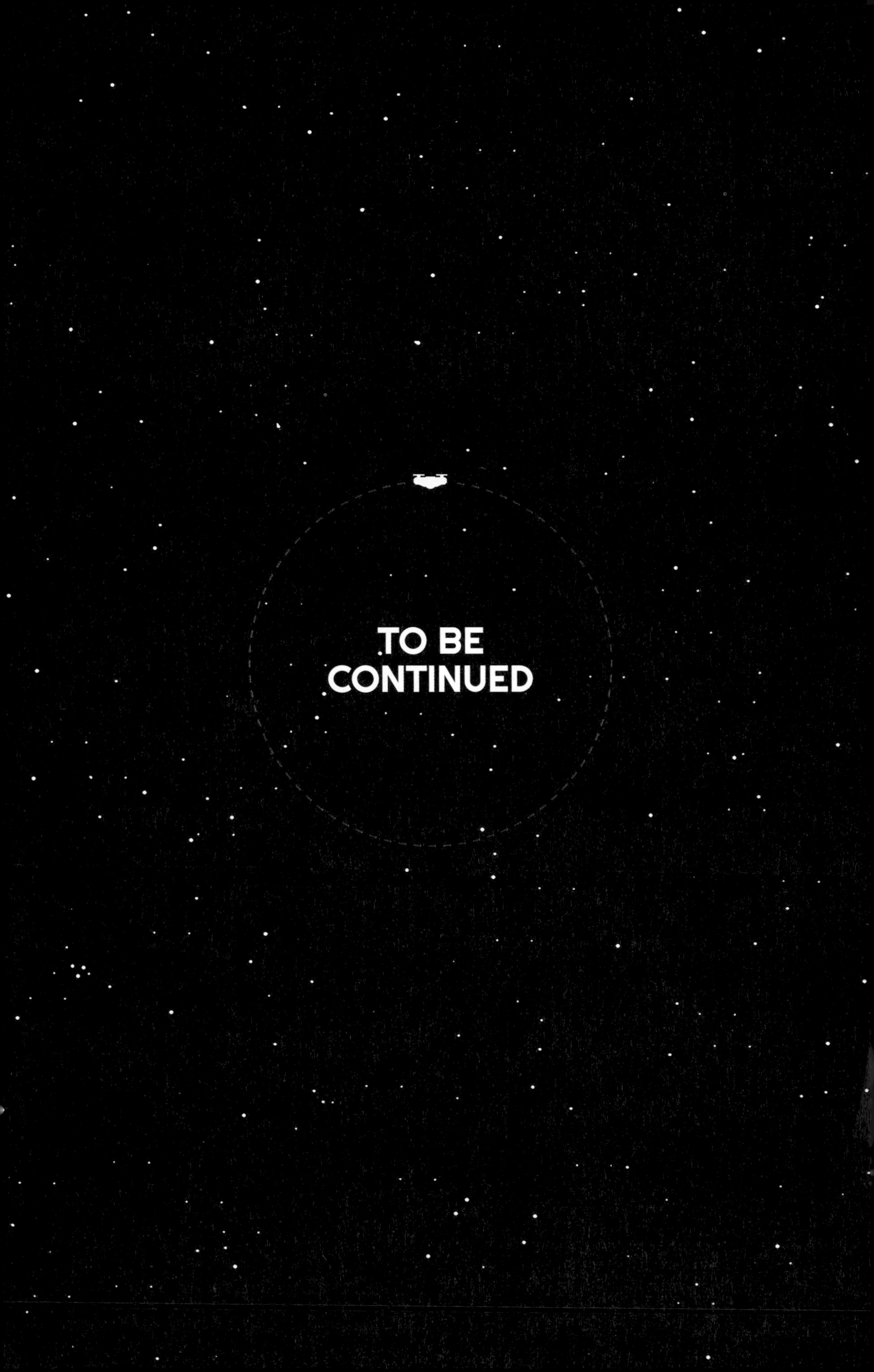
TO BE
CONTINUED

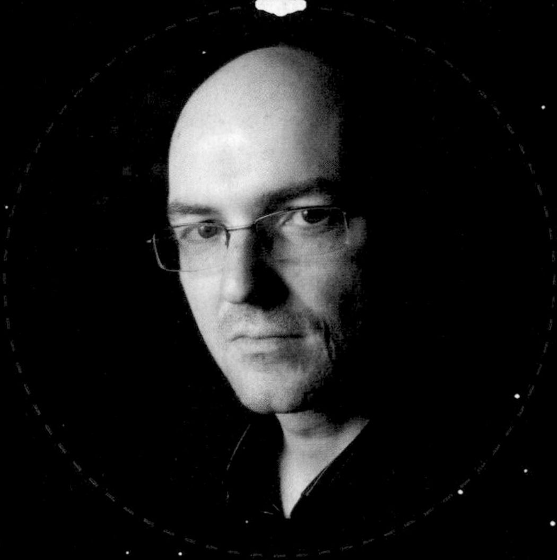

ANTONY JOHNSTON

Antony is an award-winning, *New York Times* bestselling author of comics, graphic novels, videogames, and books, with titles including *Umbral*, *Wasteland*, *Shadow of Mordor*, *Dead Space*, *The Coldest City*, *ZombiU*, and more. He has adapted books by bestselling novelist Anthony Horowitz, collaborated with comics legend Alan Moore, and reinvented Marvel's flagship character *Wolverine* for manga. His titles have been translated throughout the world and optioned for film. He lives and works in England.

ANTONYJOHNSTON.COM **@ANTONYJOHNSTON**

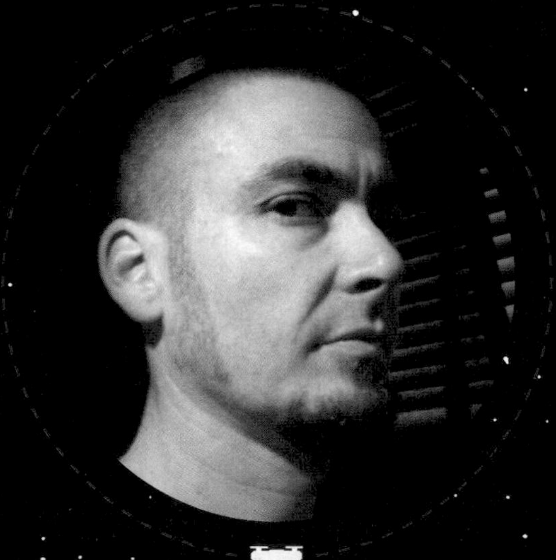

JUSTIN GREENWOOD

Justin is a finely tuned, comic makin' mammy jammy, with work on series like *Wasteland*, *Resurrection*, and *Stumptown* from Oni Press, as well as projects like *Masks and Mobsters*, *Ghost Town*, and *Continuum: The War Files* under his belt. When not drawing, he can be found running around the East Bay with his wife Melissa and their dual wildlings, tracking down small produce markets and high intensity card games with equal vigor.

JUSTINGREENWOODART.COM **@JKGREENWOOD_ART**

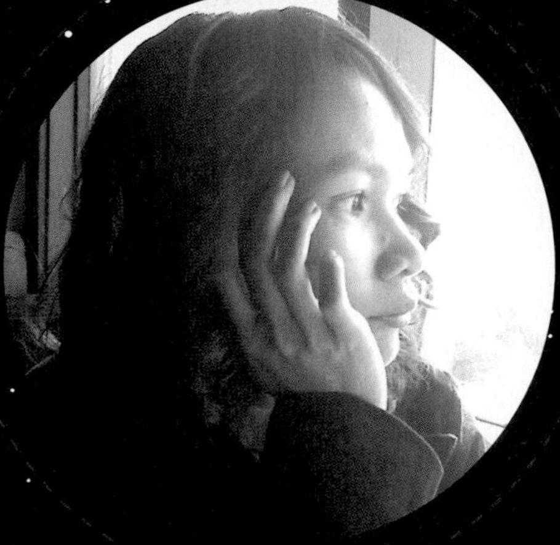

SHARI CHANKHAMMA

Shari lives in Thailand and has been working as a colorist for a while now. She previously wrote and illustrated creator-owned titles such as *The Sisters' Luck*, *The Clarence Principle*, *Pavlov's Dream*, and short stories in various anthologies. Besides comics, she enjoys wasting time on MMO and romance novels.

SHARII.COM **@SHARIHES**

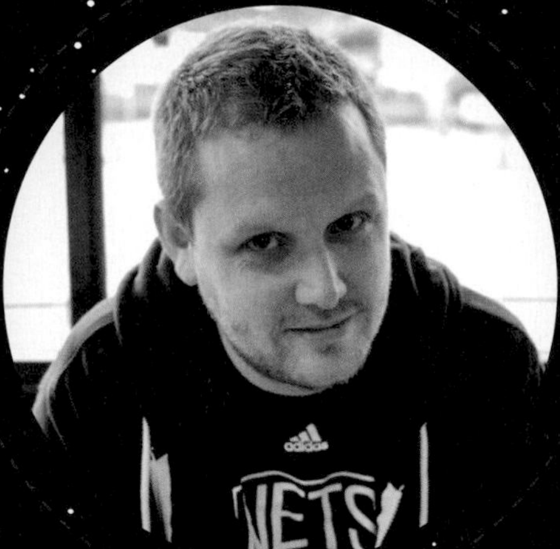
adidas
NETS

ED BRISSON

Ed is a Shuster Award nominated writer, and sometimes letterer, based out of Vancouver, BC. His work includes *Comeback*, *The Field*, *Robocop*, *Sons of Anarchy*, *Secret Avengers*, *Murder Book*, and *Sheltered*, which is currently in development as a feature film.

EDBRISSON.COM **@EDBRISSON**